D1568234

HERBS
for the
GOURMET
GARDENER

WITHDRAWN

Caroline Holmes is an author, broadcaster, and lecturer in garden history, as well as former chair of the Herb Society. Her most recent books include *Impressionists in their Gardens*, *Water Lilies*, and *Monet at Giverny*. She lives near Bury St. Edmunds, Suffolk.

The University of Chicago Press, Chicago 60637
The University of Chicago Press, Ltd., London
© 2014 Quid Publishing
All rights reserved. Published 2014.
Printed in China

22 21 20 19 18 17 16 15 14 13   1 2 3 4 5

ISBN-13: 978-0-226-17283-5 (cloth)

ISBN-13: 978-0-226-17297-2 (e-book)

DOI: 10.7208/chicago/9780226172972.001.0001

Library of Congress Cataloging-in-Publication Data

Holmes, Caroline, author.
 Herbs for the gourmet gardener : a practical resource from the garden to the table / Caroline Holmes.
   pages : illustrations ; cm
 ISBN 978-0-226-17283-5 (cloth : alk. paper) — ISBN 978-0-226-17297-2 (e-book)
 1. Herb gardening. 2. Herb gardens. I. Title.
 SB351.H5H633 2014
 635'.7—dc23
                    2014010719

♾ This paper meets the requirements of ANSI/NISO Z39.48-1992 (Permanence of Paper).

ROLLING MEADOWS LIBRARY
3110 MARTIN LANE
ROLLING MEADOWS, IL 60008

HERBS
for the
GOURMET
GARDENER

A Practical Resource from the Garden to the Table

CAROLINE HOLMES

THE UNIVERSITY OF CHICAGO PRESS

Chicago and London

CONTENTS

LEFT: Cumin (*Cuminum cyminum*) is one of many herbs that are prized for their seeds, which are used in both food and medicine.

ABOVE: The flowers of the garden nasturtium (*Tropaeolum majus*) have a peppery taste and can be used as a substitute for capers.

HOW TO USE THIS BOOK

THE HERBS

At the top of the page in large letters are herbs' common names, and in smaller italics the Latin name(s). Headings regarding plant type, climatic requirements, origins, and brief cultural requirements are beneath in bold.

BOTANICAL ILLUSTRATIONS

There is more to herbs than green leaves. The beautiful illustrations also highlight flowers, roots, and seeds.

NUTRITIONAL INFORMATION

Health benefits specific to a herb are detailed in boxes.

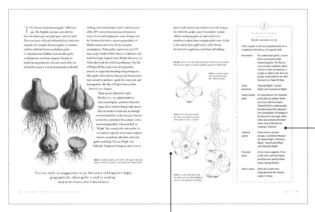

PRACTICAL GUIDANCE

Line illustrations show hands-on explanations such as how to best garden or prepare herbs.

TASTING NOTES

Look out for the boxes with the knife-and-fork icon for culinary tips to identifying different varieties or cultivars for flavor as well as simple, gourmet recipes to try.

FEATURE SPREADS

The array of parts culinary herbs can play in the garden or the kitchen are given additional detail in pages dedicated to subjects ranging from traditional designs to cocktails.

INTRODUCTION

The first foray into *Herbs for the Gourmet Gardener* will reveal beautiful botanical illustrations of 60 herbs, all of which were drawn by artists to aid identification. Herbs are ideal plants for all levels of gardeners and cooks. Many herbs are so easy to grow that the beginner gains confidence, their growing skills promoted by the taste of home-grown flavors. Conversely the gourmet cook may find themselves drawn to gardening. For the experienced gardener, the palette of the colors and scents of herbs means that their use extends beyond the herb plot into borders, lawns, and pots. Herbs are excellent short-term plants for new gardens: allow the more expensive shrubs and perennials space to develop, and while they are doing this, infill with the grays, greens, and scents of annual and perennial herbs.

The properties that herbs bring to food are those of fresh taste, fragrance, and aroma. The journey to the table just requires someone armed with a sharp thumbnail or scissors to forage the herbs for gourmet rather than gourmand use. The subtle difference between gourmet and gourmand can be counted in calories, the latter comes to play when you fold herbs into cream, butter, and seriously rich sauces.

Rather than trying to group them by use, flavor, or family, they are listed in this book by their Latin names in alphabetical order. The herbs are interleaved with feature spreads on cooking, salads, and flowers, not forgetting a short history of herbs.

LEFT: Three widely used culinary Mediterranean herbs: rosemary, *Rosmarinus officinalis*, sage, *Salvia officinalis*, and thyme, *Thymus vulgaris*.

GROWING HERBS

A GUIDE TO HOW, WHEN, AND WHERE

Each herb description includes brief growing instructions. Outlined on the following pages is more detailed information that will increase your chances of success.

RAISING FROM SEEDS

Many herb seeds will self-set when they fall from the plant if the earth is firm and they are just covered lightly with soil or leaves. Replicate this in the ground by forking the soil over, then gently pressing the soil down and raking the surface flat. Water so that the soil is moist. Decide whether to sow in rows or scatter sow and cover seeds. Lastly, cover with dry compost or soil because this seals in the moisture under the seeds and avoids unnecessary watering.

When using a seed tray, start by filling it with three-quarters of seed or fibrous potting compost. Then firm down, add more compost, water, sow seeds, and cover with the remaining compost. Such careful preparation makes it much easier for the tiny seed root to make its first foray into the growing medium before unfurling its first seed leaves. If the seed bed is poorly prepared, the seed's initial root may waste precious resources in gaining a secure foothold, resulting in weak top growth.

Seeds should be covered by their own depth in soil, so very fine seeds should have almost no soil cover. It is important to distribute them evenly because crowded seedlings will be liable to fungal infection (damping off) and difficult to manage

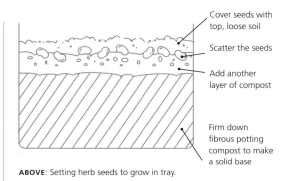

Cover seeds with top, loose soil

Scatter the seeds

Add another layer of compost

Firm down fibrous potting compost to make a solid base

ABOVE: Setting herb seeds to grow in tray.

when it comes to potting on. Label the seed tray with the name of the herb sown, since it is easy to get trays mixed up.

Germination can vary, and some seeds come up more reliable and more quickly than others. Some need the warmth of a sunny windowsill or propagator to germinate, while others will be perfectly happy on the shelf of a cool glasshouse or in a cold frame. Some seeds, especially if they are old, may show a low rate of germination. On sprouting, the first seed leaves are soon followed by the first and second "rough" leaf stages. At this stage, thin the crop, removing all the weakest seedlings and any that you do not need, in order to prevent overcrowding. This is the best time to transplant the seedlings into individual pots before growing them on and eventually planting them into their final positions. The thinned seedlings do not have to be wasted: they can be eaten as a salad or garnish.

If sowing into gravel or a wall, find crevices where moisture will be retained. If building a drystone wall, set the stones to slope upward on the outside to encourage the rain to run back into the wall to the herb roots, rather than just washing the foliage. If raising in a seed box you might also consider microsalads, i.e. sowing densely and cutting at first and second rough leaf stage. You need a great deal more seed but the resulting "mustard and cress" pickings are classed as superfoods.

Many annual herbs are available by mail order as plug plants. If space and time are at a premium this is an excellent way of stocking up your supplies. Many cultivated varieties of herbs (cultivars) are not available as seed. In these cases, only a rooted cutting, offshoot, or division will guarantee that the characteristics of the parent herb are propagated (see Propagation, p.202).

PLANTING HERBS

Most of the herbs profiled in this book are temperate hardy and are best planted in the spring. Seek out specialist growers for maximum choice. Apart from the Internet, one of the best ways to peruse the market is to go to a major gardening or flower show.

When buying, look for healthy, disease-free herbs and check that they are not root-bound, i.e. the roots are bursting out of the pot. If you do buy a herb plant like this, take it out of the pot and gently ease the roots apart, then trim back to healthy root nodes. This encourages the herb to create a new efficient root system. Soak any new herbs for up to an hour in a bucket of water (preferably of collected rainwater) before planting.

Nutrients and water are drawn from the soil by the hairs on a root. Fibrous soil or potting compost encourages their development and shortens the time for a herb to establish itself. So whatever the ground in which you choose to plant your herbs, give them a head start by creating a planting hole filled with good fibrous compost. A generous quantity of horticultural grit dug into the soil will also help to improve drainage, which most herbs appreciate. Altogether, this creates a healthier root run for surviving the two extremes of drought and waterlogging.

WHERE TO GROW

The general rule is a sunny, sheltered spot because that is what most herbs like best and it also captures their wonderful fragrances. The cook's essential and favorite herbs need to be grown near the kitchen door, either in the ground or in tubs, since only a dedicated enthusiast goes out by flashlight to gather in fresh herbs from the garden. Large and less frequently used herbs can be dotted about the garden or used to form a decorative herb garden.

A sunny site is defined as receiving seven or more hours of sun per day, weather permitting. Some herbs such as garlic and chives like their tops in the sun but their roots in moisture-retentive soil. The "Mediterranean" herbs such as basil, hyssop, marjoram, oregano, savory, and thyme as well as nasturtiums, will thrive in hot, dry summers. This will be essential if you want to grow a clipped myrtle or rosemary hedge.

Shady sites are defined as those not exposed to midday sun. Receiving no more than four hours' sunshine per day, this can be helpful with semitender shrubs like bay and possibly myrtle, although the latter flowers best in a sunny location. Other shade-loving herbs include mint, sorrel, sweet cicely, and sweet woodruff. Shade from trees is usually better than shade from buildings because it allows water to percolate down to the ground.

Large and vigorous annual herbs, such as angelica, lovage, and sweet cicely, tend to like a relatively moist but well-drained soil. Make a virtue of this by having a corner of "jungle herbs." Bergamot and mint also thrive with good levels of soil moisture.

HEDGING AND TOPIARY HERBS

Ideal for formal edible designs, any of the following herbs would be suitable grown as hedging or topiary: hyssop, lavender, myrtle, and dwarf rosemary for low hedges; bay, myrtle, and rosemary provide an evergreen backdrop perfect for larger hedges; while bay, elder, and roses could be planted in a mixed outer hedge. For topiary, many herbs tolerate clipping into a simple ball or more exotic shapes (see p.108). Regular clipping is essential to keep the hedges or topiary in good shape.

If you are prepared to live with a gappy hedge for the first two or three years, young one- or two-year plants will establish better but while you wait, interplant the spaces with annuals or biennials. Classed by its flowers, the largest "herb" in this book is *Tilia cordata*, the lime or linden tree. Apart from in grand avenues, a single specimen or row in a smaller space could be pleached (see p.197).

EDGING HERBS

There are soft, cushion-forming herbs that will edge and spill over paths or gravel. Many will also provide fresh spring leaf color and dried flower heads through the winter. For long-term interest, plant perennials; for seasonal interest, plant annuals. Good perennials include chives, dwarf hyssop (*Hyssopus aristatus*), oregano, sage, winter savory, and thyme. The tidiest annual is bush basil, but it needs a warm climate to grow well outdoors.

TENDER HERBS

These are typically herbs from subtropical and tropical regions, requiring generally warmer temperatures and freedom from all frost. Examples include cumin, fenugreek, ginger, lemongrass, lemon verbena, scented geraniums, turmeric, and Vietnamese cilantro. This may well mean growing under glass in cooler temperate climates. Their individual requirements are described under their separate entries.

ABOVE: Although this is a fig tree, the principles of encouraging a straight trunk and supporting it, can equally be applied to bay, myrtle, rosemary, and even scented geraniums.

COOKING WITH HERBS

DRYING AND FREEZING

The term gourmet evokes pictures of seeking out and sampling the finest food quality and tastes. Quite simply, fresh herbs are the first port of call. Each herb has details on its history, cultivation, and culinary use. Most can be available all year round by juggling those that are freshly available from the garden with those harvested and preserved. The making of oils, vinegars, jams, and jellies is covered elsewhere but the two simplest methods are to dry and to freeze herbs.

DRYING HERBS

In principle, herbs are at their most aromatic as they come into flower and that is the season to cut them for drying. Drying should be done in a warm, well-ventilated place—any room on a hot summer's day will be ideal. Tie up in small bunches and allow to hang where the air circulates freely. Try not to crumble before storing. The larger the stems dried, the better they will retain their flavor. Store in a dark dry place or, when perfectly dry, a large airtight jar. Crumble and break into cooking.

FREEZING HERBS

If you are freezing fresh leaves for the short term, do not blanch. As with drying, the larger the piece that is frozen the longer it will retain its savor. Fill plastic boxes—rather than plastic bags which tend to get squashed—with cut stems and then freeze. Break off pieces as and when you need them to add to favorite dishes and sauces. Chopped herbs can be frozen in butter or milk ready for use.

ABOVE: From the left, these dried herbs are the most popular and include sage, *Salvia officinalis*, rosemary, *Rosmarinus officinalis*, mint, *Mentha spicata*, parsley, *Petroselenium crispum*, and thyme, *Thymus vulgaris*.

A SHORT HISTORY OF HERBS

GRASS ROOTS FOR THE GOURMET GARDENER

In prehistoric Europe the oily seeds of *Polygonum* (knotgrass) were an invaluable ingredient for enriching pottage. We know this from evidence found in the stomach of Tollund man in Denmark whose mortal remains were preserved in a bog for over 2,000 years. The survival of indigenous peoples the world over depended on knowing what grains, leaves, and fruit could be safely eaten, which is known in Australia as "bushtucker." Wise pioneers and settlers learned to incorporate knowledge of local foodstuffs into their own repertoire of edible plants, which they then sent back to their original countries.

Although the word herbal conjures up a medical reference book, early knowledge of the plants that clothed the earth was more encompassing. Oral traditions were inscribed on clay or written on parchment, compared, and edited to ascertain a use for each and every plant—if it tasted good, so much the better. The great chronicler and observer of Roman life, Pliny the Elder, died during the eruption of Vesuvius in AD 79. The volumes of his *Historia Naturalis* (*History of Plants*) were transcribed over the ensuing centuries—sometimes spiced with sensational gossip mixed with mythological fancy, more often a sensible and first-hand observation of Roman life. For example, we learn from his writings about preserving fennel stalks and flowers, and parsley stalks in salt, then brine and vinegar in amphora for winter use.

ABOVE: Knotgrass, *Polygonum*, was used to enrich pottages. Its Asian variation, the Vietnamese cilantro, is a key ingredient in noodle curries.

The Romans brought an array of improved leaves, roots, and fruits to every far-flung corner of their Empire as well as recording new plants and their uses. Pedanius Dioscorides, a Greek military physician with the Roman army and contemporary of Pliny, recorded over 600 plants as well as 35 animal products and 90 minerals, which was published as *De Materia Medica* (*Regarding Medicinal Materials*), a five-volume reference that became the base of both European and Arabian pharmaceutical and botanical writings well into the 17th century. At a time when the term herb was interchangeable with plant, it remains a vital source of information for the identification, naming, and use of herbs.

The idealized c. AD 816 design for the Abbey of St. Gall (in modern-day Switzerland) includes the earliest surviving plans for two herb gardens—one for physic and one for pottage. Next to the physician's quarters you can see 16 rectangular beds, each dedicated to one herb and eight can be found in this book: rose, sage, curled mint, fenugreek, savory, fennel, lovage, and cumin. Apart from field crops, the Abbey residents, their dependents, and their guests were fed from a specialist pottage garden with 18 herbs, of which cilantro, savory, garlic, parsley, and chervil are listed and also found in this book.

In AD 872 when the then King of the Franks, Charlemagne, was proclaimed Roman Emperor by Pope Leo III, he issued the *Capitulare de Villis Imperialibus* (*A Decree Concerning Imperial Towns*), a part of which was a list divided into nine categories of essential plants to be grown across his extensive European kingdom. Twenty-one of the 60 herbs profiled in this book appear under five of its headings. *Flowers*—the rose; *Physical Herbs* i.e. for medicine—anise, burdock, caraway, cilantro, cumin, dill, fennel, fenugreek, lovage, rosemary, sage; *Salads*—chervil, chives, parsley, arugula; *Pot-herbs*—"Blite" (a *Chenopodium* possibly Good King Henry), mint, orach, savory; and lastly, *Roots*—garlic.

ABOVE: Page from *De Materia Medica*. Toledo in modern-day Spain became a melting pot of medieval European and Islamic knowledge regarding the medicinal properties of herbs.

The *Forme of Cury* is one of the earliest extant collections of manuscript recipes in Middle English and can be translated as "Manner of Cooking." It was written by the "chief master cooks" about 1390 at the request of England's King Richard II, who they described as "the best and royallest viander of all Christian kings." *Erbolate* was intended as a light evening snack. By the 17th century it had evolved into *herbolace*, which has been interpreted by Philippa Pullar in *Consuming Passions* as follows: "Chop three leaves each of marjoram, dittany, smallage, tansy, mint, sage, parsley, and fennel, with two large handfuls of violet, spinach, lettuce, and clary. Add a little ginger and enough beaten eggs to make two omelettes, which are fried on both sides like large cakes, strewn with grated cheese, and served." From the original recipe, herbs that can still be pleasantly used are parsley, mint, savory, green sage, fennel, with the possible addition of vervain. The pungent tastes of the others—tansy, clary, rue, dittany, and southernwood—are without the remit of this book but could be substituted with lovage, purple sage, buckler-leafed sorrel, oregano, and French tarragon.

The gardens or *herbers* around medieval castles, manors, and farms can be glimpsed in *Books of Hours*, to which contemporary poetry adds romantic pictures of fragrant and aromatic scents floating up into open windows from the herbs below. The naturalness and spirituality of the medieval landscape was reformed into order by the grand architecture of the Renaissance: structured terraced gardens in symmetry with the house, quadripartite enclosures filled with cushion herbs in ornate geometric beds, edged with clipped hyssop, lavender, or myrtle. In simple terms all gardens were "fit for use or delight" or effectively herb gardens until the mid-17th century. With the advent of dwarf box, *Buxus sempervirens* "Suffruticosa," ever more intricate parterres were formed while the ornamental kitchen garden evolved separately. Today the *potager* at the Chateau de Villandry in France provides an outstanding example of parterres as an ornamental kitchen garden, not least in details such as stepping-stone beds of chives and rectangular drifts of basil. A poetic touch is provided by the standard roses that rise in sentinel fashion, echoing the monastic belief that roses will "watch over" the plants. England's first armchair garden writer, Thomas Hyll, writing for a more domestic 16th-century market, suggested that,

space permitting, hyssop, thyme, and winter savory could be grown into an ornamental knot.

Long after the fall of the Roman Empire and before the advent of sponsored plant collectors, sailors and merchants as well as monks and pilgrims swapped herbs around the world. On a colonial scale there were the celebrated Pilgrim Fathers who sailed on *The Mayflower* in 1623 to settle in North America. The herbs they carried were a small taste of home and an important source of medicine.

A century later, the Quaker farmer John Bartram traveled around North America gathering seeds and plants that he grew and observed at his

ABOVE: Described as illuminations of the very rich hours of the *Duc de Berry*, these colorful images provide glimpses into medieval gardens from which to garner ideas for herb growing.

botanic garden near Philadelphia. He engaged in a worldwide network of botanical exchange with Carl Linnaeus in Sweden and Philip Miller at the Chelsea Physic Garden among others. Bartram's garden survives and was the first to find and raise the American native *Monarda didyma*, bergamot or Oswego tea. He observed and grew imported herbs such as the apothecary's rose, borage, chamomile, chives, dill, fennel, French tarragon, hyssop, lemon balm, lovage, mint, myrtle, pot marigold, rosemary, saffron crocus, sage, sweet basil, sweet bay, sweet woodruff, and thyme. During the 19th century, poorer immigrants from Eastern Europe and Ireland sewed seeds into the hems of the women's dresses so that they could not be stolen.

ABOVE: John Miller drew one of the earliest botanical illustrations of bergamot, *Monarda didyma*, described as *fistulous monarda* or Oswego tea in his book *An Illustration of the Sexual System of Linnaeus* in 1779.

HERB GARDEN DESIGN

When gardeners choose to create a separate herb garden they inevitably roll out the medieval or Renaissance template, and it still works. Medieval rectangular beds can be made more interesting by laying them out to form a pattern. Growing just one herb per bed serves the dual purpose of making them more attractive and easier to care for and to harvest. A Modernist take on this layout would be to look at the geometry of a Mondrian or amorphous blocks of a Ferdinand Leger painting and organize an artistic relationship between blocks of herbs, stone, gravel, and water. A raised seat with a cushion of chamomile from which to admire your handiwork sits well with most designs.

There are many designs for knots, apart from embroidery patterns—look for inspiration in wood carvings or plasterwork. The knot should be set within a square, the threads or hedges planted to intertwine unceasingly, that is without a discernible start or finish. Like true love, the lover's knot should be infinite. Working with Hyll's list of herbs, first make sure you select varieties that grow to more or less the same height, such as hyssop (*Hyssopus aristatus*), thyme (either *Thymus vulgaris*, *T. fragrantissimus* or *T. × citriodorus* "Silver Posie"), and winter savory (*Satureja montana*). They will need to be clipped in spring to ensure the knot shape, but leave them to flower as this makes a soft, colorful pattern, then clip back dead flower heads and keep reshaping through the growing season. For a larger knot, clipped rosemary and lavender with the taller hyssop, *Hyssopus officinalis*, create contrasting greens, blues, and grays to which, in protected climates, you could add the myrtle (*Myrtus communis* subsp. *tarentina*). Depending on the size of the knot, the areas within the hedges can be planted up with perennial herbs or sown with annuals. If you have time for a practice run, sow the knot pattern in three annual herbs such as dill (*Anethum graveolens*), cilantro (*Coriandrum sativum*), and summer savory (*Satureja hortensis*), or three varieties of basil (*Ocimum basilicum*). This clears the ground, gives you an edible crop, and a sense of what the pattern will look like.

The design of the open knot is less complicated than either the historic Lover's Knot or parterre patterns. Traditionally, the beds are laid out symmetrically and edged with hedging herbs or boards. This layout can easily be adapted to the shape of your plot. Lining a path to the kitchen, or any other exterior door, with herbs is simple, effective, and practical. Many herbs are as ornamental as they are useful and they can as easily be picked from a flower border, a terrace, or among shrubs, so spread them around.

Large pots provide movable feasts. If you have space, nurture them out of sight and then position by the back door when they are at their most prolific. Evergreens such as bay and rosemary are ideal; rosemary and sage both grow well together. Clipped bay gives a green elegance to any door and it is less likely to succumb to winter cold if fashioned into a ball, cone, or pyramid, rather than with a bare stem, because the foliage protects the trunk. The bushy thymes are almost evergreen, so it

is wise to grow in an old sink or trough in a sunny position. If possible, choose frost-resistant terracotta pots as they are less likely to become waterlogged or affected by weather extremes.

Starting in New York, many tall buildings have used their roof space for gardens. It was rapidly discovered that because many herbs are suited for dry, windy locations, and many are low-growing, they would provide plentiful pickings for the high-rise cook. Using wood, aluminum, modern materials, and irrigation systems, the beds and containers can be adapted to the extremes of their high life. From the start of the 21st century, Australian cities have been introducing a policy of "green roofs" to harness rainfall and ameliorate temperature extremes.

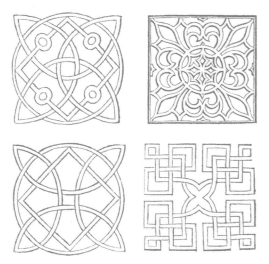

ABOVE: Hedging herbs such as rosemary, hyssop, lavender, and thyme are ideal for clipping into a woven knot with each strand dedicated to one herb. The bottom left is the simplest to replicate and requires only three herbs.

ROMAN HERBS

CLASSICAL ROOTS AND BACCHANALIAN BOUNTY

The excesses of Roman feasts are recorded in contemporary writings and colorfully portrayed in paintings such as *The Roses of Heliogabalus* by Lawrence Alma-Tadema. The Emperor Nero, who reigned from AD 54–68, started the fashion for strewing rose petals across the floor of his banqueting hall; further petals were rained gently down from the ceiling during the course of the evening. The scent was believed to enhance enjoyment and to mask the odor of wine in the guests' hair. During his four-year reign in the early 3rd century, the Emperor Heliogabalus (or Elagabalus) took excess to new heights, not least

ABOVE: *The Roses of Heliogabalus* by Lawrence Alma-Tadema. The Egyptians introduced the Romans to roses, Cleopatra had the sails of her barge washed in rose water, while the Romans had them rained on banqueters.

with roses. One fateful night he and his guests were all so intoxicated that the order to stop the gentle rain of rose petals was never given. Many slumped and slumbering inebriates simply suffocated under a deep blanket of petals. The extravagance was nearly matched by Alma-Tadema when he had regular supplies of rose petals sent from the French Riviera during the winter of 1887/88 so that he could paint the event in orgiastic detail.

Across the Roman Empire, their citizens grew and ate herbs from the shores of the Mediterranean to those of the North Sea as well as North Africa and Asia—the seeds were as important as the leaves, roots, and flowers. Roman courtyard gardens have been recreated in Europe and the United States in a typical arrangement of rectangular beds, sometimes including a vine-covered outdoor *triclinium*. This is effectively three sloping stone couches faced in concrete that are arranged to form three sides of a square. Cushions and fabrics were laid out on the couches for the comfort of the prone diners and often a small ledge was created around the inner edge for a glass of wine. The food would be laid out on a dining board that could be carried to the center for each course. In larger gardens this central area might be a water feature on which baskets of food would be floated from one diner to another—the grandest being the Canopus at Hadrian's Villa in Tivoli.

The Roman gastronomer Apicius wrote *De Re Coquinaria* (*On Cookery*), which is divided into 10 books that include many herbs. Under his instruction, "field herbs" could be served raw, with broth, oil, and vinegar, or as a cooked dish by adding cumin seeds. He viewed spiced salts, as well as the usual aromatic herb seeds, as an elixir for life. He recommended parsley seeds as a substitute for those of lovage and his recipes also included seeds of marjoram, arugula, and thyme. Both bay and myrtle berries were also used in sauces and forcemeats. The recipes for *mortaria* are preparations of fresh herb leaves pounded in a mortar such as cilantro, fennel, lovage, and mint, often with honey and vinegar or broth. Although harder work, pounding herbs, rather than processing them, does create a more aromatic taste.

TASTING NOTES

Culinary herbs mentioned by Pliny the Elder

Half of the herbs in this book appear in Pliny's *Historia Naturalis*, pictured below. Many have uses beyond the kitchen but there are some surprising omissions from his list which include the following:

Culinary	Aniseed, basil, chervil, chives, cilantro, dill, fennel, garlic, lovage, marjoram, mint, myrtle, parsley, purslane, arugula, saffron, sorrel, and thyme. Also bay, hyssop, and rose (only for wine and medicinal purposes)
Medicinal	Cumin, orache, rosemary, and violet. The following were also used medicinally: aniseed, basil, chervil, cilantro, dill, fennel, garlic, lovage, myrtle, parsley, purslane, arugula, saffron, and sorrel
Wine	Juniper, lavender, and sage

Ground elder
Aegopodium podagraria

Common names: Ground elder, goutweed, Bishopsweed, Bishopswort, Herb Gerard, ashweed, ground ash

Type: Perennial

Climate: Hardy, very cold winter

Size: 12–35in (30–90cm)

Origin: Europe, West Asia

History: The Romans introduced ground elder across their empire as part of their *Materia medica*. It was lost from written records until it was reintroduced into Britain by traveling monks before AD 1000.

Cultivation: You are likely to find ground elder already growing in your garden, introduced there by a previous occupant. Once established, it is almost impossible to weed out. Beware, just one small piece of root will rapidly recolonize.

Do not pick after flowering as this herb becomes a strong laxative. The roots are also harvested for medicinal purposes.

Storage: Best treated seasonally and picked fresh.

Preparation: Only young leaves should be used. Pick the leaves and wash thoroughly. Use as a fresh vegetable substitute for spinach—just boil the leaves in the water that clings to the leaves.

ABOVE: Once ground elder is in flower, it is too late to eat the leaves. They are both strong-tasting and a potent laxative.

When making a white sauce for fish, add shredded leaves to give a carrot and parsley flavor. Ground elder can be added as a green layer to other prepared dishes, such as between the meat, fish, or vegetarian and white sauce layers in lasagna.

Ground elder quiche

Eating the young leaves is one of the best ways of controlling ground elder's thuggish habits. Bake the leaves like you would spinach. Cook them up in omelettes if you like, but the flavor is better when baked with butter, milk, and eggs, making them an ideal ingredient for quiche.

Preparation time: 10 minutes
Cooking time: 50 minutes
Serves: 10 people

You will need:

• Handful of ground elder

• 4 eggs, separated

• 4floz (250ml) single cream

• 4½oz (125g) cheese

Preheat a conventional oven to 400°F (200°C / gas mark 6 / fan 180°C).

Roll out the pastry, line in a 10in (25cm) tin, and prick with a fork. Press parchment paper over the bottom and up the sides. Fill with baking beans. Cook for 10 minutes.

Cover the pastry with shredded ground elder leaves.

Mix the egg yolks with the cheese and milk.

Beat up the egg whites until stiff, then fold them in together.

Pour sautéed filling mixture over leaves.

Bake for 40 minutes.

The Latin generic name *Aegopodium* derives from the Greek *aix* meaning "goat," *podion* meaning "little foot," and *podagra* meaning "gout in the foot." The Romans used ground elder as a poultice to alleviate gout, later invoking the name of the Christian St. Gerard—the alternative name being Herb Gerard—as it was used for help against this affliction. The common names Bishopsweed and Bishopswort relate to the fact that having been reintroduced by monks, it is frequently found near the ruins of ecclesiastical buildings. The leaves resemble those of both the ash and elder trees, hence the origins of its other common names.

Ground elder is a traditional well-flavored pot herb but with the disadvantage of being extremely invasive. The herbal writer John Gerard bemoaned its thuggish habits. Observing the way that the seeds detach themselves as they dry, the 16th-century herbal writer William Coles called it "Jump-about" or "Jack-jump-about" because this is exactly what they do. As the choice of green herbs and vegetables improved, its status became one of a pernicious weed.

NUTRITION

Rich in vitamin C, ground elder is a mild sedative with diuretic and anti-inflammatory effects.

Thuggish herbs

Historically, herbs grown in the gardens near the castle, monastery, or cottage were the ones requiring special cultural attention, possibly newly introduced and often of great medicinal value. Pottage herbs would be grown as field crops and the rest were gathered from the wild by so-called green men or women.

Outwitting thuggish herbs' worst habits will help you not to lose the plot in every sense. Rampant self-seeders such as ground elder, burdock, lemon balm, sorrel, and vervain can be controlled by determinedly cutting off the flowering stems before they set seed. This rule can also be applied to perilla in certain American states where it has become a pernicious weed.

Herbs with seriously invasive roots are not readily contained by fencing them in with metal, wood, or terracotta. They soon outgrow their space and go on the march for new pastures. Vigorous rooting herbs such as ground elder, mint, and horseradish are best planted away from tidier, bushy, and annual herbs.

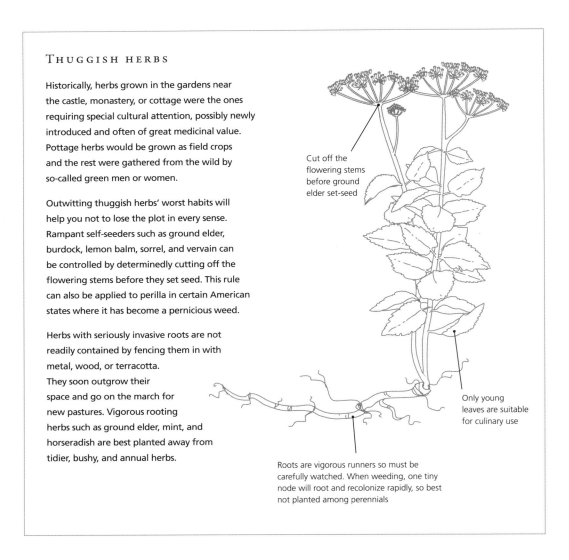

Cut off the flowering stems before ground elder set-seed

Only young leaves are suitable for culinary use

Roots are vigorous runners so must be carefully watched. When weeding, one tiny node will root and recolonize rapidly, so best not planted among perennials

The flavor is at its best when grown in moisture-retentive soil, preferably in dappled shade, so under fruit trees among spring bulbs is a possible solution. Ground elder is tough enough to take a mowing regime after you have harvested the young leaves. A good way to control it is by eating it copiously in the spring. Weed it scrupulously out of flower beds where it will be a constant nuisance, winding its roots inextricably among all the other plants. Avoid allowing it to go to seed from whence it will spread even farther. The one way of making a virtue of its enthusiastic growth is to grow the attractive white-splashed variegated form, "Variegatum." The gardeners of Monet's garden at Giverny have used this variety to line the bottom of the upper garden where it brightens up the north-facing aspect.

Garlic
Allium sativum

Common names: Garlic, Poor Man's Treacle

Type: Bulb

Climate: Hardy, cold winter

Size: 10–40in (25–100cm)

Origin: Mediterranean

History: The Roman army ate garlic for inspiration and for courage. It was associated with Mars, the god of war, and was an essential plant in their *Materia medica*.

Cultivation: Garlic is raised by separating and planting the individual cloves of a bulb. Plant cloves 4in (10cm) apart just below the soil surface between October and December or February and April and they should be ready for lifting from July onward. Usually grown in rows spaced at 6in (15cm), garlic thrives in rich, well-drained soil in a sunny position. If the garlic stem produces flowerheads, pick them off (and eat!) to focus the energy back into bulb production.

Storage: After lifting, place bulbs where the outer skins can dry, then hang in a cool, dark place until needed. Use for garlic vinegar and oil (see p.75) but remove crushed cloves after two days. Smoke whole bulbs. Slice, dry, and crush to powder.

RIGHT: In principle, every part of the garlic except the white papery skins of the cloves is edible. However, it is best to discourage the formation of flowers so that all the energies go into maturing the bulb.

Preparation: Garlic can be eaten raw if crushed or chopped finely—simply add to salads, mayonnaise, and salsa. Long used as a meat tenderizer, it is an ideal herb for marinades and slow cooking, such as daube of beef. Sit meats or poultry on unpeeled cloves of garlic for roasting; after cooking, lift out the meat and with a wooden spoon, press out the garlic and mix with the roasting juices. Thicken and add meat or vegetable broth to make delicious gravy. It is also a subtle or major ingredient in pickles and chutneys, or try garlic and chilli jelly.

The Chinese domesticated garlic 7,000 years ago. The English common name derives from the Saxon *gar* meaning "spear" and *leac* "leek." There are many wild and cultivated plants that taste of garlic, for example, Ramsons garlic, *A. ursinum*, and the wild leek known as elephant garlic, *A. ampeloprasum*. Folklore recounts that garlic would protect you from vampires. Despite its health-giving properties, the antisocial effect on the breath meant it remained unpopular in British and American cooking. Increased foreign travel in the latter part of the 20th century fostered more adventurous tastes. Travel and immigration across Europe and the Americas has led to a growing popularity of Mediterranean and Asian foods and garlic consumption. Today garlic is grown in every US state except Alaska while Gilroy in California calls itself the Garlic Capital of the World. However, it is China that leads the world in production.

There are two distinctive types. The first, *A. s.* var. *ophioscorodon* or hard-necked garlic, produces fewer but larger cloves and the thinner skin means they are harder to store but are strongly recommended for cooler climates. Varieties include the red-bulbed "Rocambole" with a stem bearing bulbils, "Chesnok Red" or "Wight." The second is the soft-necked *A.s.* var. *sativum*, typically from warmer regions, known as artichoke, silverskin, and creole garlics including "Tuscany Wight" and "Vallelado." Traditional European advice was to plant on the shortest day and harvest on the longest,

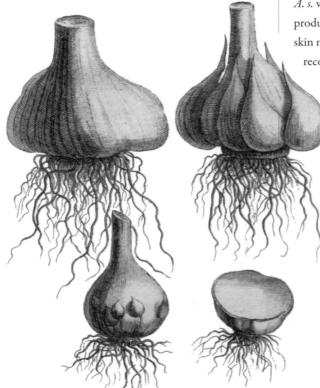

LEFT: Hardneck garlics are hardier with larger individual cloves in smaller quantities. Some have reddish skins.

"It is not really an exaggeration to say that peace and happiness begin, geographically, where garlic is used in cooking."

Myself, My Two Countries, (1936) X. Marcel Boulestin

for which the purple variety "Germidour" is ideal. *Alliums* including garlic are said to deter rose predators so plant them among garden roses. Garlic is also said to deter apple scab as well as being beneficial for raspberries, stonefruit, and cabbage.

BELOW: Garlics store well and look good if their leaves are plaited after harvest. Keep in a well-aired place, away from direct light.

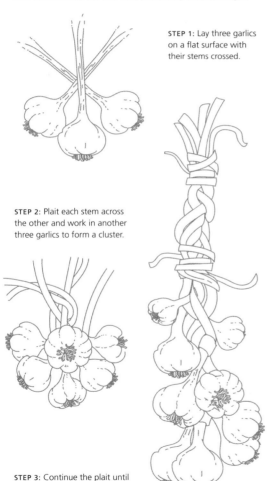

STEP 1: Lay three garlics on a flat surface with their stems crossed.

STEP 2: Plait each stem across the other and work in another three garlics to form a cluster.

STEP 3: Continue the plait until the stems run out. Wrap additional stems in two points to strengthen.

TASTING NOTES

Garlic varieties to try

Select a garlic to suit your personal taste or to complement the flavor of a specific dish.

Rocambole	The cold climate garlic, a name that is synonymous with hardneck garlics. The flavor has an earthy muskiness which is fiery if eaten raw because it is high in sulfenic acid. Best for drying. Good cultivars are "Red German" and "Spanish Roja."
Other hardnecks	"Chesnok Wight," "Lautrec Wight," and "Carcassonne Wight."
Purple striped garlic	An umbrella term for striped hardneck garlics . Tastes vary from mild to pungent. "Chesnok Red" is a deep purple skinned variety that originates from the Republic of Georgia. It has large, milky white and cranberry streaked cloves. One of the best for roasting is "Chesnok."
Softneck garlics	These thrive in warmer climates. A traditional flavor. Try "Solent Wight," "Provence Wight," "Early Purple Wight," and "Vallelado Wight."
Porcelain garlic	As the name suggests, it has a stiff neck, with skin tautly stretched over pearly white cloves. Strong flavor.
Solo or pearl	Grows as a single clove. Originates from the Yunnan region of China.

Chives
Allium schoenoprasum

Common names: Chives, chive, cive, Schnittlauch

Type: Perennial

Climate: Hardy, very cold winter

Size: 4–24in (10–60cm)

Origin: Northern hemisphere

History: The early 19th-century botanist Augustin-Pyramus de Candolle concluded that a variety growing in the Alps was the nearest to the cultivated form. Chives were used by the Romans, and it is believed that the naturalized clumps along Hadrian's Wall in Northumberland, England, are descendants from Roman fort garden escapes.

Cultivation: The common variety is easily raised from seed. Sow from spring onward and once established, it is readily self-seeding. Chives like a rich, moisture-retentive soil.

Storage: Freeze fresh spikes whole and break when needed. Freeze in milk or pats of butter for adding to mashed potato in winter.

Preparation: A key ingredient in *fines herbes* (see p.38), fresh chopped chives with their gentle onion flavor enhance salads, potatoes, scrambled eggs, or really any savory dish whether home- or ready-made. For more bite, take the fresh flowers in your hand and gently twist the florets apart and sprinkle over salads or fork through couscous or cold rice. Both common and garlic or Chinese chives can be chopped finely into soft cheeses.

Chives are listed in several early works such as Palladius c. 380, Charlemagne's *Capitulare de Villis Imperialibus* (872), Hildegard von Bingen c. 1150, Daniel the gardener c. 1375, and the Fromond List c. 1500. Chives also appear in the first Latin–English dictionary *Promptorium Parvulorum* c. 1440. John Evelyn called them "cives," "rush leeks," "civet," or "sweth." During his 41-year stint as chef of the Ritz-Carlton in New York, Louis Diat decided to add chives and cream to his mother's recipe for leek and potato soup, which he christened Crème Vichyssoise.

The most ornamental of edible alliums, they can be planted as an attractive edging or allowed to drift among flowers, especially roses. Given a rich moisture-retentive soil, chives thrive on

"A CHAPLET OF HERBS In a town … we can still have our own miniature herb garden in a window-box or tub, or even in large plant pots. These I have grown in a tiny London border … CHIVES most delicate of the lilies of the kitchen. May be employed where the robuster onion is not indicated; clip them down as you require, water them occasionally. Best of all in green salads."

Vogue's Contemporary Cookery, (1945–47) Doris Lytton Toye

regular picking. Clumps can be divided in spring or fall. After division in the fall, pot some up and keep indoors or under glass for winter picking. Apart from the usual mauve flowerheads, there are also white-flowering varieties and "Forescate" has pink flowers. "Shepherds Crook" has contorted leaf spikes. They can all be used for culinary purposes. For year-round thick, dark green leaves with a strong flavor, try "Grolau" also known as "Windowsill" because this is exactly where it can be grown though it can also be grown under glass.

When they germinate, Chinese or garlic chives, *Allium tuberosum* look like their onion-flavored cousins but as they mature they develop flatter, broader leaves. The white flowers appear later in dense flat sprays, looking like wild garlic; they too can be eaten and have an aromatic garlic taste. Curiously, they have a scent more reminiscent of roses than garlic.

A good tip is to allow chives to flower and enjoy the individual florets, which taste like tiny scallions. Always make sure to eat before the center starts to darken and dry. Then dig up the clumps, separate them into their individual bulbs, and replant as necessary—you can do this two or three times a year. Try to cut back in rotation so that you always have fresh spikes. If you want them to spread, leave the first flush of flowers on one or two plants to mature. The seeds will be ready for collection when the flowers are paper dry and the small black seeds visible. If you need to thin chives, carefully pull out individual bulbs and harvest like a delicate scallion.

The variety "Cha Cha" was introduced at the 2013 Chelsea Flower Show in England. Instead of flowers it produces mini chive heads that look like miniature hedgehogs.

BELOW: The individual florets of chive flowerheads are easy to separate and delicious scattered over salads.

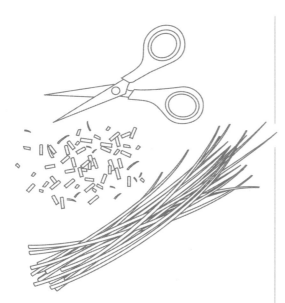

ABOVE: Once a clump of chives has flowered, harvest them and cut them back to the base to encourage new fresh spikes. Wash and use scissors for a fast preparation straight to the plate.

All are rich in sulfur. Chives are a companion plant for carrots, roses, and apples but should not be grown with peas and beans.

CHIVES FOR THE YOUNG GARDENER

Given the right conditions there can be a magic endlessness to chives, which makes them the perfect plant for a child or indeed group of children to hone their horticultural skills. Just follow the general sowing instructions (see p.8) straight into individual pots—the small shiny black seeds should be scattered over the surface and lightly covered.

The pots can be kept on a windowsill for several months before needing repotting, or be grown in a garden container, or planted out in the ground. The young gardener can then harvest the fine trimmings to add the final touches to a host of

TASTING NOTES

Herb bread

Herb bread can be made the same way as garlic bread. Delicious with soup or cheese and salad.

Preparation time: 10 minutes
Cooking time: 5–10 minutes
Serves: 1–2 people

You will need:

· 1 baguette or French loaf

· 2 cloves of crushed garlic (optional)

· ½ tsp salt

· 4oz (100g) soft butter

· Handful of chives, coarsely chopped, plus any or all of the following: chervil, fennel, lovage, marjoram, oregano, parsley, and thyme

Preheat a conventional oven to 400°F (200°C / gas mark 6 / fan 180°C).

Chop the herbs and mix in the with butter.

Make wide diagonal cuts into the loaf and spread garlic butter evenly into each cut. Any leftover butter can be spread along the top of the loaf and spread between cuts.

Wrap in foil and cook for 5 minutes or more. To test whether it is done: the butter will be absorbed into the loaf and the herbs should still be green but hot, almost falling out of the bread.

different dishes including any of their own. The flowerheads are pretty and the individual florets are a gentle introduction to the more forceful taste of scallions.

Lemon verbena
Aloysia citrodora

Common names: Lemon verbena, Herba Louisa

Type: Deciduous shrub

Climate: Half-hardy, unheated glasshouse, mild winter

Size: 10ft (3m)

Origin: Argentina and Chile

History: 17th-century Spanish explorers introduced lemon verbena into Spain from South America where it was named for Princess Louisa of Parma, hence *Herba Louisa*. The word *Aloysia* is actually a corruption of "Louisa."

Cultivation: A tender, small deciduous tree that thrives in dry warmth. Lemon verbena flowers abundantly in regions with a Mediterranean climate. It can be grown outdoors in colder regions, where it is less likely to flower.

Storage: Dry the leaves when flowering, the time of their strongest aroma.

Preparation: The leaves and flowers are not suitable for consumption but are perfect for infusing a sherberty-lemon flavor. Remove before serving,

> GROWING SUGGESTION
>
> Whether in the ground or a pot, make sure you place lemon verbena so that you gently brush past it on a regular basis. The lemon scent is gloriously refreshing.

similar to bay leaves. Pour boiling water over fresh or dried leaves for a tisane. Leave to infuse into syrup to pour over fruit or add to desserts. Add leaves to the base of a cake mixture before baking, then peel off. Add them to a finger bowl when eating seafood.

ABOVE: The flowers of lemon verbena are very similar to those of vervain but only appear in very warm, sheltered situations. Tisanes made from the leaves and flowers are often called lemon vervaine.

> "The only species of this genus known in Britain is *A. citriodora*,
> ... a half-hardy shrub, with panicles of small pinkish-white flowers,
> and very fragrant leaves, which fall off in winter."
>
> *The Ladies Companion to the Flower Garden*, (1846) Mrs. Jane Loudon

Introduced into England in 1784 as *Verbena triphylla*, it was renamed *Aloysia*, then *Lippia citriodora*, and is once more *Aloysia*. Its common name derives from the penetrating lemon scent of its lanceolate shiny leaves that is released without crushing, and verbena-like flowers. In fact, it is the source of verbena oil. Not to be mistaken for *Lippia graveolens*, Mexican oregano, and *L. micromera*, Jamaican oregano, both tender herbs with a distinctive taste of origanum.

Aloysia should be planted in a rich but light soil that is well drained, warm, and sheltered—a south- or west-facing wall is ideal. In colder areas it will grow well in a pot, but keep it virtually unwatered after the leaves drop in fall. It thrives outdoors in English coastal locations such as the Isle of Wight and East Anglia. The parchment-like quality of its

ABOVE: Lemon verbena is gloriously lemon scented. As you brush past, it releases a fragrance that is perfect for a refreshing tisane.

trunk and branches in winter make it hard to believe that it is still alive, but stay confident and you will be rewarded by the sight of the new bright green buds. As the first buds start to swell in late spring, start regular watering and, if necessary, re-pot. It roots well from cuttings of young wood taken in early summer. Be mindful to take these cuttings as early as possible to give them the maximum amount of time for root development before the fall. The newly rooted lemon verbenas will need protection until well established. Prune to shape in early summer and keep the prunings to dry—the glorious lemon scent is wonderful about the house or on barbecues.

HERBS AT NIGHT

SCENT AND SAVOR BY MOONLIGHT

A summer's evening in the garden can be enhanced in several ways. First, an area enclosed by a canopy, trees, climbers, or a courtyard ensures that the warmth lasts and contains the fragrance from scented plants. The senses of sight and smell work closely together, whether in the fading light or by moonlight—silver, white, gray, purple, and pale pink leaves and flowers radiate attractively. There are many herbs that will draw the eye and reward with their scent. At a distance both angelica and burdock add texture to the night vision. Finally, don't forget lemongrass for its mosquito-deterring properties.

DRAWING IN THE EYE

Purple sage is best planted in blocks between paving, among plantings or in pots.

Use "Blue Ice" lavender for attractive mounds with gray-green to silver of the leaves and flowers, adding architectural notes. Plant so that you brush past them to release the scent. Crush leaves around seating as the scent deters insects. Highly scented, mint and its white variegated forms are equally invaluable. Wipe wooden surfaces with leaves to deter flies.

The white mottle-leaved types of nasturtium such as "Alaska" and the pale butter-yellow

BELOW: Nasturtiums will scramble colorfully with a plenitude of edible flowers from late summer until the first frosts.

flowers of the trailing "Moonlight" will gleam at night. Also beautiful in the night garden are the white-flowering forms of chives. You can snip the leaves and flowers of chives to sprinkle over tapas or suppers.

RIGHT: Illustration from *Livre des simples medecines*, 15th century. The medieval style of raised beds is easy to maintain and decorative. Enclosed to represent the garden of Eden, each one was dedicated to one herb, beautiful and useful.

White flowers look stunning swaying in a night breeze. Search for varieties and cultivars that have white-flowering forms such as borage (which you can add to your drinks), chervil (the tiny white flowers gleam like stars and the leaves can be used for garnishing), hyssop, bergamot, and roses. There are also other flowers that should not be forgotten, such as the pinky-white umbels of cilantro, aniseed stars, or summer savory.

REWARDING WITH SCENT

Most herbs have either wafting or lurking scents, one exception being lemon verbena, which has both. When planting make sure the lurking scents are within touching distance.

Wafting scents include the herbs lemon verbena and the flowers of salad arugula. For lurking scents, plant lemon verbena, lavender, chamomile (as a seat or in wall tops or as part of the paving where the foot fall is smallest), pots of variegated scented geraniums, or rosemary, especially if trained against a wall.

LEFT: White-flowered borage has the purest candid hue that gleams in the dark. It will scramble through other plantings and you can harvest the flowers.

Dill
Anethum graveolens

Common names: Dill, dillweed

Type: Annual

Climate: Hardy, average winter

Size: 12–35in (30–90cm)

Origin: Southern Europe

History: The Romans are reputed to have introduced dill across Europe where it has been found as far north as the Scottish Antonine Wall.

Cultivation: There are a wide range of excellent cultivars available; seeds can be sown from spring onward. Dill thrives in well-cultivated, moisture-retentive soil and is tolerant of some shade.

A good tip is not to sow dill to grow near fennel, especially if you want to harvest the seeds, because they will cross to the detriment of both.

Storage: Dry seeds and store in an airtight, sterilized jar; Kilner jars are ideal. Freeze fresh leaves whole and store in a rigid container, then break off as and when you need them. For dill vinegar and oil see p.75.

ABOVE: Sow dill away from fennel. If growing for seeds let the plants mature among herbaceous flowers.

Preparation: Finely chopped dill and potatoes are a good combination. For example, try hot new potatoes with butter and dill, or cold potatoes with dill mayonnaise (see p.39) to accompany cold fish, chicken, and hard-boiled eggs. Potato and dill soup is a favorite. Dill seed is often paired with pickled gherkins or sliced cucumber.

"The seeds of the hearb Dill, bestowed in the earth, in the increase of the Moon, do (for the more part) appear by the fourth day following ... [They] come the better forward, if so be Vine branches or other boughs of trees be burned in the places, where you after mind to bestow the seeds."

The Gardeners Labyrinth, (1577) Thomas Hyll

Gravadlax

Gravadlax is a traditional Nordic dish consisting of raw, cured salmon. As this recipe freezes well, it is worth doubling up the quantities.

Preparation time: 20 minutes plus 2–5 days to marinate
Serves: 8 people

You will need:

· 31¾oz(900g) whole fresh salmon or trout, boned and filleted in two halves

· 1½ tbsp salt

· 1 tbsp granulated sugar

· 1 tsp black peppercorns, crushed

· 1½ tbsp brandy or aquavit

· Handful of fresh dill, chopped

Mix all of the ingredients together, bar the salmon, to make the pickle.

Spread a quarter of the pickle in an earthen-ware dish and lay the first fillet skin-side down onto it, then spread on half of the pickle.

Seal with second fillet and spread the remaining quarter of the pickle over the skin.

Cover with foil and press under a weight (such as a couple of cans or whatever is to hand).

Refrigerate to marinate. Turn and spoon pickle over the fish for 2–5 days.

Carve into thin or thick slices and serve on bread with a dill sauce, with salad, or in scrambled eggs.

Pliny recommended watering the ground with dill water to remove "canker worms." Like so many umbelliferous herbs, dill was originally grown for its seed; over the years the quality of its leaves has been improved. Thomas Hyll in 1577 recommended dressing the dill seedbed with wood ash to provide potash, which encourages flowering and therefore seed production.

Dill is said to derive from the Anglo-Saxon word *dillan* meaning "to lull," both in the sense of a soporific as well as soothing the digestive system and expelling flatulence. It was the key ingredient in baby's gripe or dill water and is still used in gin making. It is a difficult taste to define. Some say it is redolent of aniseed but it is actually smokier and less fragrant. Its flavor complements oily fish and potatoes magnificently (see recipe box), while the seeds are an essential when pickling gherkins or home-grown cucumbers.

If you want dill seeds, use a variety like "Mammoth" and sow it among flowers at the back of the border. The heads are magnificent—a haze of huge greeny-yellow umbels on tall gray-green stems. If space is at a premium then try the more compact, bushy "Bouquet." For dillweed or leaves, sow seeds successively from spring until late summer— "Dukat" is a personal favorite, with a high oil content and aromatic flavor. A commercial recommendation is the more vigorous "Tetra" while "Diana" is more compact and the least likely to bolt to seed.

Dill is a companion plant for cabbages but should not be grown with fennel, carrots, or tomatoes.

Angelica
Angelica archangelica

Common names: Angelica, garden angelica, archangel, wild parsnip

Type: Biennial

Climate: Hardy, very cold winter

Size: 35–47in (90–120cm)

Origin: Northern and Eastern Europe, Central Asia

History: Angelica by name and by nature is blessed with angelic qualities such as protecting against plague and witchcraft. It is an antidote to poisons as well as an aphrodisiac—uses that were revealed by an archangel, hence *archangelica*, though accounts vary as to whether it was Michael or Raphael.

Cultivation: The seeds germinate either when allowed to self-set or when freshly gathered, because they dry on the plant in summer. It is a statuesque green herb with bold foliage and long leaves on hollow footstalks. Angelica can grow to over 5ft (1.5m) tall with a similar spread in its width.

Storage: Seeds are best not stored but sown ripe and fresh. When candied and stored in airtight cans, the young stems can be kept for a year.

Preparation: The flavor and fresh green coloring of home-candied angelica is worth trying. Occasionally the end result can be a hard-boiled candy rather than soft candied stems but fear not, for they are still delicious. Young stems should be used because the older ones become stringy and chewy. Like sweet cicely, angelica is a natural sweetener and small quantities can be stewed with rhubarb to counteract its oxalic acid and sharp taste. The young leaves are delicious when gently torn into strips and tossed into a green salad.

LEFT: Angelica is a statuesque herb that likes its roots in moist soil and can tolerate a small amount of shade. Huge globular flowerheads appear in summer.

ABOVE: If possible, obtain fresh seeds from an angelica plant. Once established there is always a plentiful annual supply.

STRATIFICATION

Stratification breaks a dormancy found in seeds from the temperate regions where winters are cold. The process evolved to protect them from germinating at the wrong season. Stratification is recommended if you have dried seeds for angelica, sweet cicely, sweet woodruff, and violets—all of which self-set easily from the parent plant.

You will need to replicate the winter chill:

The amount of seeds you have forms the 1 part measurement of the following ratio: 4 parts fibrous compost wetted with 1 part water to which you add your 1 part seeds.

Mix all together. Put in a polythene bag which you leave in a *warm* place for 2–3 days.

Put the bag in the bottom of the refrigerator for four weeks. Turn and shake once a week.

The seeds should now be ready for sowing and germinating, preferably in early spring.

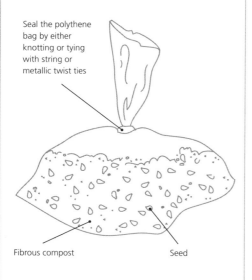

Seal the polythene bag by either knotting or tying with string or metallic twist ties

Fibrous compost   Seed

"Sucket candy" was the old word for candied orange and lemon peel that began in Southern Europe from the 16th century. Young angelica stalks, borage, and eringo roots were also candied. They were either kept in their syrup as wet sucket or dried on paper strewn with sugar. They would be set out at banquets or as refreshments for visitors. Angelica is one of the traditional aromatics in Chartreuse and Vermouth and is long associated with decorating cakes and cold cream desserts.

It likes to have its roots in moisture-retentive soil and looks best when allowed plenty of space. In the second year, the central stem rises up to support a magnificent globular green umbel. If you cannot harvest fresh seeds, it is often better to buy a plant or ensure that you give packeted seeds a period of stratification, i.e. expose to winter cold (see box).

In a small area, the large architectural leaves and seed heads of angelica add a bold touch of the jungle even when planted alone. Space permitting, mix with the similarly dramatic lovage, sweet cicely, eau-de-cologne mint, and even bergamot. Surround with spiky flowering plants in a border if seeking contrast. As angelica grows generously, there are plenty of opportunities to sample its evolving stages of taste. The young leaves are refreshing in salad. However, as they mature they become less appetizing raw and their flavoring role in many alcoholic drinks becomes more prominent. Coarsely tear mature leaves into Pimms and other summer drinks, not necessarily alcoholic. The fresh seeds can also be used for alcoholic cordials (see p.184). Last but not least, the large leaves make delightful fresh plates for picnic food.

FINES HERBES

DELICATE SOPHISTICATION

Historically the term *fines herbes* is closely associated with the preparation of mushrooms and was originally used to describe a sauce of sautéed mushrooms, shallots, and herbs that is now known as *duxelles*. The key *fines herbes* are a handful of chervil, chives, French tarragon, and parsley, whose combination infuses a subtle but gloriously fresh taste of aniseed, mild onion, and parsley.

As the name suggests, these are delicate herbs and the leaves should be young enough simply to melt in the mouth. They are the flavors of spring and summer, not to be lost or wasted on long cooking but folded in at the last moment, simply sprinkled on broiled fish or chicken or as a garnish. They are the perfect complement to the delicate sophistication of light cream soups or Dover sole. An omelette *aux fines herbes*, crusty bread, a green salad, and a glass of wine has to be one of the simplest and most enjoyable of dinners. Always remember to sprinkle the herbs just before you fold the omelette, while its center is still soft.

One way of encapsulating the flavor of *fines herbes* is to add them to pastry dough, which seals in their freshness. For example, use for quiches where they will sit comfortably with any savory filling. Put them in good olive oil to steep, then drizzle over potatoes, pizza, or pasta to ensure that fragrant freshness—only make sufficient quantity for a few days. The golden rule is to stick with fine, young pickings.

ABOVE: The fines herbes are the young leaves of parsley, chives, French tarragon, and chervil—a delicate tasting combination that lifts almost any savory dish.

However, recipe rules are there to be broken, so widen the flavors by ringing the changes with young basil, chives, and parsley leaves, with a few shavings of garlic or snipped garlic chives, in tomato-based dishes. For a scented, aromatic effect, combine sweet marjoram, lemon thyme, parsley, and chives with zucchinis or chicken breasts. In fish and seafood salads, mix fennel and parsley leaves with a twist of finely chopped lemon peel. Equal quantities of the finely chopped leaves of parsley, dill, cilantro, and basil are delicious forked through hot basmati rice.

Summer is a time when you want quick and easy meals without sacrificing good tastes—*fines herbes* provide the perfect fast-food ingredients.

A DEDICATED PLOT

Chervil, chives, French tarragon, and parsley can be grown together to good effect. All thrive in good fertile soil and sheltered conditions. Simply put one to five French tarragons in the center and edge the bed with chives—the parsley can be grown closely behind the edging of chives and the chervil scattered around the French tarragon. The minimum sized plot based on one or two French tarragons would need to be 3 feet square. To ensure good supplies this could be decanted down into three large pots, each one with a central French tarragon plus either chervil, chives, or parsley around each tarragon.

Buy plants of French tarragon and chives to set out, then scatter sow both parsley and chervil, and then thin out according to space and picking. Closely spaced in a planter they would all benefit from an occasional feed with a seaweed-based fertilizer.

BELOW: Allow sufficient space for French tarragon and chives to clump up, as well as the parsley, as it matures. Chervil is short lived so can be sown as a catch crop among the other herbs.

TASTING NOTES

Fines herbes mayonnaise

Making your own mayonnaise could not be easier, though you will need an electric whisk or food processor

Preparation time: 10 minutes
Serves: 10 people

You will need:

• 1 egg

• 1 tbsp white wine vinegar or cider vinegar

• 1 tsp Dijon mustard

• ½ pint olive or sunflower oil

• Handful of *Fines herbes*, coarsely chopped

Whisk the egg, vinegar, and mustard together in a Pyrex jug.

Hold with one hand and with the other trickle in the oil, then fold in the *fines herbes*.

Keep in a sterilized, sealed jar in the refrigerator for up to a week.

Chervil behind French tarragon; space about 4in apart

French tarragon in the center; space about 6in apart

Parsley behind the chives; can be closely spaced but 3–4in apart is fine

Chives at the front edge; can be squeezed together every inch or so

Chervil

Anthriscus cerefolium

Common names: Chervil, curled chervil, garden chervil, French parsley

Type: Annual

Climate: Hardy, average winter

Size: 12–24in (30–60cm)

Origin: Europe, North Africa, West Asia

History: Introduced by the Romans who used chervil as a pot herb and relish. Dioscorides recommended it to improve the belly, stomach, kidneys, and liver.

Cultivation: Chervil's rapid and early growth, and hardiness made it a valuable source of green food through much of the winter.

Sow from spring into well-prepared, moisture-retentive soil in a semishaded position. Chervil does not respond well to transplanting. As it goes to seed quickly, it is worth sowing successively, ensuring that a new generation is ready as another sets seed.

The young leaves of chervil look like those of cow parsley, which is poisonous. However, there are two key differences: first, chervil is smoother and greener; second, when you crush the leaves, they have the unmistakable savor of aniseed.

Storage: Freeze and break off pieces as needed. Fresh stems will keep for up to two weeks in a plastic bag or box in a refrigerator.

Preparation: One of the *fines herbes* (see pp.38–39), chervil is excellent with mushrooms or folded into an omelette or mayonnaise. It is best used fresh to fully savor the subtlety of its gentle aniseed flavor and to benefit from its antioxidants. Like dill, its flavor combines well with new potatoes. Scatter chervil leaves in a green salad where they add textural interest and refreshing savor. The tiny leaves are perfect for decorating hors d'oeuvres or appetizers. A tisane of fresh leaves is recommended to reduce the inflammation associated with headache, sinusitis, peptic ulcer, and infections.

LEFT: Dioscorides was a Greek military physician to the Roman army who noted over 600 plants and their uses. Recorded as *De Materia Medica*, his writings are still of relevance. He is seen here in discussion with a student.

ABOVE: Chervil is a prolific self-seeder. Allow new seedlings to develop naturally and pull up or transplant any that are in the wrong place.

TASTING NOTES

Herb butter

British author Roald Dahl describes in his book *Memories with Food* how he had eaten this version of herb butter with lobster in Galway Bay in Ireland.

Preparation time: 10 minutes
Serves: 6–8 people

You will need:

• 2 handfuls of fresh herbs (equal quantities of chervil, chives, and basil), chopped

• 2 tsp lemon juice

• 4oz (120g) unsalted butter, cubed

Add the herbs, lemon juice, and butter together in a pan. Heat gently.

Pour over lobster. (Delicious on any fish with the same firm flesh such as prawns or crab legs)

Chervil was acclaimed for its medicinal qualities including a remedy for bad dreams, burns, and stomach upsets. The turnip-rooted chervil, clearly illustrated in the *Apuleius Platonicus Herbarium* c. 1070–1100, has now been lost to cultivation but was much prized for candying and, when boiled, in salads. The modern chervil has small roots topped by delicate green lacy leaves that take on a pinkish tinge; the white flowers form umbels.

Chervil can reach maturity in six weeks, so in this respect it is more an ephemeral rather than an annual herb. Once established, generations of chervil will self-set throughout the growing season, providing seedlings and plants almost year round. Fresh seeds germinate in less than two weeks. It is worth doing a late summer sowing in a cold frame or glasshouse for winter supplies. It can be grown in pots but is better in boxes or larger containers. Seedlings will overwinter in temperate climates where they die back to a rosette and resume growth once the soil warms up. Fresh leaves are usually available from early spring through to heavy frosts. Always pick the outer leaves first. The richer the soil the more leaves you will harvest. The darker green foliaged "Vertissimo" is slower to go to seed and ideal for sowing in the fall.

Greater burdock
Arctium lappa

Common names: Burdock, lappa, Beggars Buttons, flapper-bags

Type: Biennial

Climate: Very hardy

Size: 5ft (1.5m)

Origin: Eurasia

History: The Latin and common names are a complex explanation of its habits: the roughness of the seeds in *Arctium* from the Greek *arktos* for "bear" with *lappa* meaning "to seize." "Bur" probably derived from the Latin *burra* for "a lock of wool"—a frequent sight on the plant where sheep are grazing. "Dock" refers to its large leaves.

Cultivation: Seeds can be sown in the spring or fall. Burdock is best grown in a semiwild part of the garden because its very stout tap-roots make it difficult to move. It has a handsome downy appearance.

A word of caution for the gardener: the burrs from burdock vigorously attach themselves to you and work their way around your clothing— under the arms and between the legs being especially popular. Check before sitting down and try to detach them.

Storage: Burdock roots will survive in the ground but the traditional storage is to brew them, often with dandelion roots.

Preparation: Harvest roots, wash thoroughly and slice. Then combine with Dandelion roots to add to vegetable broth or make root beer.

Burdock is a thuggish plant. It takes up plenty of space and its burrs or seed cases are armed with hooks that are tenacious in the extreme. The infirm in the Dioscorides quote (see right) would have been helped by the fact that burdock increases the flow of urine and perspiration as well as purifying the blood and improving skin conditions. Shakespeare used the symbolism of its unwelcome and antisocial tenacity in several plays.

ABOVE: The leaves, shoots, and roots of burdock are all edible and were prized for their health-giving qualities. The Japanese call it "gobo" and have an array of wonderful improved varieties.

NUTRITION

The roots of burdock are an excellent source of fiber, vitamin B, and minerals.

The French name *herbe aux teigneux* or "scurvy grass" relates to the fact that the leaves were historically used as a poultice on certain kinds of sores. A refreshing tisane can be made from the young leaves; it stimulates digestion and soothes inflammations of the stomach. In Scotland, the young shoots and peeled roots were prepared and eaten like salsify.

Burdock will freely self-seed. The seedling leaves are easily recognized and should either be moved or weeded out at this stage. A somewhat neglected herb, its history and potential are worth the challenge, especially with Japanese cultivars.

When it comes to interesting varieties, Japanese gobo, or Japanese edible burdock, "Gobo" as it is also known, is grown primarily for its esculent leaves. The roots are tenderer than the type and are similar to parsnips. The best varieties of gobo for roots are the light pink-brown early "Salada Musume," whose roots grow to 12in or more. The late-season and most popular Japanese variety is "Takinogawa," which has the best flavor. Another precocious variety is "Watanabe Early," which has tender roots.

Store Japanese gobo roots in soil or sand. Wash and peel at the last minute or put in vinegar until you are ready to use them, as they discolor quickly. Cut into strips for tempura and stir-fries.

> "Take four pennyweight of the seed of this wort and kernels out of pine tree nuts, pound together as thou wouldst work a dumpling, give it to the infirm to swallow; it healeth him."
>
> *De Materia Medica*, (c. AD 40) **Pedanius Dioscorides**

LEFT: Burdock's reputation as a thuggish herb in Europe lies in its strong taproot and burred seed heads that catch the gardener unawares.

MEDIEVAL HERBS

A PARADISE OF BEAUTY AND UTILITY

The so-called Middle Ages in Europe span the time between the fall of the Roman Empire and the arrival of what is now known as the Renaissance, effectively AD 400–1400. Late or high medieval gardens were herb gardens or *herbers* that developed into places of scent and savor in which to listen to music, discuss politics, make love, sew, and weave. In fact, dancing in light leather shoes on newly planted chamomile lawns was recommended to help them establish.

Key food plants including herbs were grown as crops in fields. The *herbers* were a series of garden spaces with square and rectangular raised beds, typically placed under windows and easy to replicate in more modern settings.

What was known as a *hortus conclusus* was enclosed by walls or trellis over and around which

BELOW: Painting titled *Master of the Frankfurt Paradiesgärtlein*, dated c. 1410. The medieval garden effectively only grew herbs and its enclosure recalled the garden of Eden.

ABOVE: The serpolet or creeping thyme was prized medicinally, while the more bushy common and lemon thymes provided almost year-round flavoring.

Alba, Gallica, and Damask roses and rosemary could be trained. The sweet scents and green perfection recreated Paradise or the lost Garden of Eden with an ornamental well or pool to represent the font of life. Raised turf seats were planted up with living scented herbs such as chamomile or thyme that released a pleasing fragrance as you sat. Underfoot fine grasses were planted every third or fourth year, interspersed with chamomile, marjorams, thymes, and violets to create a flowery mead. This might be constructed from brick or timber, often with a canopy overhead.

Unusual and tender herbs such as rosemary and lavender were also grown in containers and clipped into simple topiary. The medieval herb garden was a peaceable sanctuary working with nature rather than trying to control it. Today we have readily available markets for all our food needs that more than replace medieval food crops, but we can still enjoy the zests and scents of their favorite herbs.

DESIGNING A MEDIEVAL HERB GARDEN

Medieval trellis	Roses "Maiden's Blush," "Blush Damask"; common rosemary cut and trained in full sun, possibly with hyssop.
Medieval seat	In full sun, plant with creeping and cushion-forming lemon thymes; in shade, flowering chamomile—single or double.
	Around the edges where you are not going to sit, green sage and hyssop add texture and scent.
	The seat can be flanked by one or two raised flowerbeds in which a wider range of culinary herbs and flowers can be grown.
Flowery mead	You can walk across the mead but keep this to a minimum, especially if you want to pick the leaves and flowers for cooking. One way is to create a canvas of grass, bark, or gravel into which you can introduce herbs such as marjoram, thyme, winter savory, vervain, violets, and sweet woodruff. Let them flower and spread to soften the effect.
Medieval herbs	Any herb in this book except bergamot, lemon verbena, turmeric, lemongrass, scented geraniums, perilla, and ginger.

Horseradish
Armoracia rusticana

Common names: Horseradish, mountain radish, great raifort, red cole

Type: Perennial root, treated like an annual

Climate: Very hardy

Size: 12in–4ft (30cm–1.2m)

Origin: Eastern Europe

History: The date of horseradish introduction into Northern Europe is unknown but it was growing wild in northern England by the mid-16th century.

Cultivation: Horseradish thrives a soil rich in potash. Roots are the main reason for growing this plant and root crowns need to be dug up. If left in the ground in a warm, sheltered spot, horseradish will produce white flowers on long stems in early summer; more success has been had with these than good-sized roots. Prepare trenches and lay the sets horizontally, with the head (larger end) slightly raised. Cover with 6–8in of soil. This should form a 12–24in ridge. Once the leaves appear, mulch with a rich compost. The set will sucker as it grows. Left to its own devices, horseradish is a tenacious weed (for thuggish herbs, seee p.22).

Storage: Like oysters, the Illinois growers advise harvesting during any month with an "r" in it after October. Horseradish roots can be stored in a traditional clamp or left in the ground. Prepared horseradish will keep 4–6 weeks in the refrigerator and 6 months plus in the freezer.

Preparation: When grinding or grating fresh horseradish roots stand by a window or outside—its pungent aroma can be ferocious. Handling the root under vinegar helps too. Wash your hands after handling. Add to whipped cream or mayonnaise or mustard as a sauce for beef, smoked meats, fish, and tomatoes. Grate small amounts into coleslaw or smoked mackerel paté.

LEFT: If left in the ground horseradish will produce white flowers on long stems in early summer. The flowers have a pleasant light horseradish flavor, and they are delicious in salads or as a decoration for smoked mackerel.

The flowers have a pleasant light horseradish flavor and they are delicious in salads or as a decoration for smoked fish such as mackerel or halibut.

The former generic name for horseradish was *Cochlearia armoracia*, derived from the Latin *cochlear*, meaning "a spoon," which is a reference to the bowl shape of its basal leaves. The Romans used a similar plant that they called *armoracia*, which according to the Delphic Oracle was worth its weight in gold. Gerard was the first to call it horseradish; the German *meerettich* translates as "sea radish" and the French *raifort* as "strong root." It is a traditional condiment at both Jewish Passover and Eastern European Easter feasts. The first pioneers took it to the Americas in the late 17th century. Today, Collinsville in Illinois, USA, is known as the Horseradish Capital of the World. Its surrounding area produces some 85 percent of the world's production, and its biggest customers are Germany and China. There is an annual Horseradish Festival on the first weekend in June. *Wasabia japonica*, the Japanese *wasabi*, is closely related and due to its scarcity, horseradish is being increasingly used as a substitute.

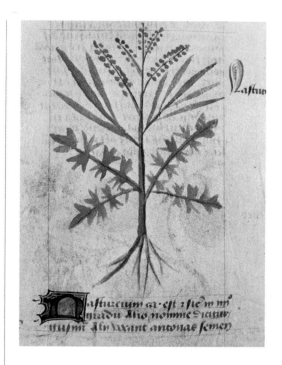

ABOVE: An illustration of horseradish from the *Tractatus de Herbis*, a treatise of medicinal plants painted in 1440.

NUTRITION

Rich in vitamin C, horseradish has both vital and essential minerals such as potassium, calcium, magnesium, and phosphorus. It also contains vitamin B6, riboflavin, niacin, pantothenic acid, and mustard oil.

The primary root is the most important part of this plant, so to encourage it to develop remove all but one or two of the leaf shoots at the top of the root as they develop. When you lift the crown, keep the side roots for sets for possible replanting. Ideally, it requires a long growing season with high temperatures through the summer, hence the need for potash, commonly known as artificial sunlight as it has the same beneficial effects. This then needs to be followed by a drop in the temperature in late summer and the fall to enhance root development. There is also an attractive variegated form, "Variegata."

Tarragon
Artemisia dracunculus

Common names: Tarragon, French tarragon, *estragon*

Type: Herbaceous perennial

Climate: Hardy, average winter

Size: 18–24in (45–60cm)

Origin: Southeast Russia

History: The *Artemisia* genus named after Artemis, the goddess of chastity, includes mugwort, *A. vulgaris*, a popular brewing herb before the introduction of hops into Britain, and wormwood, *A.absinthium*, the classic flavoring for vermouths and absinthe.

Cultivation: True French tarragon is sterile and does not set seeds. It thrives in a well-drained soil or terracotta pot with a good source of light but not full summer sun. When it dies back in the winter it is essential that it does not become waterlogged.

RIGHT: Ensure you buy French tarragon. The Russian variety can be raised from seed, is tasteless and a thug. The French is incomparably the best and only culinary tarragon. Here tarragon (left) is pictured growing beside Lords-and-Ladies (*Arum*) (right).

> "Tarragon, Draco Herba, of Spanish Extraction; hot and spicy: The Tops and young Shoots, like those of Rocket [Arugula], never to be secluded in our Composition, especially where there is much Lettuce. 'Tis highly cordial and friend to the Head, Heart, and Liver, correcting the weakness of the Ventricle."
>
> *Acetaria: A Discourse of Sallets*, (1699) John Evelyn

Storage: Add sprigs or leaves to white wine vinegar, to which it imparts a smoky, aniseed flavor (also for oil, see p.75). Tarragon freezes and dries well; break off as needed.

Preparation: The fresh and cooked flavors of tarragon leaves are very different; the former is almost lemony in its aniseed taste but when cooked it takes on and imparts a more sophisticated, almost smoky, aroma. This is what gives the classic Béarnaise sauce its distinctive flavor.

Young stems and whole leaves can be placed under the skin when roasting or boiling chicken. Chop leaves into mayonnaise or vinaigrette to serve with fish, especially monkfish or salmon, and it is good with eggs and omelettes. Tomato juice or cold summer soups are transformed by the addition of finely chopped tarragon leaves.

LEFT: Tarragon is a woody-based, upright perennial with narrowly lance-shaped, aromatic leaves and small, nodding, pale yellow flowerheads in late summer.

THOMAS JEFFERSON AND FRENCH TARRAGON

Thomas Jefferson enjoyed the subtleties of French tarragon during his stay in Paris from 1784–89. In a letter dated March 10, 1793, he notes that it was little known in America. It was April 30, 1806, before the Philadelphia nurseryman Bernard McMahon dispatched him some roots to grow at his home in Monticello in Virginia. His first crop failed but by 1812 French tarragon was well established. Jefferson produced his own *vinaigre d'estragon* by infusing three pints of vinegar with a quarter of partially dried tarragon leaves. After one week it was strained, bottled, and then corked for storage.

TASTING NOTES

Avoid Russian tarragon

Ensure you grow the true French tarragon and not its close relation, Russian tarragon, subsp. *dranunculoides*. The latter is raised from seed and will be the variety marketed simply as tarragon. Apart from the hot, dry, indifferent taste of its slightly jagged leaves, it is a garden thug with vigorous runners and because it flowers profusely, it also self-seeds with similar enthusiasm. In many respects, it looks more like its wild cousin the mugwort, *A. vulgaris*. The leaves of French tarragon are smoother with a characteristic smoky, aniseed flavor.

French tarragon's specific name *dracunculus* translates as "a small dragon," one of several "dragon" herbs that were believed to cure the bites and stings of venomous beasts and mad dogs. In cooking, it is commonly known by its French name, *estragon*, as in the classic French dish *poulet à l'estragon*. Only the leaves are used and have been since the Middle Ages for vinegar, piquant or white sauces, as well as being one of the classic *fines herbes*. Its sophisticated flavor means that French tarragon is essential in the repertoire of haute-cuisine and cordon bleu cooking.

To propagate, take tip cuttings from new growth as early as possible in order to ensure good rooting before the fall. Divide the roots of well-established plants in late spring.

Orach
Atriplex hortensis

Common names: Orach, mountain spinach, arrach

Type: Annual

Climate: Hardy, cold winter

Size: 24in–3½ft (60cm–1m)

Origin: Asia

BELOW: Apart from green there are striking red forms, such as the deep red var. *rubra*, which can be grown among flowers. Coastal varieties are more succulent.

History: The Romans noted that only cultivated varieties should be eaten. According to Pliny, wild forms could cause "dropsy, jaundice, and pallor." The leaves were cooked with meat and eaten raw.

Cultivation: Although tolerant of both high salinity and alkalinity, to ensure succulent leaves, sow direct into a rich moisture-retentive soil from spring onward, thinning along drills spaced at 24in. This can be repeated until late summer.

Storage: It is not worth storing orach; just save seeds for next year's crop.

Preparation: Orach is traditionally cooked with sorrel to counteract its acidity, and they are useful in combination for white sauces served with fish. If tender, use purple orach leaves (var. *rubra*) for a more decorative dish. Use only fresh young leaves for salads.

Hyll in *The Gardener's Labyrinth* (1577) suggested sowing in a "wel dressed and dunged earth" in December. If the soil is not frozen it would be interesting to experiment. Orach lost its popularity in Europe with the introduction of spinach in the 17th century.

The white-and-pale green-leaved varieties are the more tender, but for ornamental effect look for red- or pink-tinged varieties, such as var. *rubra*. Pinch out the tops to stop flowering. In dry weather, orach bolts rapidly and has an unpleasant taste. If you only want occasional pickings, grow as colorful border plants in rich soil and harvest fresh young leaves.

There are closely related coastal varieties that still grow wild in the UK, especially southwest Scotland, such as the spear or halberd-leaved orach, *A. prostrata* syn. *A. hastata*; frosted orach, *A. laciniata*; and Babbingtons orach, *A. glabriuscula*. They are found on and above the high tide line, typically in decomposing seaweed bands— replicating this might prove challenging if you live inland. The young leaves are succulent and salty, hence their American name of sea purslane, and are at their crunchy best at first and second rough leaf stage. Older leaves can be stripped from the stems and treated like spinach. Mark Williams of Galloway Wild Foods recommends mixing them with smoked haddock in a tart, wilted over monkfish, and with wild mushrooms. Away from the coast, *A. patula* is known in Scotland as common or inland orach.

ABOVE: The orach plant goes to seed quite readily. Its seeds should be saved for the next crop, air dried, and stored in a paper bag in a cool, dry place.

EDIBLE HERB FLOWERS

A BOUQUET GARNI OF BLOSSOMS

There are Chinese recipes for flowers as food dating back to 3000 BC. Roman cooks and writers such as Apicius used rose petals, lavender florets, and violets. Herb flower shapes and colors give texture and fragrance to the garden and to food. Edible flowers can be arranged in an "ice" plate on which you serve cold food and this is a good way of keeping the dish cool and making it attractive. Line a dish with water and submerge all or any of the herb flowers listed, freeze until thoroughly frozen to preserve, then remove from the freezer and arrange on food just before serving.

BASIL

The flower colors range from white to striated purple, depending on the variety. They also have more intense flavors than the leaves. Slice large tomatoes or put cherry tomatoes in a ramekin, then cover with basil flowers and olive oil. Bake in a hot oven for 10 minutes to infuse flavors. Also good when crystallized (see box on p.59).

ONE DO AND ONE DON'T

Do   Pick the flowers early when the dew has dried but before the bees start to forage. Freshly picked, they can be stored in an airtight plastic container in a cool place until needed.

Don't   Avoid adding flowers to the salad before dressing it, as the oils and vinegars spoil their bloom; sprinkle them over at the last moment.

BERGAMOT

The flowers can be gently infused in milk where they will impart a lightly scented orange flavor. Sprinkle over fruit salads.

BORAGE

Its sky-blue star flowers with fine black centers make them one of the prettiest to use. Flowering sprigs can be added to gin and tonic or pitchers of Pimms, sparkling elderflower, or simply water.

If you want to use the flowers in green or fruit salads, they taste best if you remove the hairy sepals, which come away easily when the flower is ready. The best way to achieve this is

LEFT: The influence of the Roman cook and writer Apicius continues. This image shows a kitchen of delights featured in a 1709 version of his recipes.

to hold the flower stem and then gently pinch the center and lift the flower off.

One time-consuming suggestion is to put the flowers in ice cubes. To do this effectively, you need to half fill the sections of an ice cube tray with water and allow each flower to float on top and place in the freezer. Once the cubes have started to freeze, top up with water and freeze again. That way you achieve a centrally placed flower. They can also be crystallized for cakes (see box on p.59).

CALENDULA

This is a herb defined by its flowers. The whole marigold flowerhead has been used as a poor man's saffron and you are better off using turmeric or the real thing. However, the golden petals sprinkled through salads make great eye candy. They can also be baked in bread.

CHAMOMILE

The flowers are the only culinary part of this herb, noted especially for their use in relaxing tisanes.

CHIVES

The best tasting *Allium* flowers are those of chives, whether purple, pink, or white with tiny firm opalescent onions at their centers.

Firmly holding the flowerhead in your hand, twist at the base and the florets will all separate. Sprinkle in salads for a delicious mild crunchy scallion taste.

Pick when young. You can tell at a glance if they are passed their best as the central florets will have darkened in color and look shriveled, and the taste will be harsh, dry, and hot.

BELOW: Marigold petals, such as the pictured *Calendula officinalis*, can be used to run red gold through salads, rice, and fruit dishes, imparting a subtle, herby flavor.

CORIANDER SEEDS

The underlying orange peel taste of the seeds is more distinct in the fresh creamy white flowers, so use them to decorate sweet orange salads or sauces. Also add to stir-fries.

DANDELION

The shaggy yellow flowerheads of dandelions are a popular sight in moist meadows or in orchards and make an excellent traditional wine.

DILL

If you find the flavor of the seeds too strong the flowers are a good, more fragrant substitute.

ELDERFLOWERS

They impart a fragrant, muscat scent and flavor with a multitude of uses.

Cut off the green stems holding the umbels and discard.

Elderflower sorbet is a personal favorite, along with elderflower cordial and champagne.

They are usually in flower when gooseberries are ripe. Harvest them together and put elderflower heads at the base of pies and cobblers or gently cook with the fruit before making fruit fools and creams. Delightful crystallized (see box on p.59).

FENNEL

Ordinary sweet fennel produces much better flowers than its bronze cousin. A great snack for the gardener, the flower clusters are a clear saffron yellow with a clean, refreshing aniseed flavor. They make a pleasant and unexpected zing in green salads but are at their best when used to decorate lemon desserts—a magically flavorsome marriage. Delightful crystallized (see box on p.59).

BELOW: Pick and brew dandelion flowers not least to stop them setting their featherlight "clocks" into flight, which are of no culinary use and produce thuggish quantities of new plants.

BELOW: The muscat scent imparted into cordials, wines, and champagnes by elderflowers makes it one of the most sophisticated home-brews. You can also let some flowerheads develop into the elderberries for later use in the fall.

HORSERADISH

The small white flowers and top stems of the horseradish are used in Japanese salads and garnishes. They are delicate in appearance, a quality which is echoed in their light horseradish flavor.

HYSSOP

The fragrant and strongly aromatic flowerheads of hyssop are best used as an infusion in syrup for fruit desserts such as apricot or peach pies. They can also be left to dry in superfine sugar where they will impart their scent; extract the hyssop before using the sugar. Delightful crystallized (see box on p.59).

LAVENDER

Pick the flowerheads in the late morning when they are dry and their aromatic oils are warm and scented.

Layer flowerheads in superfine sugar, then use for creams, ice creams, and cakes. Delightful crystallized (see box on p.59).

One of the more unusual uses for lavender flowers is recommended by Jerry Traunfeld in *The Herbfarm Cookbook* (2000) where he adds 1½ tablespoons of fresh lavender buds to 2 pounds of plums in his "Plum and Lavender Chutney."

LEMON BALM

Flowers can be used to flavor sugars or syrups. They have a less intense lemon flavor than the leaves.

MINT

Crystallized mint flowers are ideal as a garnish for mint-infused chocolate desserts or mint sorbet (see box on p.59).

The perfumed flowers of the Eau-de-Cologne (*Mentha × piperata* f. *citrata*) mint give visual and taste contrasts with fresh strawberries.

NASTURTIUM

Nasturtium flowers come in a riot of colors and their peppery taste makes them both attractive and tasty in salads.

A word of caution: check the pointed end of the flower, its "hood," because it is a popular resting place for earwigs who may well crawl out into the salad—extra protein you can do without!

OREGANO AND MARJORAM

The flowers of both marjoram and oregano are aromatic, ideal in summer barbecues or used in marinades. Both make fragrant tisanes.

PERILLA

Add the flower stems to stir-fries. Like basil, the flowers of perilla pack a bigger punch than the leaves.

ROSE

The primary object of using rose petals is for their scent. However, they can provide color in green and fruit salads. They can be crystallized (see box on p.59) and mixed into jams, jellies, and conserves.

ROSEMARY

When in flower, the leaves of rosemary have a more fragrant taste. Many flower in late winter and early spring when other herb flowers are in short supply.

Infuse flowering sprigs in white wine with redcurrants before gently cooking and use as a base for syllabub. They can also be placed under

Constant pinching out as soon as the plant starts to grow again in spring helps many herbs to stay compact and bushy, and encourages the plant to keep producing lots of fresh new leaves, rather than going to flower, after which the leaves can lose their fresh appearance.

PINCHING BACK AND PRUNING

After flowering a plant will start to set seed, which in some cases you may want to prevent. To encourage good amounts of leaves on mint, thyme, sage, oregano, and marjoram, pinch out the flowers as they start to form.

Most gardeners want a successional supply of chive spears but the flowers are both decorative and delicious. Once the flowers are harvested, cut the clump back to the ground to encourage new spears—on fertile, moisture-retentive soil you can do this several times each year.

Many woody herbs flower from spring into summer. Pruning after they have flowered will give new shoots a chance to ripen and harden before the winter. The general rule of pruning after flowering is a good one to follow.

---

lamb when roasting, chopped finely over sliced tomato salads and pizza, or liberally mixed with garlic and added to sausagemeat for a Christmas stuffing. The flowers are delightful when crystallized for winter decorations (see box on p.59).

SAGE

The clear blue flowers of green or purple sage should be gently separated from the plant and scattered through salads. Alternatively, fill small, cored dessert apples with a mixture of finely chopped sage flowerheads and onions, and roast alongside pork for the last 45 minutes.

ARUGULA

The creamy yellow, nutty-tasting flowers and flowerbuds of arugula are often overlooked. They make a delicious addition to salads or over pasta, and they are also delicious for the grazing gardener! They exude a sweet scent at night.

RIGHT: Rose petals, such as this form of the French rose *Rosa gallica*, give luxurious appeal to fruits and cups. The scent imparted into jams and jellies is truly rose-tinted.

SWEET WOODRUFF

The flowering stems are delicious infused in white wines, especially to pour over strawberries. (See the main entry on p.95 for recipes.)

BELOW: The flowering stems of sweet woodruff should be dried for a couple of hours before steeping in drinks and food to maximize their scent.

THYME

The flowers of soft-leaved thymes such as "Silver Posie" can be scattered in salads or in with new potatoes. Any of the flowers of the lemon-scented thymes are excellent cooked with chicken or folded into chicken-based salads.

VIOLET

In early spring, the new flowers of violet, purple and white, have a crisp crunchiness with an aftertaste of violet creams. They are good in salads, and delightful fresh or crystallized (see box) over cakes and desserts or among chocolates.

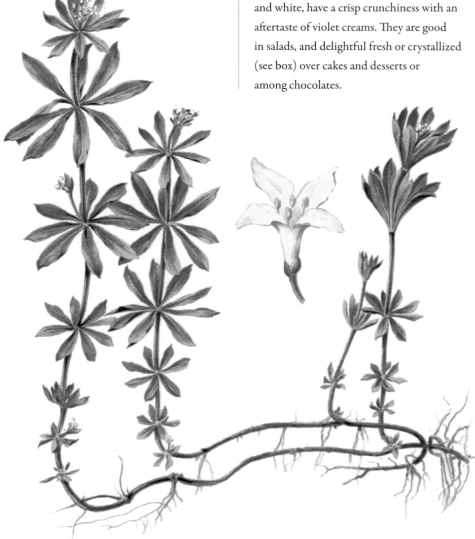

Crystallizing flowers

Armed with a small paintbrush both methods can be done at a garden table in dappled shade. Pick the flowers when dry from dew and check for insects—it goes without saying ensure that they have not been sprayed.

Quantities depend on how many flowers and spare time you have. The first method gives a greater impression of sugar coating, the second has a lighter more sparkling result.

METHOD 1

You will need:

• Handful of petals and flowers

• 1 egg, whites only

• Superfine sugar, for dipping

Lightly beat an egg white.

Thoroughly brush over petals and flowers and dip in superfine sugar.

Place to dry on a rack in a warm place until crisp and dry.

Store in layers separated by parchment paper in an airtight tin. Use within a few days.

METHOD 2

You will need:

• Handful of petals and flowers

• 1 tsp Gum Arabic

• 0.8 fl oz (25ml) rose or orangeflower water

• Superfine sugar, for dipping

Dissolve a teaspoonful of Gum Arabic in rose or orangeflower water. Use it to carefully paint each petal or flower and coat with superfine sugar.

Place to dry on a rack in a warm place until dry and crisp.

Store in layers separated by parchment paper in an airtight tin. They will keep for several months.

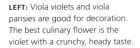

LEFT: Viola violets and viola pansies are good for decoration. The best culinary flower is the violet with a crunchy, heady taste.

Borage
Borago officinalis

Common names: Borage, bee borage, bee bread, cool tankard, star flower

Type: Leaf, flowers, annual

Climate: Hardy, average winter

Size: 27½–40in (70–100cm)

Origin: Europe

History: The Romans infused borage flowers and young leaves in wine to relieve depression and induce a euphoric state of mind. The Celtic name *bourrach* can be translated as "glad courage."

OLYMPIAN HERB

The captain of the British team at the Culinary Olympics and chef of The Elephant Restaurant, Torquay, Simon Hulstone recommends growing and using borage in its entirety—stems, leaves, and flowers—for flavor and presentation. It is important for his hallmark seafood dishes and he also adds it to cocktails.

Cultivation: Sow seeds direct in well-drained soil in spring and place in dappled shade. Transplant at second rough leaf stage, and plant out at 12–24in spacings.

As borage flowers are best when viewed from below, sow or plant on a moisture-retentive slope, if possible. Sow in drifts—both blue and white forms alongside purple, red, and white bergamot. In 1933, the American herb gardener Helen Fox suggested mixing the seeds of borage with calendula and nigella to create a flowery tapestry. Both ideas would be highly informal or "naturalistic" and possibly bordering on the untidy if not well managed. They would not suit the strict lines of a formal herb garden.

Storage: Store as crystallized flowers (see p.59) and in ice cubes. For flavoring, create borage flower and leaf vinegar (see p.75).

Preparation: The chopped leaves are a traditional component for stuffing ravioli. Borage leaves have found renewed favor in contemporary recipes: served raw with cooked fish and with pasta. Dipped in batter, deep fried and sprinkled with sugar, the leaves make a sweet fritter. The flowers and stems can be added to drinks: when crushed and added to summer refreshments like gin and tonic or Pimms, they impart a light cucumber flavor. The flowers have a taste of honey and slight crispness; they are good for decorating salads and desserts; lift off the blue star flower from the unappetizing brown fused sepals.

Pregnant and lactating women are advised to avoid borage because it can cause milk to flow.

"Those of our time do use the floures in salads, to exhilarate and make the minde glad. There be also many things made of them used for the comfort of the heart, to drive away sorrow & increase the joy of the minde. The leaves and floures of Borrage put into wine make men and women glad and merry, driving away all sadnesse, dulnesse, and melancholy ..."

Herball or Generall Historie of Plantes, (1636) John Gerard

The Celtic understanding of borage's properties was echoed some 600 years later in the words of John Evelyn: "the sprigs of borage in wine are of known virtue to revive the hypochondriac and cheer the hard student." Modern research indicates that it can stimulate adrenalin production. In 1748, Philip Miller noted that it could be found in most parts of England, often on dunghills and public roads where the seeds had scattered from gardens. He recommended borage for cool tankards in summertime—one of its common names.

Borage self-seeds easily, often prodigiously, so harvest young leaves as they appear, and weed out and compost surplus plants. Pickings will be available up to the first heavy frosts and in mild winters, often continuing to grow throughout, rapidly flowering and setting seed in the spring.

ABOVE: Despite their bristles, borage leaves are good cooked as a green in risottos or with pasta, as well as being delightful in many cold drinks.

You can manipulate this by sowing them under the shelter of winter vegetables, typically cabbages and kale, but do not let the plants get established in this position because they have deep taproots and are very difficult to weed out. Curiously, the leaves seem less bristly and more like their Arabic name of *lisan atheur* or "tongue of the bull," and can be added to winter salads. They are excellent added in strips to risottos, soups, and sauces.

Regardless of its active ingredients, it is cheering to look at the bright blue star-shaped flowers and it is also easy to grow. The Mediterranean blue of the flowers, the thick covering of short hairs on the leaves, and its statuesque growth make it an attractive subject for the border. Scatter sow the seeds among perennial vegetables such as globe artichokes, where the blue star flowers and bristly foliage of borage contrast attractively with their glaucous green dramatic leaves and spherical heads. The long taproot of borage makes it a useful green manure, drawing up nutrients into its leaves, which can be dug back into the ground.

The white-flowering *B. officinalis* "Alba" can also be raised from seed but to ensure future seedlings stay true to type (i.e. have pure white flowers), grow them separately from the common blue-flowering strains. The variegated form "Variegata" has white striations across the leaves. All varieties are good bee plants and pollinator attractants. The pretty *B. pygmaea*, which thrives in gravel, is not edible.

NUTRITION

The young leaves of borage are rich in potassium and calcium. It is a diuretic.

RIGHT: The flowers of borage, blue and white, have black centers that are said to resemble a bird's beak.

Pot marigold
Calendula officinalis

Common names: Marigold, pot marigold, ruddles, Scotch marigold, holigold, marybud

Type: Annual

Climate: Hardy, cold winter

Size: 19½–27½in (50–70cm)

Origin: Mediterranean, Macaronesia

History: Pot marigolds are among the earliest flowers noted in cultivation. The Latin name echoes the fact that they flower almost year round in their native surroundings supposedly on each *calendae* or first day of the month.

Cultivation: Sow in late spring in well-drained rich soil for maximum flower production. They prefer a sunny or lightly shaded site. Thin to 10in apart and they will flower through the summer.

Storage: Dry ray florets, but keep them out of the light when doing this, or infuse in oil (see p.75).

Preparation: Even if you can find 14 cows, there is an easier marigold cheese recipe than the Mrs.. Leyel extract, quoted on the right. Buy plain curd or ricotta cheese and pound marigold petals into it. They will create strands of gold and provide a delicate taste. When bruised, the flowers and leaves give off a peppery scent. Petals can be sprinkled over green and fruit salads. The best tisanes are brewed from the darker orange-flowered cultivars. The dried petals can be added

ABOVE: The name marigold is derived from Mary's Gold because traditionally flowers were available for her feast days in February, March, August, September, and December.

"Miss Florence White's recipe for Marigold Cheese: Mix the new milk of seven cows with the cream from the milk of seven more cows. Scald a gallon of water and add to it four handfuls of bruised marigold flowers. ... Put clean cloths round it every hour of the day."

Cinquefoil, (1957) Mrs. C. F. Leyel

to soups, and the young leaves have a salty taste and can be added to salads, but taste before using to check they are not too old and acrid.

LEFT: The young leaves of marigold can be eaten in salad. Remove petals from the flowers for salads, risottos, and tisanes.

The common name of marigold is associated with the Virgin Mary, and the flowers, subject to availability, are used to celebrate her feast days in February, August, September, and December. The golden flowers, opening and closing with the day, inspired many writers and poets, not least Shakespeare. They were valued by herbalists for their medicinal and culinary as well as ornamental purposes. The Romans used juice from the fresh flowers for warts, and calendula cream is still marketed for skin complaints. The petals were stored in barrels and sold by the ounce to cheese and butter makers to color their products a rich orange-yellow. They were also used to add color and texture to soups and casseroles, and as a "comforter of the heart and spirits."

Marigolds will grow in almost any soil. Once established they should self-seed but will gradually revert to their original form. The slightly succulent seed leaves are easily recognized and the flowers will form seeds about five months after sowing.

They have become garden escapees as can be seen in the wild populations along the shores of the Breton Glénan Islands in France. There are many cultivated varieties in a wide range of sizes, colors, (see box)—dark red, yellow, cream—and single and double flowers, all of which are edible. The whole plant is covered in little hairs that give it a sticky feeling. It is important not to confuse the culinary pot marigold, *Calendula officinalis*, with the *Tagetes* marigolds, sometimes known as African marigolds, of which only the mildly citrus *T. patula* is edible (but use this with caution as it should only be eaten in small amounts).

TASTING NOTES

Marigold varieties to try

Marigold petals have a very subtle taste redolent of a fragrant meadow, which is pleasing but indefinable. It is as much about texture and feasting the eyes as the savor. Darker varieties are favored for tea because they infuse more color.

Below are cultivars that offer what the English author, poet, and gardener Vita Sackville-West called "Summer's quick delight."

Bright yellow	"Sun Glow" or "Lemon."
Vivid orange	"Orange Prince" and "Bon Bon Orange."
Red-tinted	"Indian Prince." Also "Touch of Red Mixed" as the name suggests the reds on the orange look as though they have just alighted as a delicate edging or tip of fire.
Mixed colors	In North America the seeds "Pacific Beauty Mixed" are popular for the long-stemmed marigolds they produce, growing from 18–24in high with large, wide, double flowers. The mixed colors range through cream, bright yellow, brilliant orange, and apricot, some with dark mahogany undersides.

Caraway
Carum carvi

Common names: Caraway

Type: Biennial

Climate: Hardy, cold winter

Size: 10–24in (25–60cm)

Origin: Europe, West Asia

History: The seeds, roots, and leaves of caraway were used in classical times. The name is said to derive from the ancient Arab *karawya* with reference to the seeds. Shakespeare writes about "a pippin and a dish of caraways" where roasted apple was not cooked with caraway but rather it was served alongside.

Cultivation: Sow in a sunny spot in deep trays filled with fertile, well-drained compost either in the spring or immediately after ripening in summer when the germination rate will be highest.

Caraway grown in more northerly latitudes is richer in essential oil than those in more southern areas. The yields are higher when grown in full sun.

Storage: Harvest seed when it begins to darken and, when fully dry, store in sealed containers away from light. Kilner jars are ideal.

Preparation: A small bowl of caraway seeds is a traditional accompaniment to the French cheese Alsace Munster. The traditional English seed cake (see box) is flavored with caraway and it is pleasantly aromatic, plain rather than sweet. If you grow a variety with aromatic leaves, they can be chopped fresh into salads.

LEFT: The seeds of the caraway are most highly prized and will store for a couple of years. As it is biennial, ensure you mark its position so that it is not mistaken for a weed.

> "The seed is much used to be put among baked fruit, or into bread, cakes, etc., to give them a relish. It is also made into comfits and taken for cold or wind in the body, which also are served to the table with fruit."
>
> *Paradisi in Sole Paradisus Terrestris,*
>
> (1629) John Parkinson

Caraway comfits were sugar-coated seeds. The raw seeds have been especially popular in German cooking, flavoring cheese, cabbage, soups, and bread as well as the liqueur Kummel. Parkinson, quoted above, found that the roots tasted better than parsnips. However, they are very small. Traditionally in Britain the end of wheat-sowing was celebrated by the farmers presenting their workers with carawayseed cake. Folklore imbues it with the power of retention: ranging from an antitheft device where objects containing the seeds will never be stolen to love potions that bind lovers together.

Although the leaves are recommended for salads, many modern caraway varieties have almost none of the characteristic flavor of the seeds. This can also make it difficult when weeding. As caraway is a biennial, only flowering in its second year, ensure you clearly mark the seedbed and always crush and smell a few seeds before harvesting to ensure you don't have an umbelliferous weed.

It is a companion plant for peas. Ajmud, *Carum rosbughianum*, is an interesting Indian alternative whose seeds are used in curries, pickles, and chutneys. It requires warmer growing conditions.

Mrs. Beeton's seed cake

Seed cake was a staple of the Victorian kitchen, as were the recipes of Mrs. Isabella Beeton whose husband Sam published these between 1859 and 1861, then compiled into *Beeton's Book of Household Management*. This recipe, dated 1776, is for "a very good seed-cake."

Preparation time: 10 minutes with electric whisk
Cooking time: 1½–2 hours
Serves: 12

You will need:

· 1lb (450g) soft butter

· 1lb (450g) self-rising flour

· 12oz (350g) superfine sugar, sifted

· ½ tsp mace, pounded

· ½ tsp nutmeg, grated, to taste

· 2 tbsp caraway seeds

· 6 eggs

· 7floz (200ml) brandy

Preheat a conventional oven to 350°F (180°C / gas mark 4 / fan 160°C).

Beat the butter to a cream; dredge in the flour.

Mix together the sugar, mace, nutmeg, and caraway seeds.

Whisk the eggs, then stir into the brandy, and beat the cake again for 10 minutes.

Put it into a 10in (25cm) tin lined with buttered paper, and bake for 1½–2 hours.

Chamomile
Chamaemelum nobile (formerly *Anthemis nobilis*)

TASTING NOTES

Chamomile tonic

You can add these delicious ingredients to
a bottle of good white or rosé wine.

Preparation time: 10 minutes plus 10 days
to macerate
Serves: 6 people

You will need:

• 1oz (25g) chamomile flowers

• 1 whole orange or lemon peel (free from pith)

• 10 tsp granulated sugar

Strain and drink a wine-glassful before meals.

Common names: Chamomile, lawn chamomile

Type: Perennial

Climate: Hardy, average winter

Size: 6–12in (15–30cm)

Origin: Mediterranean

History: The spreading foliage has a fresh green
apple scent that is encapsulated in *chamae* on the
ground and *melon* apple. It was cultivated as
the "plant's physician," in that herbs and flowers
growing in its vicinity would flourish.

Cultivation: Sow seeds in late spring. Seedlings/
plants should be set 4¾–6in apart—they are
tolerant of a wide range of soils but, while
establishing, ensure they do not dry out.
The nonflowering variety "Treneague" (lawn
chamomile) should be avoided for its lack
of flowers.

Storage: Dried flowerheads should be stored
in an airtight can.

Preparation: Chamomile tea is a noted relaxant
and digestive. Make a tisane in a teapot to avoid
losing volatile oils. To do this, pour 1 pint boiling
water over 1oz flowerheads and allow to steep
for about 10 minutes.

LEFT: The leaves of chamomile have a delicious scent but it is only
the flowers, single and double, that are used for infusing into
relaxing tisanes.

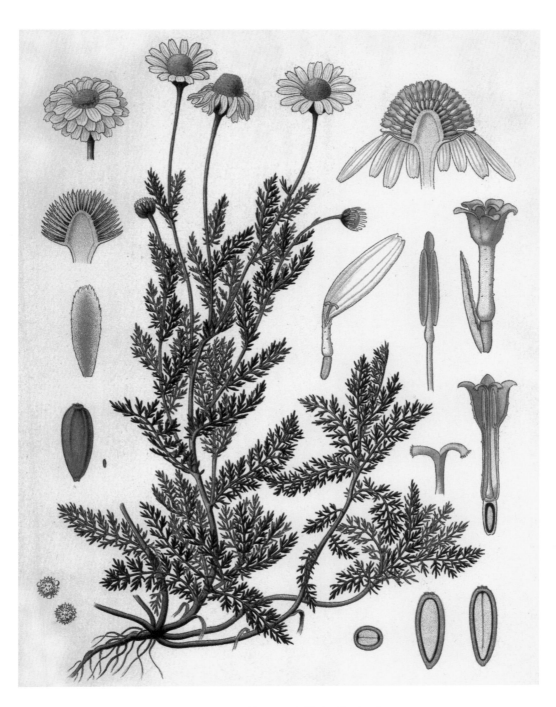

ABOVE: Rather than a lawn of chamomile, grow them as a cushion on a raised bed and let them flower.

England's first botanist, William Turner, who dedicated one of his herbals to Queen Elizabeth I, described the chamomile flowers as being "wonderfully shynynge yellow" and told of how the ancient Egyptians consecrated it to the sun and believed it to be the remedy for all sickness. In *Henry IV*, Shakespeare used Falstaff to adapt the old growing advice: "Like a Camomile bed: The more it is trodden, The more it will spread. For though the Camomile, the more it is trodden on, the faster it grows, yet youth, the more it is wasted, the sooner it wears." From the point of view of establishing a good chamomile lawn, this was when people wore soft-soled leather shoes that helped establish a smooth sward. Shakespeare's reference to youth remains relevant and valid.

"Flore Pleno," the double-flowering form of Chamomile, tends to grow more densely and should be raised from cuttings. This is best done every four or five years to replace the original plantings and thus ensure even, healthy growth. For maximum flower production, the erect, sturdy cultivar "Bodegold" is recommended. It also has a higher essential oil content. If you want to combine the lawn ideal and have flowers for tea, it is good grown as ground cover or green growing blocks in paving. The best solution is to plant a raised seat rather than lawn, as upholstered behinds are more effective rollers than modern shoes. The flowers will spring up attractively all around the edges from the springy turf cushion.

A GOURMET GARDEN SEAT

The seat structure can be in timber, brick, or stone. Make sure that the building materials are smooth—no splinters or rough rock rubbing against the sitter's legs.

Build to a height that is comfortable and possibly enclose with a trellis of scented climbing plants, such as roses or honeysuckle. The actual seat needs to be constructed like a flower bed so that there is both space for soil and good drainage. Small seats can be incorporated into a wall.

Chamomile requires light conditions but not full summer sun. The compost should be rich enough to encourage strong growth but not so nitrogenous that it does not flower.

For several years, Cambridge University Botanic Garden, England, recycled a wooden bench by keeping the back and arm rests on the edge of the scented garden and replacing the slatted seat with chamomile.

Good King Henry
Chenopodium bonus-henricus

Common names: Good King Henry, English mercury, wild spinach, Fat Hen

Type: Perennial

Climate: Very hardy

Size: 12–24in (30–60cm)

Origin: Central and Southern Europe

History: The common *C. album* can often be seen as an arable weed when in flower, resembling its common name "Fat Hen." It was a valuable early foodstuff. Archeological evidence in Scotland reveals *Chenopodium* was being eaten in the European Bronze Age (3200–600 BC).

Cultivation: Sow Good King Henry in spring and pick out growing tips to encourage it to bush and produce more leaves.

Storage: Save seeds for sowing.

Preparation: Very young, small leaves can be added to salads. Use as a spinach substitute. Like ground elder, it is excellent added to white sauces or within baked dishes like lasagna.

ABOVE: Although the young leaves of Good King Henry are more delicate for cooking, the flowering sprigs of the plant can be mixed in with them.

"The edible and virtuous Chenopodium needed distinction as the 'Good Henry.' The King in Good King Henry is our interpolation. Like the Robin in many English plant-names, this Heinrich of German plant-names may have been an elf—in this case a substitute for Hermes or Mercury."

The Englishman's Flora, (1955) Geoffrey Grigson

In his 1777 *Flora Scotica*, John Lightfoot wrote of enjoying the young leaves of Good King Henry as spring greens. Some 250 years later this advice still stands as it is when they are at their best.

Although it will grow like a weed, the flavor improves markedly if it is treated more like a vegetable and sown in well-cultivated, moisture-retentive soil and eaten young. Good King Henry will self-seed, so thin seedlings as necessary and compost young plants. It is easier to control if grown in blocks or rows.

Seeds can be slow to germinate but, once established, there should be almost year-round pickings. The more it is harvested the more young

tasty leaves will appear, though the flowering tops can be cooked like spinach.

The more pungent *C. ambrosiodes* is widely used in Mexican cooking. Known as epazote or Mexican tea, it requires tropical conditions to grow. The increasingly popular *Chenopodium quinoa* is treated like a grain, with its small nutritious seeds resembling millet. It is ground into a nutty flour and can be used for gluten-free diets.

Two others are strawberry spinach, *C. foliosum* "Strawberry Sticks" and tree spinach, *C. giganteum* "Magentaspreen."

Be aware that although not as effective as dandelion, Good King Henry was taken to "provoke urine," usually at around midday. It is not advised for sufferers of rheumatism and arthritis.

RIGHT: As a perennial, Good King Henry is useful when designing an ornamental kitchen garden and will benefit from rich soil.

MORE THAN GREEN LEAVES

SALADS TO FEAST YOUR EYES AND YOUR PALATE

Pliny the Elder advised that eating salads saved precious fuel and that, with careful watering and protection, green leaves could be available year round. In 1873, Alexandre Dumas Père published a dictionary of cookery including *"Fourniture"* (*Salad Herbs*). It is a list of 13 herbs to accompany chicory or lettuce and it included chervil, French tarragon, lemon balm "when it is young," salad burnet, flowering nasturtiums, and the flowers of the violet and borage. It is worth noting his mention of "flowering nasturtiums," because the flower stems make a crisp and cool complement to the more peppery flowers.

ABOVE: Alexandre Dumas Père wrote a comprehensive and opinionated dictionary of cookery in 1873, which included herbs for salads.

SALADING AND DRESSING HERBS

If you compare a salad to a stage set of lettuce, endive, or tomatoes, the major players are the saladings, i.e. herb leaves and flowers. Each herb provides a distinctive taste and texture to the salad. However, they need a supporting cast to enhance their performance, which is perfected with dressings of finely chopped herbs.

RIGHT: Delicious crunchy purslane tops (*Portulaca oleracea*) can be picked and put in a salad with a taste reminiscent of cucumber and okra. Older stems can be added to a stir-fry.

Salading herbs

The leaves should be coarsely chopped or torn. Old recipe books advise against cutting because so many knives were formerly made of iron—rarely a problem today. However, the advantage of tearing the leaves is that more oil is released. Of all the herb leaves, those of salad and wild arugula are as delicious served alone or scattered in quantity over food. Good candidates are the tangy young leaves of angelica, nasturtium, flat-leafed parsley, purslane, buckler-leafed sorrel, and salad burnet. If in doubt, chopped chive spears impart a light onion or garlic taste that will lift any salad. Introduce color with the variegated leaves of oregano, marjoram, mint, thyme, and basil or the golden hues of purslane, while the

LEFT: A little crushed garlic makes its presence felt. The alternative is to cook it with bell peppers and tomatoes, and serve cold.

Dressing herbs

The leaves should be finely chopped or pounded to release the flavor that lies in their oils, then added to vinaigrette, mayonnaise, and other cold sauces. A crushed clove or two of garlic is possibly the best example of this. In contrast, finely chopped chives and chervil introduce a subtle savor and the carroty freshness of moss-curled parsley is almost ubiquitous. You might strengthen the presence of a salading herb such as basil, marjoram, mint, or dill by using it in the dressing as well. The soft leaves of young thyme are fragrantly aromatic as are the anise-flavored young fronds of sweet fennel.

HERB VINEGARS

Many herbs can be infused into vinegars. Bruise the leaves and young stems of any of the following herbs—lemon balm, basil, borage, dill, sweet marjoram, mint, summer savory, salad burnet, French tarragon, and lemon thyme—to release their oils. Do not chop them into small pieces. The bruised fresh leaves, individually or mixed, should be packed into a jar. Then pour over white wine or cider vinegar to the rim. Cover tightly and leave to infuse on a sunny windowsill for two weeks. Strain and remove herbs.

It is not just leaves. The same method, without bruising, can be used for the flowers of borage, elderberry (*Sambucus*), rose petals, and violets. If you want to decant it to make a gift, add a dried sprig of the herb for decoration. Garlic crushed for vinegar should be left to steep for two days, after which it will be ready for use.

purple of young bronze fennel, basil, and thyme provide depth and contrast.

Other herbs can be used to create a taste that associates well with individual cold and salad vegetables, such as the leaves and flowers of all varieties of basil with tomatoes, dill with potatoes, summer savory with beans—green or otherwise. The creamy flesh of the avocado is a perfect vehicle for stronger flavors; slice with chopped basil, thyme, dill, or cilantro. Young sweet cicely leaves and tops of French tarragon provide an aromatically anise element. Flowers of borage, nasturtium, chives, violets, or salad arugula scattered over the salad at the last moment give the finishing touch.

"Salad. Take parsley, sage, garlic, chibols, onions, leek, borage, mints, porray, fennel, and garden cresses, rue, rosemary, purslain; lave and wash them clean; pick them, pluck them small with thine hand, and mingle them well with raw oil. Lay on vinegar and salt and serve it forth."

Recipe for salad from *Boke of Nurture*, (c. 1460) John Russell

HERB OILS

The process is very similar to that for herb vinegars. Bruise rather than chop the herbs to release their oils. The best oils to use are olive, sunflower, or grapeseed because the individual characteristics make them good for salads and to drizzle over all manner of other foods. The classic flavors of basil, dill, thyme, and French tarragon can be evoked in midwinter, as can the citrus scent from lemon balm leaves. Other good herbs are sweet fennel, sweet marjoram, lavender flowers, and the petals of marigold and roses.

Fill a jar with the bruised herb leaves and young stems or flowers, then cover with oil. After one week in a warm but not hot place, remove the herbs (use them for roasting or a barbecue), taste, and repeat if the oil is not sufficiently aromatic. Oils can be decorated with a dried sprig of the herb used. Garlic can be crushed for oil but should be left to steep for only two days, after which it will be ready for use.

The simplest way to enjoy herb oils and vinegars is to put some stems of your favorite herbs in at the beginning of the week. At the end of the week, strain and use the herbs for cooking.

STERILIZING BOTTLES AND JARS

Success when making and storing herb oils and vinegars lies with scrupulous preparation of the vessels in which you plan to keep them.

- First wash the jars and lids in soapy water and rinse in clean, warm water.

- Allow to drip dry, upside-down on a rack in the oven heated at 275°F (140°C/ gas mark 1 / fan 120°C) for about 30 minutes.

- Remove holding the sides with oven gloves.

- Fill with your preserve and cover with lid while still hot.

Cilantro
Coriandrum sativum

Common names: Coriander, cilantro, Chinese parsley, Indian parsley

Type: Annual

Climate: Half-hardy, unheated glasshouse, mild winter

Size: 18–35in (45–90cm)

Origin: Western Mediterranean

History: There is evidence dating back to the late Bronze Age (about 2000 BC) that cilantro was one of the first flavoring herbs to be introduced from the Mediterranean into Britain. The name is said to derive from the Arabic *koris* or "bed bugs." If the seeds are harvested too early or too green they do have a distinctively fetid smell. However, allowed to fully ripen they become aromatic and orange scented.

Cultivation: Scatter sow directly from spring onward, thinning to 8–12in spacings. Late summer sowings will provide pickings until the first frosts especially in a cold frame or with some protection.

Storage: Harvest seeds when paper-dry and brown, then store in airtight jars. Freeze whole leaves and break off as required.

Preparation: The distinctively aromatic leaves and young stems of cilantro add a contrasting and cooling flavor as side dishes for hot spicy foods. In Indian recipes, *hara dhaniya* and *kothmir* are the terms used for fresh leaves. Slice tomatoes with red bell peppers and cilantro leaves served in plain yogurt with or without garlic. Excellent as a "bite" in green salads or added to guacamole or houmous. Add to cold chicken. Warming carrot and cilantro leaf soup tastes and looks good.

The Indian words for whole and ground coriander seeds are *dhania*, *sabut*, and *pisa*. Apart from seasoning curries, the seeds can be added to sweet pie toppings along with finely grated orange peel. When harvesting is complete, pull up the plants and cut off the small roots to chop into soups and sauces.

LEFT: It is worth growing separate plants for seed and leaf to ensure plentiful supplies of both. The seed-bearing crop can be sown in among flowers.

All early records relate to coriander seeds not leaves, which, once dried, could be stored for year-round use and were easily carried by travelers. Fresh leaves in Britain were only available to home gardeners and were praised by Beeton during the 19th century. The name "cilantro" was originally introduced by Hispanic communities into the United States while at the same time better leaf-forming varieties became available. Other names such as Chinese parsley and Indian parsley are indicative of the popularity of its leaves in Asian cooking.

Seed varieties, as opposed to those grown for leaf production, can be sown as an annual plant among perennials. Their white umbelliferous flowers are tinged with pink and create a splendid massed effect until seed formation. The flowers become luminescent by moonlight so are ideal for the night garden. To create an ornamental haze of greens and good aroma, mix the seeds with those of caraway and chervil, then scatter sow and grow in blocks. Alternatively, mix with carrot seeds to help deter carrot root fly. Although cilantro is still a good leaf variety, the choice has widened. That said, during periods of intense dry heat all varieties will run to seed very quickly.

TASTING NOTES

Cilantro varieties to try for their leaves

The distinctive taste of cilantro is well known but it varies. The young top leaves are more strongly aromatic. As leaves mature, the texture changes and when mixed with stems will impart their flavor in cooking. The seeds must always be fully ripe or they will have a fetid aftertaste. Why not try these:

"Calypso"   British bred. Seed producers claim that it can be cut back three times and continue to supply a succession of leaves as well as being slow to bolt.

"Confetti"   Fine, feathery-leaved with a good flavor. It can be sown successionally into September. It is also recommended for windowsill pots.

"Leisure"   Popular for quantity as it is slow to bolt. It has a good flavor and its flowers, when they come, are very attractive.

"Santo"   Also slow to bolt. Has high leaf production and rapidly reaches maturity. In the right conditions it takes 55 days from sowing to harvest.

"Slobolt"   Has the most distinctly pungent flavor that is popular for Chinese, Thai, and Mexican cooking. It is slow to bolt.

Saffron crocus
Crocus sativus

Common names: Saffron

Type: Bulb

Climate: Hardy, average winter

Size: 4in (10cm)

Essex gold

The early medieval settlement of Walden, meaning "valley of Britons", in England's East Anglia became the site of a Benedictine abbey where sheep grazed in large numbers. The associated cloth trade that flourished called for a variety of dyestuffs such as saffron crocus—it was rapidly discovered that it could be successfully cultivated in the surrounding fields. By the early 16th century, Walden was a wool staple town with a very prosperous associated trade in saffron production.

Following the demise of the abbey, the wealthy citizens of Saffron Walden, as it became known, made generous donations toward building St. Mary's, which remains the largest parish church in England. A representation of their wealth in the form of a saffron crocus was carved in stone in the spandrels above the arch opposite the south porch. Although the trade died out in the late 18th century, unable to compete with Spanish and other imports, Saffron Walden continued to celebrate its namesake in Edwardian stained glass and the 1998 altar rail.

Origin: Central Asia

History: In his headlong pursuit of love for Smilax the handsome young Crocus was stopped in his tracks when she transformed him into a saffron crocus. *Krokos* is the Greek word for saffron. The radiant orange stigmas are all that is left of his undying and unrequited burning desire.

Cultivation: Plant the bulbs in the fall in well-drained soil in a sunny position. The leaves will appear in spring and a warm summer is essential for the fall flowers. Propagation is by means of offsets; these can be encouraged by crushing or breaking bulbs, which lends credence to Pliny's remarks (see quote below).

Storage: Pick flowers as soon as they are fully open and remove entire pistils for drying between sheets of white paper. Once dried they are called saffron threads. Store for no longer than a year.

Preparation: A generous pinch of saffron threads should be left to infuse overnight in 1.35 fl oz of warm water. In India, the threads are often lightly roasted before infusion in milk. The recipes for soups, fish, rice, or cakes with saffron are legion. If you cannot grow enough make sure you buy the highest quality threads, not powder. (See also Garam Masala on p.81.)

> "Saffron loves to be beaten and trodden underfoot, and in fact, the worse it is treated the better it thrives."
>
> *Historia Naturalis*, (c. AD 70 trans. Philemon Holland 1601) Pliny the Elder

The Romans ate the bulbs of saffron crocus in small quantities (nowadays this is not recommended). However, the saffron harvested from the pistils was and still is highly regarded. Apart from cooking, perfumes, and unguents, it was believed that reclining on a saffron pillow would prevent a hangover. Among many plants and foodstuffs, saffron and rice were introduced by the Moors into Spain in the 10th century; the common name derives from the Arab *za-faran*. *Zaafraan* or *kesar* is the saffron grown in the northern Indian state of Kashmir. In contradiction to Pliny's advice (see quote), Ion Gardener c. 1400 recommended planting the crocus bulb at least 3in (7.5cm) deep in beds of dung during September. Along with other herbs, The Massachusetts Bay Company imported "saffron heads" into New England in 1629. True saffron colors food with a deep yellow hue. It has a pleasant honey aroma while its unmistakable taste characterizes bouillabaisse and other Mediterranean fish dishes such as paella.

Reference is made to harvesting saffron from the pistil, stigma, and/or stamens. For botanical clarification, it is the pistil that encompasses the female organ of a flower, i.e. ovary, style, and stigma. Saffron is the vivid coating of the female stigma. The stamen is the male pollen-bearing "stalk" within the flower.

Saffron cakes and buns are traditional fare in the English counties of Cornwall and Devon in England, possibly dating back some 3,000 years

when tin was traded with the ancient Phoenicians. These Mediterranean seafarers could have used saffron as barter for other goods, creating a taste that survives today. During the 16th century 20 percent of Saffron Walden's crop was exported to Cornwall. Saffron is the only herb to rival costly spices and estimates vary, but about 500,000 pistils (the red-gold threads) are required from about 170,000 flowers for just two pounds of dried saffron. To ensure you are buying pure gold, avoid the powders, which are likely to be adulterated. Turmeric is an adequate substitute for color, or possibly marigold petals, but there is no comparison between the totally different tastes.

RIGHT: It is worth dedicating an area to saffron in your garden. If you are growing food ornamentally, it can provide good perennial interest.

Cumin
Cuminum cyminum

Common names: Cumin, comino, jeera, zeera

Type: Annual

Climate: Heated glasshouse, warm, temperate

Size: 6–12in (15–30cm)

Origin: Mediterranean to Sudan, Central Asia

History: The use of cumin as a spice appears in the Bible and the writings of Hippocrates and Dioscorides. One curious side effect was noted, which was that large consumers of cumin seeds became avaricious.

NUTRITION

Cumin seeds are a source of carotene and the minerals iron, copper, calcium, potassium, manganese, zinc, and magnesium as well as good amounts of B-complex vitamins and vitamins E, A, and C.

Cultivation: As a native of almost desert regions, sow in seed trays under glass in cooler climates. Cumin needs a warm, fertile, and well-drained soil. The seeds require a long warm season of three to four months to successfully ripen, so it is worth considering growing cumin to maturity in a glasshouse, cold frame, or on a sunny windowsill.

Storage: An important constituent of curry powder, the dried seeds should be kept whole in an airtight jar until needed.

Preparation: Like many aromatic seeds and spices, cumin is best warmed by frying in a dry pan, which provides an immediate release of its "roasted" aroma. Alternatively, seeds can be put in a sterilized, airtight container. Seeds can be put through a grinder, ground with a pestle and mortar, or placed between two sheets of brown paper and crushed with a rolling pin. Fry a small onion with cumin seeds, add basmati or brown rice, then add water or broth at twice the quantity of the rice; bring to the boil and simmer until all the liquid is absorbed; this is excellent for curries, with chicken or lamb. Fried onion and cumin with turmeric is essential for a good dal. Cumin is combined with chilli in many Mexican recipes and it is excellent in oatcakes or crackers to serve with cheese.

LEFT: Cumin is an aromatic seed, more often classed as a spice, which requires a long hot summer to ripen. The leaves have a more delicate flavor.

Garam masala

This ground spice mix is based on a recipe by Rowley Leigh that has contemporary subtleties and many elements from the herb garden.

Preparation time: 15 minutes
Serves: makes 10 teaspoons

You will need:

· 2 tbsp cumin seeds

· 1 tsp fennel seeds

· ½ tsp saffron threads

· 2 tsp cardamom seeds, removed from pods

· 1 tbsp black peppercorns

· 25 cloves

· 2in (5cm) cinnamon stick

· ½ tsp grated nutmeg

· ½ tsp mace

Roast seeds of cumin, fennel, and cardamom with peppercorns and cloves in a dry frying pan. Stir frequently so they brown without burning.

Grind with remaining spices to a powder.

Store short term in an airtight container.

According to Pliny the Elder, scholars and followers of rhetorician Porcius Latro, drank crushed cumin seeds in water in order to become unhealthily pale. Seemingly such pallor was indicative that they were deprived of sunlight owing to their dedication to continual study. Pliny also thoroughly recommended eating cumin with bread and wine as "it assuageth the wringing torments and other pains of the guts." During the Middle Ages, cumin seeds commanded high prices, although it was the commonest spice grown. It should not be confused with either the French *cumin des prés*, which is a wild caraway, or black cumin, *Nigella sativa*, also known as Roman Coriander. It is a close relative of Love-in-the-Mist, *N. damascena*; both make pretty additions to the flowering herb garden.

The slender leaves look like dill but carry the distinctive aroma of the seeds. Resist picking them, however, unless the plant is thriving. Harvest the whole plant as the seed pods ripen. Bear in mind that cumin thrives in a hot, dry climate so reaching this stage in colder areas presents quite a challenge.

It is said that eating cumin seeds depresses nervous irritability, so if you want to be like the Romans, follow Apicius's *Cuminatum in ostrea et conchylia* (*Cumin sauce for shellfish*). He simmered some cumin, honey, vinegar, and broth and added ground pepper, lovage, parsley, and dry mint. A modern take would be to cook the shellfish in the cumin sauce and add fresh leaves of lovage, parsley, and mint when serving.

"For oppression of the chest, take this same wort cumin, and water and vinegar, mingle them together, give to drink, it will prove beneficial; and also swallowed in wine, it healeth well bite of snake."

Leechdoms, Wortcunning, and Starcraft of Early England, (1864) Dioscorides, collected and edited by the Rev. Oswald Cockayne

Turmeric
Curcuma longa (also known as *C. domestica*)

Common names: Turmeric, haridra, haldi

Type: Perennial rhizome

Climate: Heated glasshouse, warm, temperate

Size: 3¼ft (1m)

Origin: India

History: A member of the ginger family, there are records in India of turmeric's culinary use dating back to 3000 BC, not least as a food colorant and preservative. By the 7th century it had been introduced into China, where its medicinal properties were recorded.

Cultivation: Sow seeds in the fall under glass. In its native regions, the highly branched, cylindrical rhizomes are divided when dormant. Cut into smaller lengths and plant 8–15¾in apart. It requires a minimum temperature of 60–64°F, ample humidity during growth, and a well-drained soil in a sunny position.

RIGHT: Turmeric root, whole or powdered, imparts a deep yellow to cooked food; it is sometimes used as a saffron substitute for color but its flavor is earthier, almost pungent.

Storage: Roots are lifted during the dormant season, then steamed or boiled before drying and grinding into powder.

Preparation: Turmeric has the coloring characteristics of saffron but not its fragrance. Its distinctive earthy aroma, taste, and color can be infused into numerous dishes. Roll potatoes in turmeric before roasting. Marinate chicken in yogurt with turmeric, garlic, and ginger (see ginger, p.213). Note that if you remove the skin of the chicken before marinating and/or cooking, the flavor of the spices penetrates the meat better. Use to color pickles and relishes. In India, the leaf is used to wrap and cook food, and in a variety of sweet dishes. Pulses cooked with turmeric become more digestible. It is sometimes listed as E100 when used as a food additive.

It is good for digestive, circulatory, and respiratory systems, though care should be taken if pregnant as it also stimulates the uterus. Eating turmeric regularly reputedly helps men with prostate problems. It is also a digestive and an antiseptic.

"Turmeric was never particularly popular in Western Europe. However, the Arabs and Persians were very fond of it and, looking no further than its brilliant color, took it for another form of saffron and called it kourkoum."

History of Food, (1987) Maguelonne Toussaint-Samat

Turmeric's large rhizomes are valued as a spice and for the yellow dye that has become characteristic of many food preparations and the robes of Buddhist monks. Tumeric is also a source of starch. It arrived in Europe via the Spice Route; the Arabs named it *kurkum* from which it gets its generic name. The English name turmeric may well be a corruption of *terra merita* meaning "deserving earth" or "worth growing." English connections with India revived its popularity in the 19th century, not least in the recipes of Beeton (see p.67). In his *Great Dictionary of Cooking* of 1878, Dumas Pére noted that one of the gastronomic diversions of the English was to put it in the pastry for rhubarb pies, a fashion that was copied by the pastry-makers of the Saint-Honoré quarter in Paris. Turmeric was grown on the French island of Réunion, Bourbon, before the 1789 French Revolution, leading to its alternative name of Bourbon saffron.

It is one of the most popular spices in Indian and southeast Asian cooking, where its color was believed to indicate its therapeutic qualities, especially in association with liver complaints. In some regions of Indonesia and Western Sumatra turmeric leaves are also used as a flavoring.

The long-valued medicinal properties of turmeric in Ayurvedic treatments are currently being researched for its potential benefits for arthritis, Alzheimer's disease, and general health-giving properties.

ABOVE: Powdered turmeric is a familiar sight in the kitchen but the roots are more fragrant and can be eaten as a vegetable, as well as being dried.

The genus *Curcuma* including turmeric has adapted to regions of seasonal drought and traditionally it was planted with the first monsoon showers. It takes 7–10 months to mature; at this stage the leaves will die back. In China, the flowering time of the bright yellow inflorescence is usually August. The roots are deep orange on the inside and in the Far East and East Africa they are eaten as a vegetable. Turmeric was introduced into the Americas and has become naturalized in Peru and the West Indies, where it features widely in Creole cookery. When fresh, the roots have a more aromatic and spicy fragrance than the distinctive flavor of the powdered, dried root. The root has a wealth of minerals and trace elements such as calcium, chromium, copper, curcumin, manganese, niacin, and riboflavin.

There are several closely related species that are of use such as the camphor-scented, bitter spice zeduoary, *C. zedoaria*, also known as Javanese turmeric root, and the mild ginger flavored *C. amada*, which is known as mango ginger and is used in pickles. Indian or Bombay arrowroot is extracted from the root tubers of *C. angustifolia*.

If you have the space in a glasshouse, the leaves make an attractive ground cover with a cone-shaped inflorescence with cup-like bracts and streaked tubular flowers. The true turmeric has pale green bracts tipped with white and rose-tinted upper bracts around the yellow flowers.

TASTING NOTES

Peelay chaaval

Attributed to the doyenne of Indian cookery Madhur Jaffrey, this recipe is for an aromatic, yellow basmati rice. Serve with curried dishes.

Preparation time: 5 minutes
Cooking time: 35 minutes
Serves: 7 people

You will need:

- 1¼ tsp salt

- ¾ tsp turmeric

- 3–4 whole cloves

- 1in (2.5cm) cinnamon stick

- 3 bay leaves

- 15oz (425g) Basmati rice

- 1.75oz (50g) unsalted butter

Add the salt, turmeric, cloves, cinnamon stick, and bay leaves to the rice, and cook for 25 minutes in 20floz (570ml) of boiling water with the pan lid on until the water is absorbed.

Leave to stand for 10 minutes. Then remove the whole spices and fork through with butter.

LEFT: The tubular flowers of turmeric are set off by white bracts, and they make an attractive ground cover in a glasshouse.

Lemongrass
Cymbopogon citratus

Common names: Lemongrass, West Indian lemongrass, oil of verbena; also *C. flexuosus*

Type: Perennial

Climate: Heated glasshouse, subtropical

Size: 24in–4ft x 35in (60cm–1.2m x 90cm)

Origin: Indonesia

History: A citral (lemon-odor) producing plant that resembles a leek, its name *kyme*, "a boat," and *pogon*, "a beard," alludes to its flowerheads. The common name "oil of verbena" refers to the similarity of its scent to *Aloysia citriodora*. A native of Indonesia, it is now cultivated in most tropical countries including Africa, South America, Indo-China, and many American states. In the early 20th century, it was used to adulterate true lemon oil.

Cultivation: Lemongrass is frost-tender. Although it requires a minimum temperature of 50–55°F with buoyant humidity, it is easily grown in a wide range of soils, preferably medium to well-drained, organically rich loam with a high nitrogen content, and in full sun. Water plentifully at the base when in full growth. Grow under glass in cool climates.

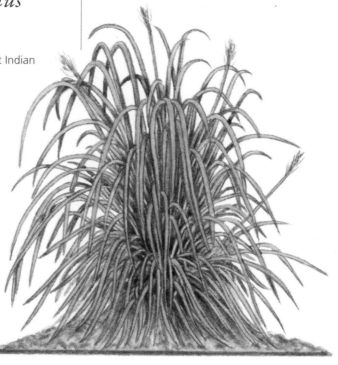

BELOW: The outer leaves of lemongrass can be used in broth but it is the softer inner ones that should be finely chopped for consumption.

Storage: Wrap lemongrass to stop it tainting other foodstuffs. Whole stems will keep for up to two weeks in the refrigerator. Stems freeze well.

Preparation: Remove the dry, fibrous outer layers and the lower bulb of the herb (these can be used to flavor broth). Use the lower 6in and interior of the stems, slicing paper-thin or pounding to a paste. If you use larger pieces, bruise them to release oils and remove before serving. Use in teas and to flavor fish stews and sauces. Lemongrass gives a characteristic fresh, fragrant, citrus flavor that is light and refreshing. It is often combined with garlic, cilantro, and fresh chillies for Thai curries.

Divide established lemongrass plants in spring and this also increases stem productivity. It is worth trying to root stems bought for cooking by soaking the bulb end in water where roots may well form. Older stems should be picked first to promote new growth, with a final harvest in the fall before the first frosts. If there are roots on any leaf sections pot them up for a sunny windowsill. This will provide a small amount for culinary uses over winter as well as doubling as an air-freshener. It would be worth trying a sky planter for this (see p.104). In turn, these can be planted out in the late spring when the soil has warmed to 55°F. Whether in the ground or in pots, plant lemongrass near where you sit out in the summer as its lemony fragrance deters mosquitoes.

To turn up the heat in stir-fries, add finely chopped lemongrass and jalapeno peppers. For an aromatic lemony syrup to pour over fruit or ice cream, mix chopped lemongrass with lemon thyme and simmer in a light sugar syrup; strain and use—it will keep in a refrigerator for a week. For extra flavor, add a dollop of maple syrup.

RAINSCAPING

This design idea promoted by the Missouri Botanical Garden mimics nature by slowing the flow of rainwater runoff to create sponge-like, rich, moisture-retentive soils. In fact, it is effectively the opposite of the Mediterranean garden that suits so many other herbs. A rain garden incorporates stone and shallow depressions that temporarily hold the water. Apart from plants such as lemongrass, planting typically features moisture-loving plants that might be difficult to grow in better-drained gardens. Other hardier herbs that could be incorporated would be angelica and mint with caution, and, with skill, ginger.

Apart from the ethereal lemon taste that lightens so many dishes, lemongrass has good nutritional benefits. It is related to many stable food stuffs such as oats, rice, sugar cane, bread wheat, and the "famine food" bandura bamboo, *Oxytenanthera abyssinica*. If you can only obtain seeds of *C. flexuosus*, the Cochin or Malabar grass form of lemongrass, the good news is that it has been the subject of research for its *in vitro* cytotoxicity against 12 human cancer cell lines. The results indicate that the oil has promising anticancer and antitumor activity.

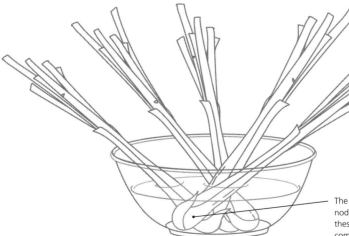

The bulbous ends of lemongrass may well form root nodules if left to soak in a small amount of water. When these embryo roots appear, carefully plant up in a fibrous compost so that the plant can develop fully.

ABOVE: If you garden in a cooler climate it is worth growing lemongrass in a greenhouse. This will greatly increase your chances of success.

The prime culinary lemongrasses, *C. citratus* and, to a lesser extent, *C. flexuosus*, should not be confused with citronella or mana grass, *C. nardus*, a powerful insect repellent, disinfectant, and cleanser that can be used for flavorings, though its strength makes it inferior to the true lemongrass.

NUTRITION

Lemongrass contains high levels of iron, vitamins C and B6, as well as potassium, calcium, and magnesium.

TASTING NOTES

Thai soup

Preparation time: 40 minutes
Cooking time: 15 minutes
Serves: 4 people

You will need:

• 2 tbsp oil

• 1 small onion

• 3 cloves of garlic

• 1½in (thumb length) ginger, peeled

• 1 stalk lemongrass, finely sliced

• 1 red chilli pepper, finely chopped

• 34floz (1l) broth, chicken or vegetarian

• 6oz (180g) Thai jasmine rice

• 7 carrots, sliced or grated

• 1 tbsp cumin seeds, crushed

• 1½ tsp cardamom seeds

• ¼ tsp ground nutmeg

• 14floz (400ml) can of coconut milk

• Handful each of cilantro and basil leaves

Heat oil in soup pan; add onion, garlic, ginger, lemongrass, and chilli. Stir-fry for one minute. Pour in broth and rice, bring to the boil.

Add carrots, cumin, cardamom, and nutmeg. Reduce heat, cover, and cook for 10–12 minutes.

Add coconut milk, stir, and process until smooth. Serve sprinkled with cilantro and basil.

Salad arugula
Eruca vesicaria subsp. *sativa*

Common names: Salad rocket, arugola, rucola, Italian cress

Type: Annual

Climate: Hardy, cold winter

Size: 24–31½in (60–80cm)

Origin: Mediterranean, Asia Minor

ABOVE: Arugula grows the best leaves as a short day plant, so sow in August and early March for fall and spring harvests.

History: Arugula was a popular herb with the Romans, who used it to flavor sauces and pickled it in vinegar. Its virtues included being an aphrodisiac, removing spots and freckles, and repelling human parasites; after floggings it was served in wine to assuage the pain.

Cultivation: Short day length suits the arugula's growth pattern so sow preferably in late summer/early fall, or in early spring. Thin out as necessary, ideally to 9–12in apart. It will be ready to harvest in 30–40 days.

Storage: Although the leaves can be frozen or kept in vinegar, they are incomparably better fresh. In mild winters there will be continual fresh pickings. Commercially the seeds are pressed to make taramira oil.

Preparation: The leaves of salad arugula have a cold-beef-meets-radish flavor, though some describe it as nutty. As the leaves mature, the taste becomes increasingly hot and peppery.

Mix arugula and fresh sliced nectarines in olive oil and balsamic vinegar with nuts, ricotta or pecorino cheese, and smoked meats. Throw a good handful over pasta, pizza, or risotto before serving. The evening-scented, creamy-yellow flowers are fragrant, nutty ,and pleasantly crunchy—a salad on their own. The young, newly formed seed pods can be eaten like snow peas. The seeds are also edible.

ABOVE: Young salad arugula leaves are delicious when liberally sprinkled whole over pizza. The plants have a habit of going to seed in warm, dry weather.

TASTING NOTES

The flavors of arugula

Both wild and salad arugula have a distinctive nutty, peppery taste, though the wild has more serrated leaves with a stronger, spicier taste.

Seedsmen offer a choice of salad arugula, some of which are slower to bolt like "Pegasus." A new variety, "Skyrocket," is described as "well-lobed." It has the vigor of the salad and the taste of the wild arugula; it is also ready to cut in 25–30 days from sowing. "Giove" and "Sylvetta" are good wild varieties.

NUTRITION

Arugula is a low calorie herb and an excellent source of vitamins A, C, and K. There are good levels of minerals, especially copper and iron with small amounts of calcium, iron, potassium, manganese, and phosphorus. Recent research suggests that the seeds possess a potent antioxidant, aid renal activity, and preclude oxidative damage to the kidney.

As a hardy herb in the brassica family that grows best in spring and fall, salad arugula was a valuable green leaf in English gardens from the late 15th to early 18th centuries. In traditional French Provençal cuisine it was served as a salad herb in *mesclun*—mixed green leaves—and used as a soup herb. The Italian island of Ischia produces Rucolino, a liqueur based on an ancient recipe where the leaves "are treated with much delicacy" and then flavored with citrus, herbs, and roots. Arugula is grown throughout the world.

A hardy, easily raised annual salad herb, it is worth setting aside a patch of well-cultivated, rich soil and allowing it to self-sow. Early fall sowings will germinate rapidly and provide pickings well into winter, then die back until spring when they will regrow then flower. Try growing year round as a sprouting seed alone or mixed with fennel seed. Late spring/early summer sowings tend to be attacked by flea beetles, resulting in arugula with more holes than leaf and a greater tendency to bolt—in short, it is not worth the effort. Salad arugula should not be mistaken for the very similar white wallrocket, *Diplotaxis erucoides,* much used by the catering trade.

Eryngo
Eryngium maritimum and *E. foetidum*

Common names: Sea holly, eryngo, eringo, sea holm; and culantro, Mexican cilantro, long cilantro; spiny or serrated cilantro, *shado beni*, and *bhandhania* in Trinidad and Tobago; *chadron benee* in Dominica, *coulante* in Haiti, *recao* in Puerto Rico; and fit weed in Guyana. *Jia Yuan* in China, Ngo Gai in Vietnam, and ketumbar jawa in Malaysia.

Type: Short-lived perennial; biennial

Climate: Hardy, cold winter; heated glasshouse, subtropical

Size: 12–18in; 24in (30–45cm; 60cm)

Origin: Europe, Continental Tropical America, West Indies

History: Traditionally, the candied roots of the sea holly were considered an aphrodisiac and made into kissing comfits or candies. The former Roman city of Colchester was noted for "oysters and eringo root." Their hardiness along the shores of Great Britain led to their symbolism of austerity.

Cultivation: Sea holly, *E. maritum*, is tolerant of a wide range of soils, including poor gravelly soils, and it thrives in maritime conditions. Sow seed in the fall in a cold frame when it is fresh. Their glaucous, silver blue-gray, spiny foliage and architectural stature makes them an attractive garden or ornamental kitchen garden plant.

Storage: Dry or candy two-year-old roots of *E. maritimum*. Dry the leaves of *E. foetidum*; they retain their flavor better than true cilantro.

Preparation: Lift, peel, and remove pith from the roots of *E. maritimum*, then candy in syrup (p.59). Experiment with young shoots early in the season before they become stringy; like many herbs the flavor is subtle, tasting like asparagus.

For *E. foetidum*, harvest the entire rosette by cutting the leaves with a knife at soil level to grow new leaves. The leaves are similarly flavored to cilantro but more pungent and can be used as a substitute. The leaves are chopped over soups, noodle dishes, and curries. A digestive tea can be made by pouring boiling water over 6 chopped leaves and leaving to infuse for 15 minutes.

NUTRITION

E.foetidum is rich in calcium, iron, carotene, and riboflavin. It is an excellent source of vitamins A, B2, B1, and C.

Linnaeus recommended eating the new young shoots as a substitute for asparagus. In the kitchen the old European *E. maritum* has been superseded by its tropical cousin, *E. foetidum*. The latter was widely used as a cure-all in Carib medicine and is one of the herbs that give Caribbean foods their distinctive flavor. Merchants and travelers introduced it into southeast Asia, where it is popular in Vietnam, Thailand, and Korea. Its Thai name *pak chi farang* can be translated as "foreign cilantro." It is also widely grown in West Africa and India.

Culantro, *E. foetidum*, is raised from seed sown in spring. Germination takes about 30 days. It is also available as plugs (the best way to start) which should be planted in spacings of 3¼–5ft apart in the row and 5ft between rows.

TASTING NOTES

Puerto Rican salsa

A simple, spicy salsa to complement tortilla chips.

Preparation time: 15 minutes
Cooking time: 10 minutes
Serves: 4 people

You will need:

• 1 tbsp oil

• 4 tomatoes, chopped and sliced

• 4 cloves garlic, chopped

• 1 onion

• 1 tsp lemon juice

• 2 chillies, chopped

• Handful of culantro, finely chopped

Fry the tomatoes, garlic, and onion in oil with lemon juice and chillies. Simmer for 10 minutes.

Mix into a smooth paste.

When cool, sprinkle on culantro.

BELOW: The old advice was that only eryngo roots below a depth of 4½ft were worth candying, but it is worth preparing very young shoots early in the year.

Culantro grows naturally in shaded, moisture-retentive sandy soils rich in organic matter, and it likes to be well-irrigated. Although it will grow in full sun, shady sites produce larger, greener leaves, and a significant delay in flowering. In temperate climates, grow under glass or in the house—a steamy kitchen or bathroom—and view its cultivation as short-term. The leaves need to be picked before flowering. In nontropical regions it will bolt in high summer when the days are longer.

Fennel
Foeniculum vulgare

Common names: Sweet fennel, *sonf* (seeds in Indian cookery); also bronze fennel comes from the cultivar "Purpureum"

Type: Perennial

Climate: Hardy, cold winter

Size: 5ft (1.5m)

Origin: Mediterranean

History: According to legend, Prometheus carried fire from heaven down to earth in a fennel stem. Gladiators ate fennel to give them stamina and courage. The Roman writer Lucius Junius Moderatus Columella's reference to "threatening fennel" relates to the use of the mature stems for caning naughty schoolboys.

Cultivation: Sow seeds in spring in well-drained soil in a warm sunny position. For regular pickings, thin plants to spacings of 12–14in and keep cutting back to encourage new feathery growth.

Fennel is promiscuous and will cross with other umbelliferous herbs, especially dill, to the detriment of their individual flavors.

Storage: Freeze feathery leaves and break as required. Preserve mature stems in oil (see p.75). Store seeds that have been allowed to air dry on the plant in a sterilized, airtight container. See also recipe for Garam Masala (see p.81).

Preparation: Fennel has a pronounced aniseed flavor. The fresh, young leaves look and taste delicious in salads. Young, bronze fennel leaves look good with purple-leaved lettuces or in contrast to the pale green of avocadoes. Chop finely in sandwiches or into mayonnaise. As fennel matures, the stems become woody but strongly flavored. Place fennel stems inside whole fish when baking or under chicken when roasting. The green fennel has attractive yellow flower umbels and a clean, fresh aniseed flavor that look and taste good with lemon-based desserts or scattered in a fruit salad. Crystallize them to decorate cakes and desserts (for method see p.59).

The seeds of fennel have a reputation for quelling hunger, so it was used as an early slimming aid by the Romans, chewed by Christians in times of fast, and used figuratively as a symbol of deceit by Shakespeare—the deceit being that it makes you feel you have eaten when you have not.

ABOVE: Pound herbs in a mortar using a pestle either to extract the oils or create a paste. The resulting extract will have a far better flavor than when chopped.

LEFT: The herb sweet fennel does not produce a bulb, unlike Florence fennel (var. *azoricum*). The leaves, flowers, and seeds all have an excellent aniseed taste.

"A CHAPLET OF HERBS ... FENNEL Would seem to belong exclusively to fish. Set fronds of it on top when baking fish, or on a fish cutlet cooked *en papillotte*. Serve fennel sauce with boiled salmon or mackerel. The sharp piquancy of the herb corrects the oiliness of the flesh."

Vogue's Contemporary Cookery, (1947) **Doris Lytton Toye**

What is true is that if you are tempted to eat between meals, chewing a few seeds provides a pleasant, calorie-free taste that stops you snacking.

The Italian salami, *finocchiona*, is flavored with fennel seeds. According to English writer, gardener, and diarist John Evelyn, fennel expelled wind, sharpened eyesight, and "recreates the Brain." Stems were used when cooking fish, their warm flavor counteracting the cold of fish.

Sweet and bronze fennel should not be confused with the less hardy vegetable Florence fennel, which produces an edible bulbous stem. An attractive tall herb with feathered leaves on long stems, sweet fennel is worth planting among herbaceous perennials in borders rather than the herb garden. The early leaves of bronze fennel make an attractive dark foil for spring bulbs. In summer the sunshine-yellow umbels, set against the bright green of the sweet fennel, strike an architectural note; the bronze is more weedy and

TASTING NOTES

Fish flambée with fennel

This light and refreshing recipe is ideal for use with whole sea-bass, red mullet, or mackerel.

Preparation time: 5 minutes
Cooking time: 7–10 minutes
Serves: 6 people

You will need:

• Whole fish, gutted

• 2–3 short fennel stems

• 6–8 fennel stalks, dried

• 6floz (175ml) Armagnac

Place the stems of fennel in the body cavity.

Make two or three incisions in the skin.

Brush oil over the fish and then either bake or broil on a grid for about 7 minutes, turning once.

Lift the grid onto a fireproof dish lined with dried fennel stalks.

Set alight to a glass of Armagnac and pour it flaming over fish. This will ignite the fennel, which in turn flavors the fish and gives out a gorgeous scent.

the umbels are less interesting. Fennel readily self-seeds, and as the seedlings are easily recognizable, they can be moved or weeded out accordingly. Established plants can be lifted, divided, and moved in spring.

Sweet woodruff
Galium odoratum

Common names: Sweet woodruff, wuderove, wood-rova, Our Lady's Lace, sweet scented bedstraw

Type: Herbaceous perennial

Climate: Hardy, cold winter

Size: 12–18in (30–45cm)

Origin: Europe, Northern Africa

History: The Old English name of *wuderove* was derived from the French *rovelle*, meaning "wheel," and descriptive of the spoke-like arrangement of the whorled green leaves. The French name *muge-de-boys*, meaning "musk of the woods," evokes the gentle fresh grass scent that it infuses both into the air and food, which increases markedly when dried.

Cultivation: Best sown from fresh seed in late summer. If using packeted seeds ensure they have a period of stratification, i.e. exposure to winter cold (see p.37). Divide established clumps in spring.

Storage: Dry the whole plant and store in a sterilized, airtight jar.

Preparation: Use the top 6in of plant; when crushed the leaves exude the scent of freshly mown hay. These aromatic properties become far stronger when dried. Dried or fresh, steep for a few hours in fruit juice, white wine, or punch to impart an aromatic yet cooling flavor.

There are two traditional Germanic recipes designed to be spring tonics. The first is *Maibowle* or *Maitrank,* where fresh or dried flowering tops are steeped in still white wine, preferably a dry Palatinate; it is important to keep tasting for strength because woodruff rapidly imparts its scent. Keep chilled, then top up with an equal amount of sparkling white wine before serving. For a less alcoholic version, add sparkling water. The drink was used to toast May Day. American recipes add orange and pineapple juice. The second is *Waldmeister*, where strawberries served in white wine, preferably a Moselle, are infused with fresh flowering woodruff. The latter can also be adapted into a cold soup.

BELOW: Sweet woodruff is at its most aromatic when in flower. Allow to dry slightly, but only infuse for a short time.

Woodruff contains a useful crystalline chemical called coumarin, also found in melilot and tonka beans, which fixes the scent of other plants. It is still invaluable in herbal mixtures such as pot-pourri and in its traditional use as part of the "hay" used for stuffing mattresses. Dried stems were stored with bed linen to impart a fresh scent. It was also used to disguise unpleasant odors both in medicine and domestically as an air freshener. It was one of the ingredients added to "fancy" snuff. English botanist and herbalist John Gerard recommended steeping it in wine to "make a man merry, and to be good for the heart and liver ..." Woodruff's close relation, Ladies Bedstraw, *G. verum*, was used for curdling and coloring cheese; it too contains coumarin.

Woodruff thrives in dappled shade. Grow under shrubs and small trees where it will carpet the ground in late spring. Its tangle of whorled leaves provides a bright emerald-green underlay. Late spring and into early summer, it is studded with small white four-petaled, star flowers that are lightly fragrant.

Grow in loose, moist, leafy soils. Like its close relation the weed goosegrass, the seeds will attach themselves to passing humans and animals to aid their distribution. If it naturalizes too successfully it can be cut by a rotary mower on a high setting. It will suffer and die back in long, hot summers.

The scents and flavors of sweet woodruff increase as it dries so do not infuse immediately after picking but enjoy fragrant wafts—described variously as rose, vanilla, summer, and citrus—in the room for at least a couple of hours or overnight. The traditional popularity of Germanic woodruff cocktails has taken a modern twist by infusing the half-dried flowering stems in schnapps or vodka for about half an hour as

SWEET WOODRUFF—A HARD-WORKING GARDEN PLANT

Ideal for allowing to naturalize under the shade of deciduous shrubs or a small tree as long as the soil does not dry out.

Its starry flowers will light up the ground as the shrubs or trees break into leaf, then continue as a green mat under their canopy. Underplant with late winter bulbs such as crocus or snowdrops and, as they die back, woodruff's attractive ruffled leaves will cover their tracks.

Woodruff also provides an attractive foil to white tulips, just as long as you don't harvest the flowers or stems of the latter for consumption with the former.

a straight drink. An alternative is a gloriously lucid lime-green sweet woodruff vodka jelly. Infuse in hot syrup for no longer than half an hour and then, with the addition of gelatine and vodka, follow the usual method for an adult jelly. In France, the half-dried flowering stems are used to flavor cold soups and palette-cleansing sorbets served between courses.

Hyssop
Hyssopus officinalis

Common names: Hyssop, hyssope, Herbe de Josephe

Type: Perennial

Climate: Hardy, average winter

Size: 18–24in (45–60cm)

Origin: Southern Europe

History: Prized as *azob*, meaning a holy herb, it was used for cleaning sacred places echoed in the Old Testament: "Purge me with hyssop and I shall be clean." There are arguments that the plant in question is actually *Origanum syriacum*. However, hyssop's essential oil is antiseptic and is also still used in the perfume industry.

Cultivation: Hyll's 1577 cultural advice remains valid: "Isop may be sowed of seeds, or you may part the roots, or set the Slips." He also recommended it as a hedging herb for knots. Hyssop will be hardier in a well-drained, sunny situation that is dry during the winter. Sow direct in spring.

Storage: Air dry the leaves on their stems (see p.11), then crumble off as needed. They can be frozen but there are fresh supplies almost year round.

Preparation: See *Herbes Provençales* (p.138). As well as with cooked tomatoes, the resinous and fragrant leaves are good with roast and stewed pork and wild boar. Infuse in syrup when cooking peaches or apricots, then serve these fruits chilled or placed in a pie. Flowers can be scattered over, or incorporated in, the finished dish or folded into an accompanying crème fraiche. Flowering sprigs are used for tisanes. Eating hyssop was long believed to warm the body and protect against colds. Recent research in Canada has indicated that it could be a valuable antiviral for HIV sufferers.

LEFT: Whether blue-, pink-, or white-flowering, sprigs or leaves of hyssop add a resinous flavor. Plant in well-drained situations as this aids successful overwintering.

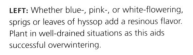

"The leaves have a spicy taste a little like mint with a bitterness. Hyssop is used in Gascony as one of the herbs in a bouquet garni for flavoring a concentrated puree of tomatoes that is to be preserved for the winter. A sprig of the leaves gives a pleasant flavor to a sugar syrup for fruit."

Recipes from a French Herb Garden, (1989) Geraldene Holt

The Romans noted wild and garden varieties, and its value as a bee plant. They also stewed figs in honeyed water flavored with hyssop and rue. Hyssop mixed with wormwood and mint gave absinthe its characteristic green color. English botanist and herbalist John Gerard recommended it for relieving bruises, for which it is still used.

Hyssop flowers can be blue, white, or pink, so if you want to guarantee one color, buy plants only when they are in flower. The blue- and white-flowering forms typically have narrower leaves and tighter florets, while the pink-veering-toward-purple flowers are more voluptuous and the plant tends to be more bushy. Cut back the flowering stems in late fall to stop wind rock in winter, and in spring cut back to the lowest buds on the collar of the main stems. This will stop the bushes becoming leggy. Hyssop is a short-lived perennial but self-sets easily. Cuttings can be taken in the spring or fall. Although not as tidy as lavender, it is a good hedging herb. In a knot garden, keep it in shape with regular trimming but allow it to flower. Subspecies *aristatus* is a compact form with purple-hued blue flowers, which makes it an attractive, scented edging plant. It grows well in a pot and can be trimmed into a globe.

TASTING NOTES

Herbelade

This recipe is reminiscent of 17th century-style leftovers. *Herbelade* is a delicious sweetly aromatic way of using leftover roast pork.

Preparation time: 15 minutes
Cooking time: 45 minutes
Serves: 8 people

You will need:

· 1lb (450g) leftover pork, minced

· 3 tbsp hyssop, sage, and parsley

· 4 dates, pitted and chopped

· 2 tbsp raisins and nuts

· 2 tbsp pine nuts

· 4 egg yolks, beaten lightly

· 1 tsp ground ginger

· 1 tsp salt

· 1 tsp superfine sugar

· 1 pinch of saffron

· 4floz (110ml) pork broth

· 8floz (240ml) water

Preheat a conventional oven to 400°F (200°C / gas mark 6 / fan 180°C).

Put the pork, herbs, water, and broth in a pan, bring to the boil, and cook for 15–20 minutes.

Drain, cool, and mix in the rest of the ingredients.

Pour into a pastry case and bake for 45 minutes.

THE BOUQUET GARNI

GENTLY IMPARTING HERBAL FLAVORS

A well-chosen bouquet garni equates with an artistic and balanced flower arrangement. Rather than the texture, tone, and color of flowers, the garni requires an understanding of aromatic balance and piquant subtleties. The keynote lies in the leaves of the sweet bay: when fresh they are gently aromatic, and when dried they take on an almost smoky flavor. Although not part of a bouquet garni, garlic crushed and wiped around earthenware cooking pots imparts an extra dimension.

The herbs used are different from the *fines herbes*. They need to be woody, matured by the sun, so that their savor is not lost during the long slow cook or marinade. Unlike fresh-cut young herb leaves and flowers, whose individual tastes are there to be enjoyed, the herbs in the bouquet garni gently impart a compound aromatic flavor.

Key herbs in order of importance are:

Sweet bay (*Laurus nobilis*)—only use leaves, fresh or dried.

Parsley (*Petroselenium crispum*)—take off the leafy tops and only

use the stems. Just before serving, finely chop the parsley leaves and fold in or use as a garnish. Good in accompanying pie crusts or dumplings.

Thyme (*Thymus*)—two or three sprigs, fresh or dried. Good when finely chopped in accompanying piecrusts or dumplings.

Oregano or marjoram (*Origanum*)—two or three sprigs, fresh or dried. The flavors change during the year: fragrant in spring and summer when the stems and leaves are still soft, highly aromatic as the stems harden in the fall. The leaves are good in accompanying piecrusts or dumplings.

RIGHT: The leaves of sweet bay are an essential part of most bouquet garni mixtures. In the winter, pick some small branches and bring them into the house to have to hand.

THE YEAR-ROUND BOUQUET GARNI

The most convenient place to grow favorite herbs for cooking is near a house door. This is especially useful in the winter. A decorative traditional herb garden can be created with the key herbs: bay, thyme, marjoram, rosemary, fennel, and parsley.

Bay can be trimmed into a variety of shapes or used as a boundary evergreen. Bush thymes thrive in terracotta pots, which make them truly a movable feast for both the garden and the kitchen. The bright leaf color of golden marjoram, *Origanum vulgare* "Aureum," especially in the spring, can be used to create drifts through borders as well as soft path edgings. Rosemary can be trained as an evergreen wall shrub or clipped as a hedge, with its flavor becoming increasingly resinous during the winter. Parsley pots provide regular small pickings throughout the summer, but if grown with vegetables in rich soil and with some protection you

TASTING NOTES

Tailoring your bouquet garni

Meat	A bay leaf, parsley, thyme, and marjoram
Fish	A bay leaf, parsley, fennel stems, and/or lemon balm
Poultry	A bay leaf, parsley, lemon thyme, and marjoram or a bay leaf, parsley, and French tarragon. An equally good combination placed in the bird's cavity before roasting
Game	A bay leaf, parsley, rosemary, and juniper
Provençal	A bay leaf, parsley, crushed garlic, and orange peel
Winter stews and pulse soups	A bay leaf, parsley, and winter savory. Finely chop the parsley and savory leaves into accompanying dumplings

should be able to have fresh leaves almost year round. Apart from parsley, these herbs all dry well.

When the days are shorter, it is worth picking a large bouquet of fresh mixed herbs and keeping them in a pitcher to hand in the kitchen.

LEFT: Stems of flat-leaved parsley, a bay leaf, and a generous sprig of thyme form the simplest bouquet garni for a huge range of savory dishes.

HOW TO TIE THE BOUQUET GARNI

The model of high culinary art is to wrap your chosen herbs up in a leek leaf and secure like a parcel. The whole process will take about 10 minutes (see below). The practical cook will tie up the stems with plain cotton string (make sure it is not colored as the dye will run). This method accords with the translation of bouquet garni— a faggot of herbs. This method is ideal if you have a plentiful supply of fresh herbs, as you can make a really generous bouquet. This system makes it easy to remove the bouquet garni before serving. Avoid the temptation just to throw in all the herbs and leave the diner to sift out unwanted twigs. The garni can be frozen or kept in a fridge for the short term if it is not for immediate use.

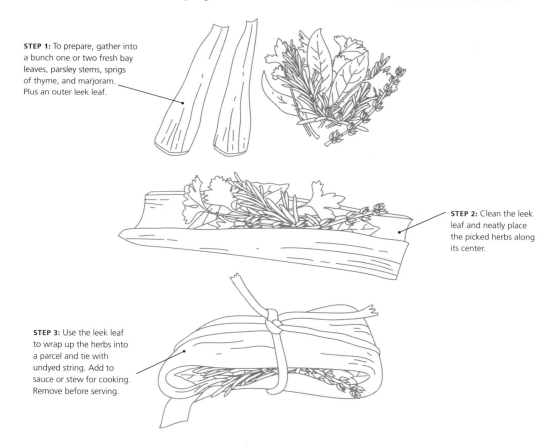

STEP 1: To prepare, gather into a bunch one or two fresh bay leaves, parsley stems, sprigs of thyme, and marjoram. Plus an outer leek leaf.

STEP 2: Clean the leek leaf and neatly place the picked herbs along its center.

STEP 3: Use the leek leaf to wrap up the herbs into a parcel and tie with undyed string. Add to sauce or stew for cooking. Remove before serving.

"Bay Leaf. In cooking, only the *laurier franc*, or Apollo's bay leaf, is used; and it is frequently. It is put in all bouquet garnis, which are an obligatory seasoning for all stews. But it must be used in moderation, and preferably dried, so that its flavor is less strong, and less bitter."

Le Grand Dictionnaire de Cuisine, (1873) **Alexandre Dumas Père**

Juniper
Juniperus communis

ABOVE: The only edible part of the juniper is its berries and their distinctive taste is redolent of gin and aromatics. The berries take 18 months to ripen.

Common names: Juniper, bastard killer, horse saving

Type: Evergreen shrub

Climate: Very hardy, very cold winter)

Size: 6½–33ft (2–10m)

Origin: Eurasia

History: Virgil wrote of the incense of juniper wood and this can still be enjoyed on an open fire or barbeque. Herbalists from earliest times prized it as a counterpoison and resister of pestilence. It was believed to be a powerful force against devils, elves, witches, and other evil incarnations.

Cultivation: The common variety can be raised from seed sown under cover in spring or fall. Propagate from heel cuttings in the fall.

Storage: Dried berries (fruits) can be kept in an airtight jar for up to two years.

Preparation: Use dried berries in which a gin-like aromatic can be discerned. See bouquet garni for game (see p100). The gently crushed berries can be added to coarse textured pork or game terrines. Cook with wild duck.

Juniper is described as a "bitter" aromatic herb that is antiseptic and diuretic. It aids digestion but also stimulates the uterus. Pregnant women are advised to avoid eating it in any quantity.

The flavor of true Holland gin is derived from juniper, as is the name a corruption via the French *genièvre* to geneva and thus to gin. A readily available berry in the mountainous districts of Provence and Corsica, as well as central and eastern France, juniper is a key flavoring for cooking game, pork, and their associated stuffings and pâtés.

Numerous cultivars of *J. communis* are available in different forms and habits from columnar to weeping and prostrate. It tolerates a wide range of soil types. Harvest by shaking the berries off the branches onto a ground sheet, or pick them off bush forms.

RIGHT: There are many cultivars of edible juniper suitable for a variety of climates, and its resinous wood exudes a fragrant smoke when burned.

"The appearance of juniper berries in a list of ingredients often puzzles English people, which is odd considering that they constitute one of the main flavoring agents of gin, which gets its name from the Latin *Ginepro* or juniper, and juniper berries were commonly used in England in the spicing of beef and hams."

French Provincial Cooking, **(1960) Elizabeth David**

CONTAINERS

PLOTS IN POTS

Containers provide versatility, seasonal variation, and decoration both outside and in, and have a long history of use. The Romans used terracotta pots, ones that closely resembled the modern strawberry or parsley pot, to transport herbs and plants around the Empire. Old amphoras would be set in the ground and used as plant containers—a good way to recycle old pots.

LEFT: Lilac flowers of *Petunia* Surfinia Pink Vein "Suntosol" (Surfinia Series) displayed here as an example of a hanging basket on an outside garden wall. Try planting herbs such as parsley, marjoram, or woodruff this way.

Other examples of containers include the paneled wooden container known as the Versailles box. It is associated with orange trees, but was equally used for myrtles and bay trees in historic orangeries. The wood acts as an excellent insulant for the inner pot and is worth considering for any of the larger perennial herbs. The inner pot should be lightweight plastic rather than clay. Try to replicate this if using a window box by leaving the plants in pots, but setting them in potting compost.

Glazed terracotta pots are best for herbs. Being porous, they are able to insulate against extremes of heat and cold, dry and wet, to a greater degree than unglazed pots and are less likely to crack in frost. Generally avoid plastic pots as they are poor insulators. Most gardeners will grow herbs in pots on patios and windowsills or in hanging baskets (see left) or planters.

If space is at a premium, particularly on a balcony or indoors, ceramic sky planters are worth experimenting with. They are designed with a unique reservoir that allows the planters to be grown upside down, seeming literally to hang from the sky, and they are recommended for mint, parsley, and scented geraniums, as well as fennel. However, fennel would need to be grown as an annual or it would become too large.

POT GUIDANCE

Large pots are usually expensive, so need to be well cared for. Italian Terrace are among the best. Line the pot with a porous material that will protect the interior and make lifting out established herbs for repotting much easier, without inhibiting growth.

Traditional advice is to fill the base of large pots with crocks to allow drainage, a good idea in principle, except all the potting compost rapidly drains all around them. By lining the pot as above, the crocks and compost are kept separate.

When it comes to strawberry or parsley pots, buy as big as possible. Many herbs will grow well in the top but the side pockets are only suitable for parsley, the finest-leaved basil, small thymes, and violets. Depending on what you grow in the top, you could underplant with a few saffron crocuses—just ensure you do not eat the leaves.

If pots have to be left outside in regions with hard winters, insulate them by either wrapping in bubble wrap (unsightly but effective) or sinking in the ground.

Large specimens do not need annual repotting. Simply scrape away the top soil and add new compost in the spring.

For moisture retention, mulch the pot surface with gravel, stones, or shells. Compost should also be fully moistened so make sure to water, though a good soak is of much greater value than light daily watering, which rapidly evaporates.

During the festive season, potted bay, juniper, myrtle, and rosemary can be decorated as substitute Christmas or party trees.

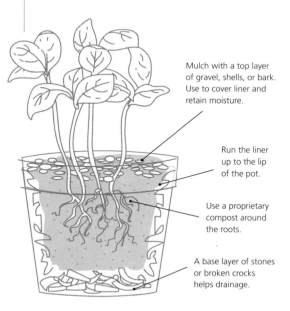

Mulch with a top layer of gravel, shells, or bark. Use to cover liner and retain moisture.

Run the liner up to the lip of the pot.

Use a proprietary compost around the roots.

A base layer of stones or broken crocks helps drainage.

ABOVE: Sky planters seem counterintuitive but are perfect for growing herbs in well-lit kitchens. It gives a whole new meaning to herbs to hand as the pots can be hung from the ceiling.

ABOVE: Lining ornamental pots with a porous material keeps the compost out of the crocks and helps you lift out perennial herbs without damaging them or the container when repotting.

Sweet bay
Laurus nobilis

Common names: Sweet bay, bay, true laurel

Type: Evergreen tree

Climate: Hardy, average winter

Size: 10–49ft (3–15m)

Origin: South Europe

History: Bay was introduced across the Roman Empire, and many centuries later pioneers introduced it into the Americas and Australia.

Cultivation: In colder climates, plant bay in a position that does not get the morning sunlight. Partial shade is tolerated.

Storage: Bay leaves can be picked fresh all year round. Dry small branches, keep in a dust free place, and use the leaves as required.

Preparation: A key herb in the bouquet garni, soft new leaves can also be used in the summer to be chopped into cream cheeses. Dried leaves have a subtle, almost smoky flavor and are ideal for long, slow cooking in casseroles and stock pots. The fresh kind are more fragrantly aromatic and will lift a béchamel sauce or savory or sweet custard. Press them into the tops of fresh pâtés and terrines where they will be both decorative and impart a gentle flavor.

ABOVE: Bay leaves can be used whole in sauces (from which they must be removed before serving), or finely ground in soups and broths.

The origins of bay lie in a story of metamorphosis. The god Apollo, overwhelmed by love, was chasing the nymph Daphne with less than honorable intentions. She called for protection from her father, the river god Peneus, who transfigured her into a bay tree. Apollo embraced her leafy limbs and vowed to wear them as chaplets of honor. They became a Roman symbol of victory and peace, which has echoed through history in architecture, statues, garlands, and nomenclature such as Poet Laureate. In addition to its many culinary uses, cooks placed small leaves under cakes when they baked them, and it was used in the packing of dried figs to deter weevils. It is said to alleviate indigestion and wind.

Bay can be grown as a tree or clipped bush in a large pot. If creating a cone- or pyramid-shaped topiary bay, remember that it will be hardier if the branches are left on the trunk. In sheltered locations or in a movable pot, it can be trained into a "lollipop." Ensure a stout trunk by identifying the central straight stem, supporting with a cane if necessary, and only gradually removing the side branches. Young, flexible stems can be trained around a sturdy cane to create a spiral trunk. Trim the bushes in spring or fall. A severe winter can cut a bay tree to the ground; if this happens, wait at least three months before removing as they often reshoot from the base. Female bay trees have small scented yellow flowers, and if you grow male and female clones, they will set viable seed in temperate climates. The golden-leaved variety "Aurea" can be planted in a sunny position and is hardier than the species form.

ABOVE: Antonio Pollaiouolo's horticulturally accurate painting of Apollo desperately trying to grasp Daphne as she metamorphoses into bay. Her arms depict the bay's natural form.

TASTING NOTES

Herb cheese

This recipe is based on a 1955 one by British cookery writer Elizabeth David. She suggested using homemade milk cheese, but ricotta is a good alternative for the modern kitchen. Great when eaten simply with brown bread.

Preparation time: 10 minutes
Serves: 6 people

You will need:

• ½lb (250g) tub of ricotta

• 5 tbsp fresh lemon thyme, chopped

• 5 tbsp fresh sweet marjoram, chopped

• 1 fresh bay leaf, chopped

• Salt and pepper

Into the ricotta, stir the lemon thyme and sweet marjoram then add the bay leaf.

Season with salt pepper.

Pile the cheese up in a dish and leave for several hours before serving to give the flavor of the herbs time to penetrate the cheese.

TOPIARY

CLIPPINGS, CLOUDS, AND CHARACTERS

ABOVE: A printed chromolithograph depicting topiary in "The Alhambra Garden" Elvaston Castle, from The Gardens of England by Edward Aveno Brooke (1821–1910).

Pliny the Younger, the nephew of the oft-quoted other Pliny, used the term *topiarus* to describe the man who trimmed his plants into mottoes and other such delights. Topiary can be scaled and fashioned to any space available, and can be as sober or as quirky as the gardener might wish.

In herbaceous perennial flower beds, the formality of clipped evergreens gently brings the scheme into focus, a focal point to admire or amuse. The shapes can be in the singular; a series such as single, double, or triple lollipops; or balls on one stout stem. A combination of any of the following add sober balance or gentle humor: sentinel cones, pyramids, spirals, wedding cakes, or Japanese cloud pruning, not forgetting peacocks or squirrels. Rather than a lavender hedge, pot up a larger form like "Grosso" and trim it into spheres or cones but allow it to flower. In fact, put any of the above shapes in an attractive container and you can create a scene wherever you wish, not least having ready-to-pick herbs flanking an outer door.

STANDARD TOPIARIES

Regular topiaries are trained on one trunk and need it to be stout. Identify the main straight stem, then gradually prune away the side branches. Remember that the side branches help to feed and strengthen the trunk. A strong trunk will support a healthy plant that will not need staking. Once established, rub out any side shoots that appear on the trunk. If you start with a young, whippy stem, you can train it around a cane to form a spiral main trunk and follow the instructions above.

If larger stems or branches need to be removed from the main trunk, make sure the cut is not flush with the central stem but cut to the branch collar; this will gradually disappear as the topiary grows. When it comes to cutting back branches, note that every bud is at a different angle on the branch; identify which direction you want the new shoot to grow and cut to that bud. Cuts should slope away from the bud so that water drains away.

AIMING FOR EVEN GROWTH

A balanced shape can be achieved by attending to the cultural needs of the plant, such as soil type, watering, feeding, and availability of light. Topiary in small containers can be turned regularly to ensure an even exposure to sunlight.

WHEN TO PRUNE

For foliage-only topiary, trimming should take place in mid-spring and again in mid-fall. Occasional extra trimming may be necessary to maintain the shape, but try to combine that with harvesting for cooking. For flowering topiary,

ABOVE: From left to right: lavender, bay, and rosemary lend themselves to being trained into a globe; bay can be trained to form a lollipop; while the branches of rosemary can be cloud pruned.

such as lavender, bushes should trimmed once the display is over. A further, closer trim can be made again in early spring before growth recommences, but check the individual pruning requirements of your plant before you do the spring trim.

FRAMING UP

There are a good selection of topiary frames available, which makes the job of shaping topiary much easier. Place these over the herbs, allow them to grow through, and then just trim to shape.

WINTER CARE

It may be unsightly, but wrapping up the exposed trunks of ball and lollipop topiaries with bubble wrap during the winter will help their survival. If grown in containers, it is worth wrapping the container as well, which will not only insulate the roots but will also protect the container. Decorative as it looks, heavy snow can damage topiaries so shake off any that settles.

Lavender
Lavandula angustifolia

Common names: Lavender, English lavender, true lavender—there are myriad cultivars of the old English variety, *Lavandula angustifolia*, ranging in size and flower color. There are celebrated names such as "Hidcote," "Hidcote Pink," and "Munstead."

Type: Evergreen shrub

Climate: Hardy, average winter

Size: 19½–40in (50–100cm)

Origin: Atlantic Islands, Mediterranean

History: The Greeks named it Nardus, believing it came from the Syrian city of Naarda, and it is one of the plants also known as Spikenard. The Egyptians used it for mummification and perfume. *Lavandula* is derived from the Latin *lavare* meaning "to wash." Not only did the oils in lavender add fragrance to the wash, but they are also an insect repellent.

Cultivation: Lavender can be raised from seed but sometimes does not come true to type. Sow seeds in spring, direct into the soil or seed boxes, then thin or transplant to 12–19½in apart. Alternatively buy named varieties from a specialist nursery.

Storage: Lavender leaves and flowers dry excellently. Dry in sugar (see box) or store in an airtight can or jar away from the light. Flowerheads can be infused in oil or vinegar (see p.75).

Preparation: The leaves can be used as a substitute for rosemary when cooking lamb with garlic. Use both leaves and flowers in ice cream, sorbets, and cookies. Chop finely and add to marzipan candy. The flowers will give a highly scented flavor. A tisane of lavender flowers is said to ease headaches, insomnia, and gum problems.

LEFT: The lavender-covered hillsides of Provence in France are seas of purple when in flower and the heady scent is an integral part of the local cuisine.

The Romans used lavender to deter bed bugs. English lavender started to be developed commercially in the 17th century, at the same time as plants were taken to America, where the Quakers farmed lavender and other herbs. The English Romantic poet John Keats poetically captured the scent and blue flowers with the joy of deep sleep in clean sheets: "And still she slept an azure-lidded sleep, In blanched linen, smooth and lavender." Old writers praise its virtues as a decorative plant for the garden as well as attracting bees and smelling sweet. Historical recipes for distillation, oils, and comfits were intended for medicinal use. On a culinary note, Napoleon would drink a hot cocktail of coffee and hot chocolate sweetened with lavender sugar before going to his first wife, Josephine. In the past *L. angustifolia* has been known as *L. vera* and *L. officinalis*, all more commonly called Old English Lavender. The oils and flowers are used to scent soaps, bags, and perfumes.

TASTING NOTES

Lavender-scented sugar

Lavender-scented sugar is an easy way of infusing a perfumed tone into desserts.

Preparation time: 5 minutes, plus 1–2 weeks for standing
Serves: makes 10oz (280g) Kilner jar

You will need:

• 2oz (55g) lavender flowerheads

• 8oz (225g) superfine sugar, plus some extra for topping up

Mix the lavender flowerheads with the sugar.

Select a dry glass jar and simply layer the flowers and sugar alternately.

Cover tightly and leave in a warm room for 1–2 weeks, occasionally giving the jar a shake.

Before using, sift the sugar, then return the flowerheads, and top up with more sugar.

"Hot lavender," 12.

ABOVE: The taste of lavender has a zest and fragrance that matches Crane's portrayal of Perdita in *A Winter's Tale*. Lavender flowers on cakes and desserts can make an equally dramatic stance.

Lavender varieties to try

The leaves and flowers of the lavenders listed below can be used in cooking, for both their scent and flavor.

L. angustifolia Traditional gray-green bush with rich lavender-blue flowers. Leaves evergreen in warm winters, foliage and flowers highly aromatic, growing up to 4ft.

"Alba" Smaller lavender with gray-white leaves and white flowers. Sweetly fragrant but more tender, growing to 24 x 24in.

"Blue Ice" The flowers appear to be frosted with their pale mauve florets peeping out from woolly sepals. Ideal for a white or night garden. Grows to 24 x 29½in.

L.a. "Elizabeth" The dark lavender-purple florets have a royal blue appearance, sometimes described as "shocking violet," are very fragrant, on strong stems set against evergreen silvery foliage appearing in late summer. Good for hedges, as a specimen, or clipped into a cone. Grows 18 x 24in.

"Hidcote Giant" Deep purple flowers; as the name suggests, it is taller than the original compact "Hidcote"; also there is the supposedly improved "Hidcote Superior," growing to over 3¼ x 3¼ft. Ensure you keep it well pruned to stop it becoming woody.

"Loddon Pink" Soft pink flowers, growing to 18in, drought hardy, good for hedges. Space at 12–15¾in. Introduced in the 1950s.

"Munstead" Introduced in 1902 and named for the Munstead wood gardens of Miss Gertrude Jekyll who made quantities of pot-pourri from her scented roses and lavender in the early 20th century. Large, blue-lilac flowers contrast with small leaves. Flowers good for lavender sugar. Grows 24 x 24in.

L. × intermedia "Grosso" Also known as Fat Bud French Lavender—popular on both sides of the Atlantic with a naturally globular habit; trim after flowering and then in spring for shape. Flower spikes unusually plump. Both leaves and flowers are highly aromatic. Good for topiary, spot planting, and containers. Grows to 18–29½in x 18–29½in.

L. × intermedia "Seal" Old-fashioned, tall elegant lavender; strong, long stems and pale well-scented lavender flowers. Ideal as a specimen or for tubs and pots. Grows to 35 x 35in.

As a native of Mediterranean hillsides, lavenders like sunny, well-drained sites and calcareous soil. In England, the low rainfall of Norfolk seems to meet these requirements, assisting with the successful production of commercial lavender. However, lavenders do not like summer humidity, extreme winter cold, or winter damp, which can make growing lavender difficult in some areas.

The *L. angustifolia* forms are the best for culinary purposes and can be grown as a low hedge or path edging in a sunny position. There are many more decorative species but they are neither as aromatic, nor suitable for consumption. If you want to ensure the variety, propagate from tip or heel cuttings, which will root well. The former in early summer and the latter in early fall. Lightly prune the bushes as soon as the flowers start to fade, then trim back again in early spring, being careful not to prune into old wood because lavenders do not reshoot readily from the bare stems. Lavender will also tolerate air pollution, but be careful to clean the leaves and flowers of plants growing in polluted areas before consumption. Lavender and roses grown together evoke the traditional English garden.

RIGHT: *Lavandula angustifolia* is the traditional highly fragrant lavender and parent of many cultivars. The leaves infuse an aromatic, summer taste into barbecues or cookies.

FIELDS OF LAVENDER

Between 1946 and 1989 Deeside Lavender could boast that it had the most northerly lavender fields in the world. They were planted and developed on two acres in Banchory, northeast Scotland, by Andrew Inkster. Inkster was a chemist and entrepreneur. He established that the light, sandy soils of Deeside—near the River Dee in Aberdeenshire—probably in conjunction with the very long summer days, produced a lavender oil that was superior in quality to other commercial extractors, but yielded less in quantity.

In its heyday, over 25,000 visitors a year flocked to walk along Scottish fields of purple lavender mirroring those of Provence. The British National Collection of Lavenders is held at the University Botanic Gardens, Cambridge; in their taxonomy of *The Genus Lavandula*, its former Director Tim Upson and Susyn Andrews identified a cultivar of lavender that is specific to Banchory, which had been developed commercially by Inkster. In 2001, an especially hardy lavender from Banchory was named for Inkster's old home, *Lavandula* "Torramhor."

Lovage
Levisticum officinale

Common names: Lovage, love parsley, sea parsley

Type: Herbaceous perennial

Climate: Hardy, very cold winter

Size: 24in–4ft (60–120cm)

Origin: Mediterranean

History: The Roman taste for strong flavors made celery-tasting lovage a popular pot herb. It was used in sauce for pigeons and other small birds. Lovage appears on Charlemagne's *Capitulare de Villis Imperialibus* of AD 872 as a physic herb, for which the root would have been used.

Cultivation: Lovage can be grown from seeds, ideally sown ripe from the plant in late summer. Grow at minimum 12in spacings. Cut back regularly to encourage fresh, more palatable shoots.

Storage: Seeds can be dried for flavoring. Candy the stalks as for angelica (see p.75).

Preparation: Young leaves give a great "bite" in green salads and here you can enjoy its strong flavor in isolation. Stems add a distinct celery flavor to soups and casseroles—the younger the plant the more aromatic and subtle the savor. As older stems become hollow, they can be used as natural straws for cocktails such as Bloody Mary. Seeds can be added to savory cookies and bread, and can be ground to make a salt substitute or used as celery salt. Make a creole ratafia cordial by steeping 2 tablespoons of lovage seeds in 8½floz of brandy for 30 days. Strain and mix with a sugar syrup, cinnamon, and lemon juice to taste. Drink hot or cold. After the third year, roots can be lifted and cooked or grated raw. Eating lovage is said to freshen your breath.

LEFT: Lovage is a hardy, green herb with a strong taste of celery. Its habit marries well with angelica and sweet cicely.

> "The Lovage joyeth to grow by waies, and under the Eeves of an house, it also propsereth in shadowy places, but especially delighteth to grow near to a running water. This in the growing sendeth up a long and slender stemme..."
>
> *The Gardeners Labyrinth*, (1577)
>
> **Thomas Hyll**

ABOVE: It is best to keep lovage cut back to encourage new fresh shoots, but if allowed to flower it will set seeds.

A Roman recipe called for honey, dates, pepper, lovage, cilantro, caraway, chopped onion, mint, the yolk of an egg, vinegar, sweet wine, and oil to be pounded together. The seeds were pounded together. In medieval love potions, the seeds were part of the mix, which is supposedly how it derived its common name. In Britain and across Europe it continued to be used for ales, cordials, and homemade wines, and as a bath herb and deodorant. Lovage was among the first herbs taken by the early settlers to America and is still growing at Thomas Jefferson's home, Monticello in Virginia (see French Tarragon box on p.49). During 1775, the great dictionary compiler, Dr. Samuel Johnson, was suffering from rheumatism and almost as much from the prescription medicine. However, he washed it down each time "... drinking a quarter pint of the infusion of the root of Lovage. Lovage in Ray's *Nomenclature*, is Levisticum: perhaps the botanists may know the Latin name." It was used in veterinary medicine as a purgative for calves and for sheep with a cough.

A hardy, vigorous grower almost anywhere, it is best in a rich, moist soil in a sunny position.

An advantage of growing lovage in a damp spot is that the celery flavor will be less overpowering and the leaves have an attractive burnished appearance. It grows well with angelica and sweet cicely. The flowerheads are a dull yellow, neither ornamental nor edible, but they are attractants for beneficial insects.

The hardier Scotch Lovage, *L. scoticum*, is found around the coasts of Scotland and Scandinavia, formerly gathered from the rocks and eaten raw or boiled as a vegetable, and eaten by sailors against scurvy. Unlike its English cousin, the flavor is harsh and can no longer compete with the better alternatives that are available. Neither variety should be mistaken for black lovage or alexanders, *Smyrnium olusatrum*, which look more like angelica.

Lemon balm
Melissa officinalis

Common names: Lemon balm, sweet balm, balm mint, honey plant, blue balm

Type: Herbaceous perennial

Climate: Hardy, very cold winter

Size: 12–31½in (30–80cm)

Origin: Mediterranean

History: Lemon balm has been cultivated for over 2,000 years. The name Melissa derives from the Greek word for "honeybee," and it has long been associated with them. Traditionally, their skeps, boles, and hives are rubbed with the leaves to stop the bees swarming.

Cultivation: Sow seeds in spring, although the plants are readily available. Balm grows freely—many say it is a thug, and it self-seeds prodigiously, so cut off the flowering stems as they appear.

Storage: Dry young leaves when they are at their most lemony before flowering and brew with tea. The leaves can also be preserved in vinegar and oil (see p.75). Try also lemon balm wine, a traditional way of harvesting its citrus flavor for winter.

Preparation: In spring, the young leaves give a zest of lemon to salads, or can be added to cold chicken dishes. Put sprigs of lemon balm with bay leaves in the cavities of whole fish before baking. Bruise young fresh leaves, put in a large pitcher, and fill with water. If you do the same with wine, it was believed the leaves could then be used against the bites of venomous beasts. Good as a soothing tisane (which when applied externally is used to alleviate cold sores) or mixed with other herbs such as chamomile or tea.

LEFT: The young leaves of lemon balm are the best for salads and cooking, but the flavor is most intense just at or before flowering.

Balm is a corruption of "Balsam," meaning honeyed sweetness. Evelyn's remarks quoted below appear in much the same form from the Roman herbals onward and modern research has shown that lemon balm does have antidepressant qualities. Balm was the primary ingredient in Carmelite water or *Eau de Melisse de Carmes,* which also contained lemon peel, nutmeg, and angelica root. Lemon balm was used in Renaissance gardens as a close-clipped cushion herb within knots and parterres such as the late 15th-century designs for the Chateau de Blois in France. Colonists introduced it to North America and, when facing the isolation and strange climate, found it invaluable for counteracting their low spirits. Later, Jefferson grew lemon balm at Monticello.

In a *Modern Herbal (1931),* Mrs. Grieve recounts historical cases of people who drank lemon balm tea every day and reached a grand old age, such as John Hussey of Sydenham, who attained an age of 116, and Llewelyn, Prince of Glamorgan, who died in his 108th year.

Today lemon balm is grown throughout the world as a garden plant, while commercial quantities are raised for medicine, cosmetics, and furniture polish manufacture. On a small scale, rub leaves across wooden surfaces in the house and garden for its lemon fragrance, which deters flies and mosquitoes. With regular clipping it can be shaped into an attractive globe with a ready supply of young leaves. Prune back hard in the fall. If grown in a pot, split and cut back annually to ensure a healthy, soft plant. Do the same every three to five years in the ground, discarding the woody center and roots after lifting and splitting. Leave the tiny white flowers to mature to attract bees, but cut back before they set seeds.

Arguably the most lemon-scented cultivar is "Citronella." The golden forms "Gold Leaf" and "All Gold," as well as the gold-variegated form "Aurea," make attractive alternatives especially in shady corners. "Compacta" is a smaller form for edging and pots.

NUTRITION

Lemon balm contains Vitamin C and the B vitamin thiamin. Research suggests that the tannins present are responsible for many of its antiviral qualities. Lemon balm also contains eugenol, which calms muscle spasms, numbs tissue, and kills bacteria.

"Cordial and exhilarating, sovereign for the Brain, strengthening the Memory, and powerfully chasing away Melancholy. The tender Leaves are us'd in Composition with other Herbs; and the Sprigs fresh gather'd, put into Wine or other Drinks, during the heat of Summer, give it a marvellous quickness. This noble Plant yields an incomparable Wine, made as is that of Cowslip-Flowers."

Acetaria: A Discourse of Sallets, (1699) John Evelyn

Mint
Mentha

Common names: Mint

Type: Herbaceous perennial

Climate: Hardy, very cold winter

Size: 12–35in (30–90cm)

Origin: Eurasia, Africa

History: Legend recounts that a young nymph, Menthe, caught the eye of Pluto, the god of the underworld. Pluto's jealous consort Persephone took prompt action to put a stop to such attentions. She metamorphosed Menthe into a scented herb thriving in the damp soils around the entrance of the underworld.

Cultivation: Mint is rightly classed as a thug. Given a good, moist soil it will rampage across your plot. However, it is an invaluable culinary herb. So either grow it alone in suitable conditions, or lift it every other year, cut back to new vigorous roots, and replant. Grow mint in a large pot and submerge in soil up to just below its rim.

Storage: Pot up some roots for the glasshouse or windowsill to have fresh leaves in winter. Dry or freeze leaves before flowering. Use flowering stems for mint vinegar (see p.75).

Preparation: Sprigs of mint can be used in pitchers of cold drinks, as a digestive tisane, or boiled with new potatoes. The many scents of mint can be infused to make a refreshing mint sorbet (see p.184) and finely chopped fresh mint transforms a chilled summer pea soup and provides aromatic contrast in hearty ham and dried-pea soups. The classic cooling side dish for hot curries, *Raita*, combines cucumber, mint, and yogurt. Added to blackcurrants after cooking, mint acts like a secret ingredient that magically enhances the flavor of the fruit; sprinkle over a salad of fresh orange slices; or add to cold chocolate mousses or ice creams.

LEFT: All parts of mint above the ground can be used. Classic combinations are young, fresh leaves in salads and in yogurt, or bruised stems for infusions and vinegars.

TASTING NOTES

Mint varieties to try

The distinctive taste of mint can also strike up interesting variations from fruity to confectionery, sweet scents to high perfumes that match its wide selection of leaf and stem colors.

M. australis — Native Australian mint has a strong peppermint scent and was used for tea by Aboriginal peoples. Colonial settlers used it in lieu of European varieties.

M. × gracilis — Known as Gingermint or redmint—attractive, red-tinged stems and leaves with a sweet scent, ideal for sorbets. There is also a yellow striated form "Variegata."

M. × piperita — Digestive peppermint with purple-tinged leaves from which oil of peppermint is extracted.

M. × piperita "Chocolate" — A sweet-scented foliage that literally shines in a sunny situation in moisture-retentive soil. It is also said to be deer resistant.

M. × piperita f. *citrata* — Known as lemon mint, *M. Eau de Cologne* mint and bergamot mint. As the common names suggest, this cultivar is highly scented and perfect for sorbets and Indian desserts.

M. × smithiana — Red raripila mint with attractively purple-tinged ovate leaves that are sweetly scented. Good for tisanes and sorbets. Attractive in salads.

M. spicata — Formally *M. viridis*, the spearmint for classic mint sauce, it has long, bright green leaves. The variety *crispa* is more ornamental and equally useful in sauce and salads.

M. suaveolens — Downy-leaved applemint, as the name suggests, has a gentler minty, slightly fruity taste. It is preferred by many for mint sauce but is too downy for salads. "Variegata" has marginal white markings.

"'Do you mean to say,' said my father, 'that they really eat mint with lamb?' I said they did, and that it was delicious. He shook his head thoughtfully. 'What a funny country,' he said."

Myself, My Two Countries, (1936) X.M. Boulestin

M int thrives in moist soil and partial shade. The Roman poet Publius Ovidius Naso called mint the "herb of hospitality," a perfect description for a plant that infuses refreshing coolness into hot or cold water. Along with this, the Romans believed it increased intelligence and stimulated the appetite. The Old Testament records that tithes of mint, anise, and cumin were paid by the Pharisees. The flavor of mint itself seems able to metamorphose to suit its culinary host, from mint sauce with lamb, to peppermint tea in North Africa, to Vietnamese salads.

Two mints that are no longer used for culinary purposes are the best for deterring flies and insects when eating—very important for enhancing the gourmet experience of meals al fresco and inside where there are no fly screens. Pennyroyal, *M. pulegium*, appears regularly in old recipes but it is a strong abortifacient and has other contraindications; its overwhelming peppermint scent has a detrimental effect on the flavor of foodstuffs. Its virtue lies instead in its deterrent value: flies simply avoid any area where pennyroyal has been crushed. It likes a shady moist spot. Gather some leaves and wipe them over the table or gently crush the stems before arranging them in small jars near the food to be served. It is short lived but vigorous, low growing with attractive mauve flowers set against purple-tinged green shiny leaves. The tiny leaved Corsican mint, *M. requienii*, will colonize gaps and joints in paving, forming a green "mortar" covered in a haze of tiny mauve flowers. Like pennyroyal, it prefers shade and will certainly not thrive in full sun, and has a strong peppermint scent.

LEFT AND ABOVE: Watercolor of mint by Pierre François Ledoulx, c. 1790. There is a vast variety of mint to explore—try peppermint (*Mentha × piperita*), spearmint (*M.spicata*), applemint (*M. suaveolens*), or *Eau-de-Cologne* mint (*M. × piperita* "Citrata") to give a subtle twist to the flavor of food and drinks.

Bergamot
Monarda didyma

Common names: Bergamot, bee balm, monarda, Oswego tea

Type: Herbaceous perennial

Climate: Hardy, average winter

Size: 24–59in (60–150cm)

Origin: North America

History: The common name relates to the leaves, which have the fragrance of the bergamot orange, the zest of which is used to flavor Earl Grey tea. The American botanist John Bartram recorded plants growing by Lake Oswego in 1744. He sent seeds to the merchant Philip Collinson living in London, where its scarlet shaggy flowers soon made it a popular garden plant.

Cultivation: Sow the perennial herbaceous species in spring in a cold frame; transplant when large enough to handle. Established plants can be divided in the fall. It will thrive in any soil, preferably in full sun, but grows best if the ground is mulched and dug over with manure or garden compost, as this improves the moisture retention. Divide every three years.

Storage: Dry leaves and flowers, then store in a dry place away from dust and light.

ABOVE: Bergamots are excellent for flavoring drinks—hot and cold, water, milk, or punch. The scent is redolent of the bergamot orange for which it is named.

Preparation: Pour boiling water over fresh or dried flowers to make Oswego tea; it yields a deep red color. Alternatively, steep in syrup and pour over red fruits. Pour hot milk over leaves, stand for 5 minutes, strain, and drink. Leaves add a fragrant seasoning for game and other meat dishes, including goat. The gently fragrant lemon bergamot (*M. citriodora*) makes a good tisane or infusion for fruit salad.

"[The Indian women in Oneida] engaged in carefully collecting and preserving the flowers in baskets. They use them in the shape of a tea, and call the plant O-jee-che—the fiery or flaming plant."

Professor Benjamin Smith Barton of Philadelphia, (1807)

from *Plants of Colonial Williamsburg*, (1979) Joan Parry Dutton

LEFT: Oswego tea made from bergamot was a popular North American alternative to black tea, especially following the uprising known as the Boston Tea Party in 1773.

Nicolás Monardes (1493–1588) had been the first to publish details of the medicinal flora of North America in 1571. The lengthy title was shortened to *Joyfull Newes out of the New-Founde World* in its 1577 English translation. Bartram was also in correspondence with Carl Linnaeus, who decided to immortalize Monardes's contribution by creating the name *Monarda*. The common name of Oswego tea stems from its use as a brew by both the Native Americans and colonists. The popularity of Oswego tea increased after the 1773 American nonviolent protest against the British, known as the "Boston Tea Party." Jekyll recommended drifting the red forms of bergamot through summer herbaceous borders for additional color.

The annual, tender, lemon or lemon-scented bergamot, *M. citriodora* (sometimes also known as lemon mint), should be sown directly into the ground in spring and they prefer sandy soils. The plant has paler green leaves with soft purple flowers and luminescent, almost white, bracts. It is especially attractive to bees and butterflies. Bergamot leaves are subject to powdery mildew, so ensure the bergamot is not under stress by keeping the soil moist and mulching with well-rotted organic matter; some varieties are more resistant than others. The wild bergamot, *M. fistulosa*, has a much broader growing range that makes it invaluable for many American gardeners. The mint-leaved bergamot or Oregano de la Sierra, *M. fistulosa* var. *menthifolia*, as the common name suggests, has a strong flavor of oregano and is popular with chefs in the southwest United States. It has gray-green foliage and pale lavender flowers.

TASTING NOTES

Bergamot: a feast for the eyes

The flavor of bergamot is more or less a constant, but the range of flower colors provide decorative choices.

Red	"Adam" has red flowers, fragrant foliage, and withstands dry conditions better. Grows to 35in tall.
	"Cambridge Scarlet" is a reliable old variety.
	"Fireball" has deep red globe-shaped flowers set against dark green fragrant foliage. Compact 14 x 24in.
	"Jacob Cline" has showy, large, long flowering red blooms. The fragrant foliage is one of the best for mildew resistance. Pinch or cut back in early summer to get a second flowering. Grows to 47in tall.
Pink/ Purple	Favorites are "Beauty of Cobham" which has pale pink flowers, while those of "Croftway Pink" are deeper.
	"Blaustrumpf" or "Blue Stocking" has deep lilac to purple-colored flowers and fragrant foliage. Grows to 5ft tall.
	"Purple Rooster" is an American cultivar with imperial purple flowers set against clean, mildew-resistant foliage. Grows to 35in tall.
White	"Schneewittchen" or 'Snow Maiden' has whorls of long-lasting, tufted white flowers set against green bracts.

Sweet cicely
Myrrhis odorata

Common names: Sweet cicely, sweet chervil, myrrh, sweet humlick, sweet bracken, sweet fern

Type: Herbaceous perennial

Climate: Hardy, very cold winter

Size: 24in–4ft (60cm–1.2m)

Origin: Europe

History: *Myrrhis* is derived from the Greek word for the biblical myrrh, *Commiphora myrrha*. The Roman writer Columella wrote that it caused joy and gladness. He termed it *Chaerophyllum*, classing it with the bulbous chervil, a name that is apt as it means "pleasing leaf." It has since been placed in the carrot family.

Cultivation: Sweet cicely germinates best from fresh seeds and, once established, they will seed themselves annually. If using packeted seeds ensure they have a period of stratification, i.e. exposure to winter cold (see p.37). A moist, humus-rich soil is preferred, but they will self-seed into gravel. Space at 24in apart.

    If they do not have the characteristic aniseed scent they could be cow parsley or hemlock seedlings, both of which are poisonous and not to be digested. Remove these plants, wearing gloves.

Storage: Freeze stems to add to rhubarb and other tart fruits as a natural sweetener. Dry seeds and use as a sweetener in stewed fruits or custards.

ABOVE: Older leaves can be used as a natural sweetener especially with rhubarb, though remove the stems before serving.

Preparation: The older leaves are downy, so the young smaller ones are best for salads. The fresh, aromatic, aniseed-flavored green seeds can also be added to salads, but be aware that they look like small caterpillars, which can be unnerving. They are best eaten on the spot when newly formed, before they start to dry and become stringy. The young roots can be lifted, boiled until soft, and chopped into salads. The older leaves are excellent for presentation so spread out across serving plates for mayonnaise-based salads—chicken, fish, or potato—or for antipasti drizzled with pale green olive oil. Stew chopped young stems with rhubarb and gooseberries to counteract their sourness.

> "It is used very much among the Dutch people in a kinde of Loblolly or hotchpot which they do eat, called Warmus. The leaves of sweet Chervill are exceeding good, wholesome and pleasant among other salad herbs, giving the taste of Anise seed unto the rest."
>
> *The Herball or General Historie of Plants*, (1633) John Gerard

All parts of sweet cicely were and can be eaten. The anise flavor can be savored in the leaves, cooked roots, and fresh seeds. Gerard (above) praised the fresh seeds as being "wholesome for the cold and feeble stomacke." The roots were used as an antiseptic for snake and dog bites.

The white umbels will light up a shady garden corner as long as the soil is not too dry. Another characteristic is that some leaves are a ghostly white as though the green has been bleached out of them and this led to the legend in Yorkshire, England, that the "White Lady" had touched them. Sweet cicely enjoys much the same conditions as angelica and lovage and the varied heights and leaf shapes complement each other in a moisture-retentive soil.

Sweet cicely's delicate fern-like foliage and creamy white umbels make them attractive additions to the early border although be aware that each plant requires a space of up to 3 sq ft. The easily identifiable young plants can be weeded out of inappropriate places and eaten. After flowering, cut back because the late summer regrowth will provide foliage interest until the first frosts. This secondary growth also provides fresh aniseed leaves and flowers to add to fall and early winter salads.

NUTRITION

This sweet, aromatically anise-tasting herb aids digestion and, by lessening the amount of sugar you need to sweeten fruits, is also good for the waistline. Like ground elder, sweet cicely is reputed to ease gout.

ABOVE: All parts of sweet cicely have a clear, pleasant anise flavor. The seeds make an enjoyable snack when gardening.

SEASONAL HERBS

A WINDOW OF OPPORTUNITY

The excitement that gardeners can have for the first arrival of seasonal favorites has been slightly diminished by the ready availability throughout the year of fresh herbs on supermarket shelves. Some of the more obscure herbs in this book have a small seasonal window of opportunity when they are at their best. Their unappetizing reputations are often gained by being used well past their eat-by date.

Several pages of this book are seasoned by quotes from John Evelyn's *Acetaria—A Discourse of Sallets* of 1669, because he understood how just a week or two can alter the taste of a salad. The seasoned gatherer of herbs also knows the importance of factoring in the weather, sun or snow, rain or drought, which advance or delay them being at their best. Evelyn's original edition is available on the Internet; engaging and opinionated, it still makes an interesting and informative read. Evelyn wrote at a time when close observation of tastes and uses of fresh leaves was of great interest for survival and for intellectual stimulation.

The taste of most perennial herbs differs with each season. In principle, they are at their most fragrant when in flower and largely in the summer months when the levels of volatile oil are at their greatest. Plant them where the eye and nose can still enjoy them once their culinary peak has passed.

SPRING

This is the most important culinary season. You can imagine the relief to our ancestors as they watched the green blades rising and were once more able to get out to gather vitamin-packed fresh herbs.

Asparagus was (and still is) a luxury vegetable and readily harvested substitutes were appreciated before they became stringy and established, such as the young spring shoots of sea holly. The first herb in this book, ground elder, is at its best from the appearance of its green leaves until the flowering stems appear. During its prime season, it provides a vigorous, healthy spinach substitute; not only does the taste diminish as it approaches flowering but it also becomes a powerful laxative. It is much the same story, without the side effects, for Good King Henry—harvest young or not at

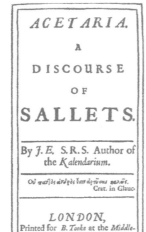

RIGHT: John Evelyn's discourse on salads encompasses far more than this book. His writing exudes the first-hand experience of an enthusiastic gourmet.

ACETARIA.

A

DISCOURSE

OF

SALLETS.

By *J. E.* S. R. S. Author of the *Kalendarium*.

Οὐ φαϲὶϲ ἀνδρὸϲ ἔϲτ᾽ ἀρϧῦουϲ ϧελῶϲ.
Crat. in Glauc.

LONDON,
Printed for *B. Tooke* at the *Middle-Temple* Gate in *Fleetſtreet*, 1699.

> "Culinary and afterwards medicinal herbs were the object of every head of a family; it became convenient to have them within reach, without seeking them at random in woods, meadows, or on mountains, as often as they were wanted. When the earth ceased to furnish spontaneously all these primitive luxuries, and culture became requisite, separate enclosures for rearing herbs became expedient."
>
> *On Modern Gardening*, (1770) **Horace Walpole**

all. The delicate leaves of salad burnet are only enjoyable in salads for about the first two to three weeks of their spring appearance. They have a subtle flavor and sit prettily among other green leaves. Francis Bacon recommended salad burnet as an edging to a herb garden. However, within a month their leaves become dry and papery to taste, at which point they are only fit for wine cups.

You can keep nettles cut back, but the flavor of the first tops is incomparably better than secondary growth. Traditionally, and today, nettle soup is a superb spring tonic. Celebrate mid-spring with sweet woodruff whose mass of flowers contribute to its aromatic, freshly fragrant flavor in infusions and wine cups.

SUMMER

The gloriously citrus leaves of the tender lemon verbena are at their fragrant best in the summer. Place them where you can brush by on a regular basis—picking leaves for tea and just to rub on your hands. Angelica stems should be harvested for candying in early summer before they become too stringy. Only the very young leaves are good for salads, becoming increasingly unpalatable as the days grow hotter and dryer. The young leaves and stems of lovage have a deliciously strong

ABOVE: You will soon know when the nettle tops are too old for cooking: instead of a glorious green the resulting soup turns out a dreary brown.

celery taste from spring into summer, after which they become dry and acrid. If grown in moist soil, keep cutting lovage back to ensure young tender stems. If you fail to harvest the young purple and green leaves of orach, just leave them to play an ornamental role.

ABOVE: Saffron is among the prettiest of herbs. The flowers bearing the saffron threads appear in the fall and the leaves appear with them or shortly afterward.

Beeton advised: "From the month of July to the end of September is the proper time for storing herbs for winter use." Item 445 in *Beeton's Book of Household Management* on drying herbs is as apt today as it was then; herbs should always be gathered on a dry day. With Victorian preciseness, she wrote, "It is very necessary to be particular in little matters like this, for trifles constitute perfection, and herbs nicely dried will be found very acceptable when frost and snow are on the ground." That said, she opined that fresh herbs always tasted better, on which all cooks would agree.

FALL

The leaves of salad arugula are at their best when the days are shorter, so sow to have pickings from September to April/May. The amounts available will diminish or even disappear in mid-winter. The saffron crocus flowers and yields her golden threads in fall. If you have left some blossoms on the elder it will now produce its vitamin C-packed berries to add to vinegars, to make syrup or to brew a rich port wine. Harvest some rosehips for jellies and syrups and leave the rest for colorful interest.

WINTER

Be grateful for evergreen herbs such as bay and rosemary; just make sure that the branches are not damaged by the weight of heavy snow. On the other hand, snow acts as a wonderful protective blanket for many herbs. Myrtle berries will stay on the bushes during early winter. The white-flowering bergamot, *Monarda* "Schneewittchen" or "Snowmaiden," will not be in flower, but the stiff vertical stems that are left look distinctly architectural when outlined in frost and emit a gentle fragrance when the sun is on them. Apart from "Schneewittchen" and other bergamots, leave some of the old, tall-flowering stems of burdock, fennel, and marjoram to be etched by frost and add ornamental interest and structure to the winter garden.

Myrtle
Myrtus communis

Common names: Myrtle, sweet myrtle

Type: Evergreen shrub

Climate: Hardy, average winter

Size: 6½–10ft (2–3m)

Origin: Mediterranean, Northern Africa

RIGHT: Myrtle is related to the allspice berry tree and its black fruits can be used as a substitute, while the flowers and leaves make for spice scented table decorations.

History: Legend recounts that when Adam and Eve were expelled from Paradise, they were allowed just three plants. They chose wheat, dates, and myrtle, the last for its fragrant flowers. Since earliest classical history myrtle has been associated with peace, love, and immortality.

Cultivation: Myrtle is best planted in spring after the last frosts. It requires well-drained, neutral to alkaline, moderately fertile soil in a sunny, sheltered position. Sow fresh myrtle seed direct in the fall. It should eventually attain 8ft in height.

Storage: Harvest berries and dry, then keep in sterilized, airtight jars.

Preparation: The leaves can be used to impart a gently spicy scent to meats and to barbecues. Aromatic and sweet, the spicy black fruits can be used fresh or dried with game. In southern Italy, Sardinia, and Corsica they make Mirto, a dark red aromatic liqueur. The flowers are used to make the lighter, in all senses, Mirto bianco. For a homemade version, bruise myrtle berries and put in a glass bottle or jar, cover with vodka, and leave for six months, then strain and drink.

Raised on nectar and ambrosia, Apollo's son Aristaeus was taught useful arts and mysteries by the myrtle nymphs such as beekeeping, cheesemaking, and training the wild olive tree to bear fruits. Myrtle's black fruits were prized by the Romans as a spice; featuring in many of Apicius's recipes. *Myrtus* are closely related to the allspice family, *Eugenia*, and so allspice berries can be used as a stronger tasting substitute. Tradition also has it that Sir Walter Raleigh and Sir Francis Carey reintroduced myrtle to England, as well as orange trees, from Spain in 1585. Along with sweet bay, their evergreen leaves and stature meant they went well with tubbed oranges in and around orangeries. There is also an attractive myrtle-leaved orange, *Citrus myrtifolia*, which produces small fruits. Sprigs of flowering myrtle were included in bridal bouquets, as they are redolent of feminine symbolism and harbingers of happiness. A myrtle tree rooted from a cutting from Queen Victoria's wedding bouquet still grows at Osborne House on the Isle of Wight.

In colder areas, plant myrtle where it is protected from the morning sun in a south- or west-facing aspect, thus avoiding early sun after frost and the deleterious effects of rapid thawing. Protect from drying or cold winds, which easily damage myrtle leaves, causing brown spotting and dieback. Plants root well from semihardwood cuttings taken in late spring or fall. Leave them to form good rooting systems before planting out in spring.

All varieties respond to pruning, cutting out dead wood, and shaping in late spring after the last frost. They are excellent subjects for topiary (see p.108), and the delicate white, 1in-wide flowers with golden anthers appear in late summer. With sustained sunshine they are followed by small, black fruits that can be harvested fresh. Like the sweet bay, *Laurus nobilis*, a severe winter can cut the bush to the ground. However, by summer they should reshoot and re-establish.

Two final thoughts: first, having a myrtle on either side of a door ensures peace and love to those who dwell within; second, a Roman culinary tip from Apicius for storing and preserving sorrel—

trim and clean sorrel leaves and stalks, place them in a glazed pot, sprinkle myrtle berries between, and cover with honey and vinegar. The result is a prototype Worcestershire sauce.

TASTING NOTES

Myrtle varieties to try

After flowering, these varieties will produce firm, dry, blue-black berries that will infuse allspice into cooking or marinades.

"Flore Pleno"
As the name suggests it is double flowered. It was first noted in Britain by John Parkinson in 1640.

"Variegata"
Has narrowly margined creamy-white variegated leaves; the flowers are the same as the sweet myrtle but it only grows to 5ft.

Subsp. *tarentina*
Introduced into Britain by John Tradescant the Younger. Growing to only 3¼–5ft it is ideal for topiary or containers and, in milder areas, as an evergreen hedge. The flowerbuds are attractively tinged with pink. It is also known as *Tarentum myrtle* and is sometimes sold under any of the following synonyms: "Jenny Reitenbach," "Microphylla," 'Nana,' subsp. *tarentina* "Microphylla," and "Tarentina."

Basil
Ocimum basilicum

Common names: Sweet or Genovese Basil

Type: Herbaceous perennial, often grown as an annual

Climate: Half-hardy, unheated glasshouse or mild winter

Size: 8–24in (20–60cm)

Origin: Old World Tropics

History: *Ocimum* takes its root from *okimon*, the name given to it by the Greek polymath and gardener, Theophrastus, c. 300 BC. Such were its munificent healing and aromatic qualities that it was described as *basilicus*, meaning "princely" or "royal."

Cultivation: A tender perennial, most grow it as an annual under glass. Sow seeds thinly under glass or protection until early summer; cover lightly with soil or compost. Once all fear of frost has passed, start sowing successively directly in the soil. Basil grows well in a pot. Transfer seedlings when large enough to handle into 3in pots, harden off, and repot when fully established into the final container.

Storage: Freeze or dry stems; break off as required. Oil-rich basil leaves are ideal for infusing in oils and vinegars (see p.75).

Preparation: The stems and flowerheads have a stronger flavor, so use for cooking or chopped up

ABOVE: Basil is synonymous with Italian, and especially Neopolitan, cooking. The scent and flavor are at their best in high summer.

small for a basil buzz. Classic sauces are *pesto*, where basil is pounded or processed with garlic, pine nuts, and olive oil with salt to taste for pasta and risotto; and *pistou*, where basil is pounded with oil, garlic, and freshly grated Parmesan or Gruyere cheese to stir into hot soups. For a warm salad, gently sautée yellow and red bell peppers in basil oil, add some pine nuts, allow to cool a little, then add lemon juice and finely chopped or shredded basil. Hot or cold, basil and tomatoes are the perfect culinary marriage, a combination that captures the summer's warmth and sun. Lightly oil skinned chicken pieces (removing the skins allows the aroma to be absorbed) or monkfish, then wrap in fresh basil leaves before baking. Serve warm with a fresh, tomato-based sauce.

Roman farmers fed their horses and asses basil as an aphrodisiac when they were on heat. Curiously, despite its royal name, basil also came to symbolize poverty, hate, and misfortune, so it was advised that you hurl abuse at the seeds as you sowed them to drive want away. Remember this when you are bothered on those first really hot days in late spring because this is the moment to sow basil.

Although it germinates readily, a night in cool, damp soil often irretrievably damages basil seedlings, so wait for the warmth of late spring to penetrate the soil before sowing. Even better start in a seed tray on a warm windowsill or in a glasshouse. After germination, try to keep as dry as possible. For example, water in the morning so that the soil is dry overnight. Always ensure that you do not overwater; erring on the side of drought. Pinch out and harvest new shoots and flowering stems to encourage basil to bush out.

A ROYAL BOX OF BASILS

If you decide to raise basil from seed, the varieties available are legion. The traditional "Napoletano," which as the name suggests is from Naples, has a very sweet fragrance and large, light green leaves. It is a must-have for antipasti or over pizza, and its flavor is prized over the larger "lettuce-leaved" basil by Italian cooks such as Giorgio Locatelli.

However, the leaves of the latter are indeed the size of small lettuce leaves, so are perfect to present finely chopped tomatoes in oil and garlic, a miniature Salad Niçoise or smoked mozzarella. Use to wrap skinned chicken pieces or fish before cooking.

"Crispum" has a good clear basil flavor but, as the name suggests, it has ruffled edges, so beware when tearing into strips for salads as it looks like a green caterpillar. Basils are excellent windowsill herbs but the best is *O. minimum*, the so-called bush or Greek basil. It is a very small-leaved, compact variety but productive and one of the easier basils to raise. In the garden it makes an attractive, low, annual edging plant. The variety "Minette" is even more compact.

ABOVE: Illustration of various forms of basil showing the species form, var. *purpurascens* and Greek basil (*Ocimum minimum*).

A citrus zest enhances several varieties: lemon is predominant in the tender *O. × africanum* (syn. *O. × citriodorum*) with pale green, lemon-scented leaves. It is prone to wilt and suffers on cold nights. For lime, try the highly lime-fragranced narrow bright green leaves of the Thai lime basil *O. americanum*, whose clusters of small cream flowers are very free flowering.

There are shades ranging from matte purple to striated pink, often with the spicy allure of cinnamon, liquorice, or aniseed. The original var. *purpurascens* was grown for the perfume industry. With smooth dark inky-purple leaves, it is fragrant and colorful in pasta or salads. The "Purple Ruffles" has dark inky-purple crinkled leaves that are ruffled like perilla (there is also a "Green Ruffles" with a mild anise flavor). "Dark Opal" is another purple form. In cooking, these purple leaves make a great contrast with yellow tomatoes or with sautéed yellow bell peppers. Grow them as an ornamental foil for pale green and golden plants around the garden. "Red Rubin" is similarly good tasting and ornamental.

"Cinnamon" has oval spice-scented leaves in shades of green and purple topped by clusters of small pink flowers. Originating from Mexico it is one of the most attractive basils and it is good in stir-fries. "Horapha" is known as the anise basil; it has reddish purple leaves and flowers that taste of aniseed. It is popular in Thai and Indian cooking. There is also a dwarf form "Horapha Nanum." Lastly the Thai basil, var. *thrysiflorum*, tastes like a cross between cinnamon and liquorice varieties. A good range of basils are also available in pots and readily adapt to being planted out in early summer or moved into larger display pots. Many

TASTING NOTES

Tricolor canapé

This recipe is inspired by the red, green, and white colors of the Italian flag.

Preparation time: 10 minutes
Serves: 8 people (2 each)

You will need:

• 8 cherry tomatoes

• 1 large mozzarella ball

• Handful of basil leaves

Cut the mozzarella into small cubes.

Slice each cherry tomato in two.

Thread a cherry tomato half onto a cocktail stick, then a basil leaf, then the mozzarella. Repeat process.

supermarkets stock potted basils, where an increasing variety are often on offer. It is worth transferring these into a permanent pot or the garden for continuous pickings. Basil reputedly enhances the culture of tomatoes so grow it alongside them and as tomatoes need constant moisture it will ensure that the basils are never too damp. If you have spare seeds of different varieties mix them and grow as sprouting seeds or as a microsalad.

Marjoram
Origanum majorana

Common names: Wild marjoram, oregano, pot marjoram

Type: Herbaceous perennial

Climate: Hardy, very cold winter

Size: 18in (45cm)

Origin: Europe

History: A hardier northern form of the oregano of ancient Greece, Egypt, and Rome, this native marjoram was known in English as "Organ" or "Organy". Seeds of this hardy herb were among those taken to North America to be made into a tea that was said to cure all ills.

Cultivation: A very hardy herb that thrives in dry soils. Seed can be sown in spring or summer. Once established and allowed to flower, it will freely self-seed. Clumps can be split in spring or fall. As with oregano (*O. vulgare*), buy a plant or ask for a cutting, but smell the leaves beforehand to ensure you have a well-fragranced herb.

Storage: Dry leaves and store in sterilized, airtight jars. They can also be preserved in vinegar and oil (see p.75).

Preparation: One of the *herbes Provençales* (see p.138), this traditional English herb can be mixed in breadcrumbs with parsley, thyme, and lemon as a forcemeat for chicken. Fill the cavity of a chicken with fresh leaves (and flowers) before roasting for a lighter-on-the-stomach option. Strip leaves off stems for pizza toppings and sprinkle young leaves onto salads. After boiling Brussels sprouts, drain and toss in butter and marjoram. Add to most "Mediterranean" recipes.

BELOW: 14th-century women harvesting a sweet marjoram in a treatise on the preservation of health. Also known as pot marjoram, this herb thrives by an outer door or in the kitchen.

John Gerard, the English botanist and herbalist, noted that when drunk in wine marjoram was a sovereign remedy against venomous bites and stings and a cure for poisoning by opium and hemlock. Before the introduction of hops, marjoram was used as an aromatic and preservative in beer. It was believed to protect the body from poisons by withdrawing them from all parts. In *The Compleat Angler* (1653) Isaak Walton recommended cooking freshly caught fish with marjoram, probably readily to hand growing wild along the dry river banks. When thunder threatened, marjoram and thyme were gathered and laid by milk in a dairy to prevent it curdling.

When grown in drifts, marjoram can fill the air with its aromatic scent particularly after rain in the fall or when a cool night is followed by sunshine. It has a higher proportion of thymol than *O. vulgare*, hence its taste being more akin to thyme. Either can be used in recipes calling for marjorams. Most are freely self-seeding but it is best to propagate by cuttings, division, and layering so that you retain an exact clone. In many respects this profile and the last for *O. vulgare* are interchangeable, as is their use in French, Italian, and Greek dishes.

RIGHT: The fragrant leaves of the pink-flowered wild marjoram were used to leaven the flavor of pottage as well as suet and pastry crusts. Oven roast in oil or sauté in butter with zucchinis.

Oregano
Origanum vulgare

Common names: Oregano, Greek oregano, pot marjoram, Cretan oregano, Turkish oregano, rigani

Type: Herbaceous perennial

Climate: Hardy, very cold winter

Size: 24in (60cm)

Origin: Mediterranean

History: Apart from cooking, because of its strong, pleasing perfume, the Romans liked oregano as a garland and strewing herb. Cultivated first in ancient Egypt, it was then introduced across the Roman Empire, noted by Dioscorides for its many medicinal properties.

Cultivation: Oregano thrives in sunny, well-drained soil. Plants are hardier in winter if not subjected to damp. Sow seeds directly in spring; thinning to 12–15¾in spacings. Treat as an annual in colder climates. Buy a plant or ask for a cutting having smelled the leaves beforehand to ensure you have selected a well-fragranced specimen.

RIGHT: Handcolored copperplate engraving from Dr Friedrich Gottlob Hayne's *Medical Botany*, 1822. When oregano comes into flower the stems take on a more fragrant savor. Use them whole when oven roasting and remove before serving.

Storage: Dry stems just before flowers open. They can also be preserved in vinegar and oil (see p.75).

Preparation: One of the *herbes Provençales* (see p.138), the strongly fragrant, aromatic scent brings the taste of summer and Italy or Greece into tomato, garlic, and onion-based dishes. It is an essential herb for flavoring the meat sauce for moussaka. For an easy summer soup, process with peeled and seeded tomatoes and garlic, then chill and serve. Apart from being arguably more aromatic and tender, its use is interchangeable with the *Origanum majorana*.

The genus *Origanum* has many species, varieties, and naturally occurring hybrids. Most are freely self-seeding, but it is best to propagate by cuttings, division, and layering so that you retain an exact clone. In many respects this profile and the previous for *O. majorana* are interchangeable in terms of their use in French, Italian, and Greek dishes. In addition, *O. onites*, the more highly scented knotted, sweet, or Italian marjoram of southern Europe, is also used in Portuguese and North African cuisine. Legend has it that the latter offers good luck and good health to mankind. Opinions differ on which species has the best flavor.

In October 1631, the ship *Lyon's Whelp*, having safely crossed the Atlantic, docked in Boston harbor. Passengers included the Winthrop family, who were armed with seeds of 59 different plants, of which 29 were herbs, including *O. vulgare*, *O. majorana*, and *O. onites*. Over two hundred years later, Beeton advised Victorian cooks that the sweet or knotted marjoram was preferred but that all varieties were favorite ingredients in soups and stuffings. Up until World War Two, an oregano was cultivated in Tunisia and exported to Marseilles under the name of *Khezama*, meaning lavender. This is unsurprising as the Provençal herbs share a distinctive highly fragrant aroma and in areas where it grows wild its bouquet scents the air—the smell of the *terroir*, the garrigue. These native herbs are grazed by stock and imbibed by the vines. They give the local foods and wines that discernible heady characteristic that is redolent of dry sunshine.

Oregano will be more highly scented in a sunny position. If it forms a dense mound, pinch it back to encourage bushiness. As the flowers fade the tops take on a deep purple hue and exude a heady perfume.

TASTING NOTES

Oregano varieties to try

The flavors of oreganos and marjorams range from highly perfumed to aromatic and scented. The delicately flavored young spring foliage can be used in generous quantities. Rub between your fingers and smell to ascertain just how much may suit your tastes. Below are some different forms to test out.

Subsp. *hirtum*	Recommended as having the best classic pungent, aromatic flavor. It is also known as Greek oregano or winter sweet marjoram. It has a low creeping habit, about 8 x 12in, with highly aromatic, dark green leaves with tiny white flowers appearing during the summer.
"Compactum"	Forms a small green globe. It is smaller leaved, and is ideal for pot growth.
Subsp. *gracile*	Russian oregano is also good for cooking and free flowering from summer into the fall. It has a sprawling habit with dark green leaves that have the best flavor just before flowering.
Subsp. *glandulosum*	A native of North Tunisia that can also be used for cooking.

HERBES PROVENÇALES

A TASTE OF THE MEDITERRANEAN

Provençal—an adjective that conjures up visions of herb-scented hillsides, dry sunny heat, and robust food. The Provence region stretches from a rural, traditional, alpine hinterland to the market gardening-soils of the River Rhône and down to the rocky shores of the Mediterranean Sea. The cheeses may change, but its gloriously perfumed herbs are ready to adapt for every setting.

Wild thymes and rosemary thrive in poor, well-drained soils, their spiky leaves accumulating tasty volatile oils as summer passes, and garlic and basil grow in prodigious quantities. Together this merry quartet transforms any summer barbecue, dull pizza, or oil drizzle into a gourmet treat. Subtle and harmonious, fresh or dried bay leaves, oregano (which equates with the Provençal wild marjoram *origan*), and fennel can also be added. Stalks of the latter are a must with fish, while

LEFT AND BELOW: Garlic and basil grow in prodigious quantities and form the basis of many dishes.

TASTING NOTES

The herbes Provençales

Allium sativum	Garlic
Ocimum basilicum	Basil—purple-leaved forms add color and scent
Laurus nobilis	Bay leaves
Foeniculum vulgare	Fennel—stems are mainly used in Provençal cooking
Hyssopus officinalis	Hyssop—gives a gently resinous perfume
Juniperus communis	Juniper berries
Lavandula angustifolia	Lavender—leaves and flowers
Origanum onites	Greek oregano or the annual sweet marjoram, *O. majorana*
Rosmarinus officinalis	Rosemary
Salvia officinalis	Sage—in late spring
Satureja hortensis	Savory—the annual summer savory is best
Thymus	Thyme—the wild thyme of Provence is known as *farigoule* or *frigolet*

juniper berries have the spirit to nestle in terrines or with beef or game. Like rosemary and thyme, the green and purple sages grow wild in Provence. However, they are best used in late spring as the taste can be overpowering when the oils build up in the leaves during the summer. Like basil, the annual summer savory, traditionally grown alongside fava beans, thrives in hot summers. Winter savory is a hardy substitute but lacks the aromatic delicacy. The more fragrant hyssop and lavender can be added to this herbal bouquet, as well as being used individually for infusing into cooling foods such as fruit pies, ice creams, and sorbets. With the exception of garlic, dry branches and sprigs of any one or all of them can be used to rekindle memories of sunshine when you are cooking in the depths of winter.

TASTING NOTES

How to perfect chicken cooked with whole garlic cloves

"This is a simple dish but a difficult one to do well. With the chicken you must cook some cloves of garlic as large and as round as hazelnuts. They must be as saturated with the juices as 'rissolées' and (this is of capital importance) as tender and sweet as new potatoes. To bring about this miracle, you must have heads of garlic from Provence, which have matured quickly and so have not had the time to become too impregnated with their special aroma."

La France à Table, Paul-Louis Couchoud

Hyssop

Lavender

Rosemary

Sage

CULTIVATION

If you do not live in a Mediterranean climate, choose a site that is sunny and well drained. This is most important in the winter as waterlogging is more lethal to these herbs than frost. Their natural habitat makes them ideal subjects for large terracotta pots in a sunny spot or in window boxes. Rosemary and sage grow excellently together . The silver of lavender and green of hyssop grown together look splendid in the summer. This theme could be picked up by including, or growing in an adjacent pot, the silver thyme, *Thymus* "Fragrantissimus." Both bush basil, *Ocimum minimum*, and sweet knotted or Italian oregano, *Origanum onites*, are ideal candidates for trimming into globes. Bay, juniper, and fennel are best grown in separate pots adapted to their needs; the first two are shrubs so not suitable for windowboxes, and the latter needs a taller container if you want stems.

Lemon-scented geranium
Pelargonium crispum

Common names: Lemon geranium, scented pelargonium

Type: Herbaceous perennial

Climate: Frost tender—heated greenhouse

Size: 12–18in (30–45cm) or more

Origin: South Africa

History: During the 16th century, Portuguese and Dutch merchant adventurers brought plants back from the Cape to Europe. In time, they were introduced into the Americas and Australia.

Cultivation: Being natives of South Africa they thrive in sun and low humidity. Species can be raised from seeds at 70°F. Named cultivars should root well from tip cuttings in late spring, early summer, or early fall; keep at a temperature of 70°F. Do not allow pots to dry out but never leave standing in water.

Storage: In sugar (see below). Keep plants in frost-free conditions for year-round pickings; fresh leaves have more bouquet.

Preparation: The fragrant flavor of lemon- and rose-scented geraniums will gently infuse into cakes if placed at the bottom of the tin before baking, but remove from the base of the cake before serving. Chopped fresh, young leaves can be added to a wide range of sauces for fish or pork. A leaf or two are ideal for scented infusions of tea or syrup, mix a handful of leaves with white sugar, then store and use as an alternative to lavender sugar. The rough texture and scent of the leaves make them ideal for finger bowls.

LEFT: The variety "Crispum" has tight, crinkled foliage that is especially lemon scented. It is excellent for placing under cake mixes before baking to infuse them with citron.

The popularity of scented geraniums soared in the mid-19th century with the advent of cheaper glass for public and private glasshouses, as well as domestic conservatories. In these warm, propitious climes, space permitting, they could be arranged into spectacular, scented displays and centerpieces. In 2006, the Herb Society of America made lemon-scented geranium their "Herb of the Year." Celebrating its many varieties and their uses, the accompanying book identified 23 varieties for cooking alone.

Scented geraniums are ideal for large pots and can be planted out and/or stood outside during warmer months, when there is no fear of frost.

LEFT: The rough leaves of the scented *P. tomentosum* release a strong peppermint scent. There is even a variety called "Chocolate Peppermint"—excellent for sweet dishes.

PELARGONIUMS WITH CULINARY ZEST

Enjoying full sun, *P. crispum* has an upright habit with small crinkled leaves that have an intense lemon scent as well as a clear lemon flavor for sauces, batter, salad, and garnish. It has delicate lavender-pink flowers. There are also more decorative cultivars such as "Large Flowered Crispum," which, as the name suggests, has showy flowers; the shrubby upright "Prince Rupert Variegata," aka "French Lace," is good for topiary; and the striated golden-leafed *Variegatum Aureum* "Well-Sweep" has pink flowers. Lemon scent is not confined to varieties of *P. crispum*: the "Frensham" has a strong lemon flavor for grains, fish, poultry, liqueurs, and salads. It is similar to the cultivar "Bitter Lemon," with excellent pink and mauve flowers.

There are rose-, lime-, orange-, fruit-, and mint-scented geraniums that can be used in the same way as *P. crispum*. For example, commonly known as rose-scented geraniums, *Graveolens*

varieties such as "Rober's Lemon-Rose" and "Lady Plymouth." The former has a lemon-rose flavor for sweet or savory culinary use. It has scalloped, fuzzy, gray-green leaves with pale pink flowers. The more lemon- than rose-scented form "Lady Plymouth," with variegated leaves, dates back to 1800 and is a personal favorite. Planted in large pots, it is ideal to flank a garden bench; in the evening the cream variegations on the leaves and pale lavender flowers enhance its fragrance. It grows well in borders during the summer. Scent is a subjective experience and reports vary on Lady Plymouth—apart from lemon, nurseries write of rose and mint fragrances.

The leaves of the strongly peppermint-scented and -flavored *P. tomentosum* are used for confections, sauce, and tea. Vigorous with many branching stems, the emerald, densely hairy leaves are velvet-soft, readily yielding their scent. The flowers are small and white. There is also a cream variegated form. The last word lies with the variety "Chocolate-mint," whose scent needs no description.

Perilla
Perilla frutescens

Common names: Perilla, Japanese basil, beefsteak plant, shiso

Type: Annual

Climate: Half-hardy, unheated glasshouse, mild winter

Size: 24in–4ft (60cm–1.2m)

Origin: India to Japan

History: A native of the Himalayas and eastern Asia, the leaves and seeds have been used in Chinese medicine to boost the immune system since c. AD 500. It has long been used in Japanese cuisine, not least because the leaves were wrapped around raw fish, as an antidote to the associated potential food poisoning.

Cultivation: Sow undercover or when the soil has warmed up, in late spring. It needs well-drained, organically rich soil and will survive drought, but this mars its flavor. It is a sun-loving annual that will self-seed following a good summer.

Storage: Properly cleaned, the seeds can be dried. Freeze leaves whole and break off as needed.

Preparation: Wrap around raw fish, sashimi, and sushi—decorate with buds or flowering tops for an extra spicy taste. Tear leaves into strips and add to salads for color and bite. Leaves and flowers can be added to soups at the last minute to maximize the flavor. Fry leaves in oil with garlic and/or ginger. Steep leaves in rice vinegar to make Japanese shiso vinegar. Add leaves to Japanese pickled plums to infuse red coloring. Like mustard seeds, those of the perilla are a condiment—roast and grind them with salt, chillies, and tomatoes as a fresh chutney.

NUTRITION

The volatile oil in the leaves of *P. frutescens* contains perillaldehyde. Research indicates it is 2,000 times sweeter than sugar and up to eight times sweeter than saccharin. It is rich in omega-3 fatty acid alpha-linolenic acid. The leaves are a valuable source of vitamins A and C, riboflavin and calcium, iron and potassium.

Perilla is closely related to both basil and coleus. Long prized for its spicy scent, which is reminiscent of cinnamon, the green leaves leave a gingery aftertaste. The deep sanguine red of the purple-leaved variety, var. *purpurascens*, are the origins of its common name of beefsteak plant as well as purple *shiso*. The term *umeshiso* on Japanese menus indicates the inclusion of the red-leaved perilla or *shiso*. It is also known as *aka jiso, aka shiso*, and *oba*. The yellow oil that is extracted from perilla seeds has been used as a substitute for linseed oil and is used in the making of artificial leather.

Apart from seeds, varieties of perilla are readily available as plug plants. It flowers from late summer so if you do not want flowers, pinch out the buds and encourage it to bush out. It will grow to 24in–4ft tall by 12–18in wide. If potted up and protected, it can

"I have no idea why perilla (aka *shiso*) remains comparatively unknown as it is fabulously flavored—imagine the earthy but bright child of mint and cumin parents. It looks wonderful too, with soft crinkled leaves, in deep purple and vivid green varieties."

Mark Diacono (2013)

be treated as a short-lived perennial, and in warmer climates you can propagate from cuttings. The lime-green or purple-black leaves make an attractive foil for other annual flowers so consider growing it as a dual-purpose ornamental and culinary plant. The var. *crispa* has especially attractive crinkled leaves that are broad with a silky, deep purple hue and a serrated edge. It is also known as var. *nankinensis* or curly perilla.There are closely related varieties in China, Korea, and Vietnam that feature in their cuisine, known respectively as *gee so, zi su; dulketip, kkaenip, kkaenip namul, tulkkae*; and *rau tia to, tia to*.

There are also exciting ornamental varieties. For example, the "Magilla" has spectacular hot pink, deep burgundy with green variegated leaves that are very like coleus but without the fragrance and flavor of the species form. Equally, despite its name, "Magilla Vanilla," introduced in 2006, is flavorless but with green leaves with a central cream variegation and it is attractive to butterflies.

LEFT AND ABOVE: Green and purple leaved perillas are known as Japanese basil because their taste is similar. The generous leaves are ideal for wrapping sushi or raw fish. The mature stems and flowers can be finely chopped and added to sauces.

Vietnamese coriander

Persicaria odorata (syn. *Polygonum odorata*)

Common names: Vietnamese coriander, Rau Ram, Vietnamese mint, hot mint, Asian mint, perennial cilantro, laksa leaves (formerly *Persicaria odorata*)

Type: Subtropical herbaceous perennial

Climate: Tender, heated glasshouse

Size: 12–18in (30–45cm), spreading

Origin: Southeast Asia

Cultivation: Needs temperatures above 32°F (0°C). It is sterile and cannot be raised from seed. The former genus name, *Polygonum*, derives from the Greek *poly* meaning "many" and *gonu* "joints." It is these many joints that produce a ready supply of edible leaves, making it best planted and grown as an understory plant in the glasshouse.

Storage: Freeze young fresh leaves. Do not break up until needed.

Preparation: Use young leaves as the older leaves become tough, leathery, and bitter. It can be used as a substitute for cilantro or mint in many Vietnamese recipes.

Try using it as a dipping herb in beef noodle soup, *Pho Bo*. Each person is given a bowl of hot broth into which they add thin strips of raw beef, bean shoots, lime wedges, noodles, and a selection of fresh herbs such as *rau ram*, basil, mint, or cilantro, from a central platter.

RIGHT: Vietnamese coriander has an amalgam of tastes so it is widely used in Asian cooking as an alternative to cilantro and mint. Young, tender leaves are best.

The deltas of the Mekong and Red Rivers are key to the development of rice and Vietnamese cuisine. The country is quite a melting pot—from the Chinese with their chopsticks and stir- and deep-frying, to neighboring Laos, Cambodia, and Thailand with their flat egg noodles, spices, chilli, and coconut milk. Explorers and traders added potatoes, tomatoes, and snow peas into the mix. Vietnamese coriander can be used in any of these traditions, less so with the final influences of French colonization and the US military years, whose legacy is baguettes and ice cream. However, this cilantro variant has been exported into France and the United States via the growing market for Asian cooking.

> "In Singapore, Vietnamese coriander is know as *laksa plant* (also *laksa herb* or *laksa leaves*); in Singaporean Cantonese, there is the equivalent name *laksa yip*. These names reflect the usage of Vietnamese coriander for the Chinese-Malaysian noodle 'curry' *laksa.*"
>
> ***Exotic Spices*, (2011) Gernot Katzer**

Parsley
Petroselinum crispum

Common names: Parsley

Type: Biennial

Climate: Hardy, average winter

Size: 10–31½in (25–80cm)

Origin: Southern Europe

History: Legend recounts that parsley sprang from the blood of Archemorus, the forerunner of Death. According to Homer, warriors fed their chariot horses with parsley, presumably so that they could outrun death. Garlands of parsley were worn as an emblem of joy and festivity.

Cultivation: Seeds can be sown successively from spring onward directly into the soil or into pots. Thin seedlings (use leaves) to 12in or more spacings. If necessary, transplant before the second rough-leaf stage; any later and parsley is likely to bolt. It grows successfully in well-watered pots of rich compost, even in hanging baskets. Parsley is much enjoyed by rabbits, but it is poisonous to parrots.

Storage: Freeze whole leaves; break off as required.

Preparation: When chopping parsely, avoid using a parsmint (a parsley and mint grinding tool) as it just tears up the herb and diminishes its flavor. When cutting with scissors or chopping with a knife, make sure the leaves are dry or they will stick to everything.

Its addition lessens the need for salt. A fresh leaf is a great mouth freshener as it also helps to counteract the smell of garlic on the breath. The moss-curled varieties are best finely chopped for sauces such as béchamel. Tear or add the plain-leaved variety whole to risotto, cold collations, or salads. Chopped stems provide a stronger, sustained flavor. Put fresh chopped leaves and grated cheese on the table

LEFT: Plate 17 from *Flowers from Shakespeare's Garden: A Posy from the Plays*, illustrated by Walter Crane. Dated 1906 and published by Cassell & Co Ltd. Shakespeare frequently made reference to herbs and it is very likely that the herbalist John Gerard was among his London friends.

when serving hot pasta. Whole leaves, deep fried briefly in hot oil, become crisp and an iridescent green.

For persillade, finely chop parsley with shallot or garlic and add in the final stages of cooking to any savory dishes that need an extra zest. For a pesto alternative, process parsley, walnuts, and sunflower oil together, season to taste, and fork through rice.

NUTRITION

Rich in vitamins A and C, parsley contains apigenin, a flavonoid that reduces allergic responses and is an effective antioxidant.

The Romans grew at least three varieties of parsley; apart from culinary use it was put in ponds to cure ailing fish and was dedicated at funeral feasts to the memory of the dead. Charlemagne enjoyed cheese flavored with parsley seed. It was used as an early green food coloring, recommended c. 1390 in *Forme of Cury*: "Take parsel and grynde with a cowe mylk. Medle [mix] it with ayren [eggs] and lard ydyced [bacon diced]. Take mylke after that thou has done, and myng [mix] therwith, and make therof diverse colors." Until more modern times, only the stalks of *P. crispum* var. *neapolitanum*, the flat-leaved or Neapolitan parsley, were used by cooks.

There are over 20 cultivars of moss-curled and flat-leaved parsleys, as well as the turnip-rooted Hamburg parsley, var. *tuberosum*. They are notoriously fickle in germinating, so sowing small amounts frequently is a way around this. Parsley requires well-worked, moisture-retentive soil with partial shade. If you have a cold frame or glasshouse, sow a last crop in mid-summer for winter use. "Bravour" is a good cultivar. Always harvest outer leaves first. Parsley plants will self-seed in the fall of their second year.

The Ancient Greeks used parsley and rue, *Ruta graveolens*, as a garden edging. The textured green acts as an excellent foil for *Rudbeckia, Helenium,* and *Anthemis*.

LEFT: The plain-leaved parsley has a less intense flavor than the moss-curled variety, but its clear carroty, fresh taste is excellent in green salads.

VICTORIAN HERBS

TRADITION AND INNOVATION

The word 'Victorian' is a legacy of Queen Victoria's long reign from 1837–1901, not just in Britain but across her extensive empire. In 1851, over six million people flocked to The Great Exhibition in London's Hyde Park, housed in what *Punch* magazine nicknamed the Crystal Palace. It was a showcase and inspiration for an activities including gardening. Throughout her reign, the Royal Botanic Gardens, Kew and nurserymen like Veitch's in Chelsea and Exeter introduced, exchanged and cultivated plants from the four corners of the Earth. For the domestic gardener, there were magazines to read, garden clubs to join, and cheaper improved domestic glass structures to buy. Herbs and tender exotics such as ginger were a small, but important, part of this home garden revolution.

When choosing gourmet herbs for the Victorian garden, where better to delve than into Beeton's *Book of Household Management*, where one can find many illustrated notes. A drawback of 19th century urban living was the level of air pollution, so those residing in town were instructed to procure fresh herbs from the greengrocer or herbalist. Apart from traffic fumes, pollution is no longer such a problem for the retro-Victorian herb gardener, so whether in town or country, design to evoke the eclectic choice of building, manufactured and garden goods advertised in contemporary catalogues for homes of taste. Enhance the herbs in 19th century style

ABOVE: Following the repeal of glass taxes in 1845 and the Great Exhibition in 1851, glasshouses and glass in the garden both improved and became available to a wide range of gardeners.

with plain and glazed terracotta such as tiled paths, rope-edged beds and chimney pots; decorate further with ornate metal seats, wirework plant holders and hanging baskets and do not hesitate to clip some topiary. Enjoy the revival of the knot garden and slip into the more propitious clime of the glasshouse.

SOME VICTORIAN HERBS

Beeton listed the sweet herbs as thyme, sage, mint, marjoram, savory, and basil for sauces, soups, and forcemeats. A line drawing of basil was used as illustration. Among the herb forcemeat recipes are ones for baked pike, boiled calf's udder, and turtle soup—not frequently seen on menus today. Many recipes call for a faggot of savory herbs to be included as flavoring for all manner of dishes, with parsley being the key agent. Her "Indian Curry-Powder, founded on Dr. Kitchener's recipe," included coriander and fenugreek seeds as well as ginger and turmeric.

These are the key herbs that Beeton recommended for country gardens. Sadly, she felt that urban pollution was such that town gardeners should avoid growing foodstuffs:

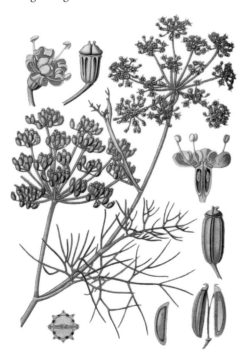

Bay—care is taken to differentiate between the ornamental cherry laurel and this, the classic laurel. Leaves are used in many recipes and with the additional suggestion that putting one under your pillow would procure pleasant dreams.

Cilantro—for its highly aromatic, tender leaves in soups and salads. Seeds suitable for distillation.

Fennel—for fennel sauce for mackerel notes. This is the only sauce where the British use fennel.

Garlic—although described by her as having the most offensive smell of all alliums, there is a recipe for Bengal mango chutney that includes ¼lb (150g) of fresh garlic.

Ginger—a line drawing for ginger was accompanied by a recipe for pickling eggs and the history of ginger production in Jamaica.

Horseradish—the plant is illustrated with the root and flowers. Beeton advised that it should never be dried (as it would lose its volatile oils), but stored in sand, and always grated fresh for sauce that was to be served hot. It was also used to flavor vinegar, Indian pickle, and pickling gherkins.

Marjoram—there is a preference for the sweet-knotted marjoram from Portugal, as well as oregano and pot marjoram for soups and stuffings.

LEFT: The aromatic, fresh herb fennel (*Foeniculum vulgare*) is a common plant that can be grown in traditional herb or vegetable gardens, raised beds, containers, or the mixed border.

Mint—"has an agreeable aromatic flavor." Beeton recommended including it in pea soup as a "stomachic and antispasmodic."

Nasturtium—seeds were pickled as caper substitutes and included in "Mixed Pickle."

Parsley—a favorite for her table—fresh for sauces or deep fried. If there were no leaves in winter she advised tying up the seeds in calico for flavoring.

Purslane—is classed as a form of parsley.

Sage—green and red varieties are described, with a preference for the leaves of the red or purple sage.

ABOVE: Beeton recommended adding fresh mint to pea soups. This is equally delicious whether you are serving this verdant soup hot or cold—add a dollop of sour cream with mint for a final touch.

ABOVE: Mrs. Beeton recommended that the red or purple sage has a better flavor for cooking. The flowers are a clear blue in pleasant contrast with the darker foliage.

Sorrel—illustrated in flower, Beeton refers to the writings of Pliny and Apicius, suggesting it could be stewed with mustard, oil, and vinegar. She notes that the French used it widely but it has a pronounced acid taste. She suggests it for a green sauce for geese or ducklings.

Tarragon, French—to be made into vinegar.

Thyme, lemon—"usually find a place in the herb compartment of the kitchen-garden." The illustration is accompanied by a recipe for lemon white sauce, for fowls and fricassess. She preferred it to garden thyme, which was to be used to flavor soups, sauces, and stuffings.

Anise
Pimpinella anisum

Common names: Anise, aniseed

Type: Annual

Climate: Hardy, average winter

Size: 18–24in (45–60cm)

Origin: Eurasia, Northern Africa

History: The plant has been prized for its aromatic seeds since earliest times. Cultivated by the ancient Egyptians, it was also known to the Greeks and cultivated in Tuscany in Roman times. It appears in Charlemagne's *Capitulare de Villis Imperialibus.*

Cultivation: The seeds require a long warm summer to ripen, so sow from mid-spring, in full sun, in a light, well-drained soil. Scatter sow seeds in blocks in flower beds to enjoy the creamy white umbels before the aromatic seeds form. Harvest the seeds as they turn brown on the plant.

Storage: Dried seeds will keep for over a year in airtight jars.

Preparation: Roll the seeds in or around cream cheeses—anisé is the speciality cheese of Lorraine, France. Seeds are excellent rolled into pastry, or added to bread dough and cookie mixtures. The leaves are both ornamental and anise-flavored so they can be added to salads or served with boiled carrots. When boiling carrots or cabbage, drain just before they are cooked and finish in a little butter with aniseeds. A tisane of the seeds not only sweetens your breath, but is also beneficial for bloating, wind, digestion, heartburn, and is reported as being "the comforter of bowels."

LEFT: Although the leaves can be used, anise is famed for its seeds, which give a distinctive flavor to breads, cheeses, and drinks—not forgetting that it lay at the heart of the British candy, the aniseed ball.

The Romans served small meal cakes, *Mustacae*, flavored with aniseed and cumin, as a digestive at the end of rich meals, which is said to be the forerunner of the wedding cake. It was baked as part of the bottom crust of bread, which is still worth doing and has evolved into Italian *pizzelle* and Norwegian *knotts*. During the medieval period its popularity spread to Central Europe where the hot summers help the seeds ripen. A real seed lay at the core of the original boiled candy, the aniseed ball. The Chinese aniseed known as *badiane* is used to flavor the anisette liqueur of Bordeaux, but it should not be confused with star anise, *Illicium verum*, or Japanese star anise, *I. anisatum*. As the production of *Illicium* is easier, the star anise has replaced aniseed in commercial production of the essential oil. However, an array of alcoholic drinks are still flavored with true aniseed. There is *arak* in the Middle East to *aguardiente* in Colombia, *pastis* in France to *raki* in Turkey, and *Jagermeister* in Germany to *mastika* in Bulgaria.

If seeds are sown in a seed tray, transplant them as soon as they are large enough to handle and before the taproot has formed. In good conditions anise will grow over 3ft tall. The white flowers form dense umbels that are decorative in the border or for a night garden. It can be grown among vegetables and is recommended for beans and cilantro, but not with carrots. It attracts predatory wasps and repels aphids.

TASTING NOTES

Anise cookies

This recipe is based on one by Australian cookery author Rosemary Hemphill. These cookies are a meal in themselves.

Preparation time: 15 minutes
Cooking time: 12–15 minutes
Serves: makes 12–15 cookies

You will need:

· 4¼oz (120g) soft butter

· 6¼oz (180g) demerara sugar

· 1 egg

· 4¼oz (120g) wholemeal flour

· 1 tsp baking powder

· Pinch of salt

· 3oz (85g) rolled oats

· 4¼oz (120g) desiccated coconut

· 2 tsp aniseed

Preheat a conventional oven to 350°F (180°C / gas mark 4 / fan 160°C).

Cream the butter and sugar.

Add the egg and beat well.

Mix in sifted flour, baking powder, and salt, and add the rolled oats, coconut, and aniseed.

Roll into small balls, flatten in circles, and place on a greased baking tray. Bake for 12–15 minutes.

Leave to cool; store in an airtight tin or freeze.

Purslane
Portulaca oleracea

Common names: Purslane, green purslane, pussley, little hogweed; var. *aurea* is known as golden purslane

Type: Annual

Climate: Half-hardy, unheated glasshouse, mild winter

Size: 8–18in (20–45cm)

Origin: India

Cultivation: Sow in a sheltered, warm position in drills when the soil has warmed in late spring, and later thinned out to 8–10in apart. The soil should be light but moisture retentive. It will yield small succulent, mucilaginous leaves and culinary stems.

There are a range of large-flowered ornamental cultivars but they are acrid to taste and not suitable for culinary use. Along with the similar *P. umbraticola* they are good plants for poor, dry soils. Unfortunately in many parts of the world, purslanes are viewed more as "weed it, not eat it."

Storage: Best eaten fresh so sow successively. It does not freeze well but older stems can be pickled in vinegar like a poor man's samphire.

Preparation: An excellent addition to salads for color and texture, it is crunchy like cucumber; the Italian gourmet Castelvetro recommended adding black pepper and finely chopped onion to "counteract its coldness." Purslane with chives, leaves, and flowers makes a delicious and attractive side salad or refreshing garnish. At its best in summer, its cool crispness is a welcome addition to salads. Cooked, it is a traditional ingredient in *Soupe Bonne Femme*, and it is good for stir-fries, where it can be used as a substitute for okra.

NUTRITION

Purslane is a rich source of omega-3 fatty acids and iron.

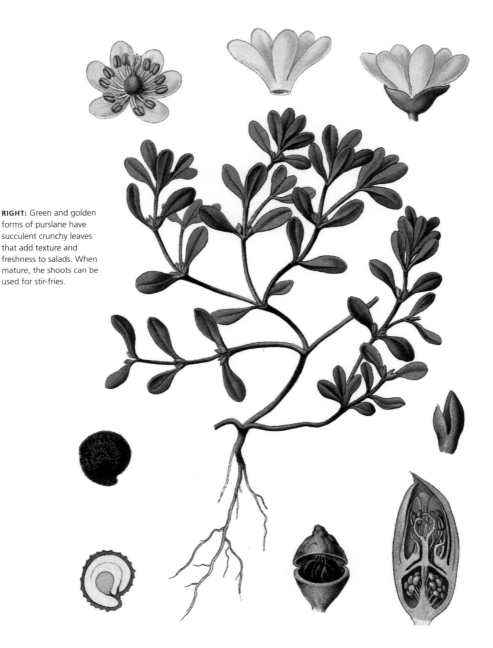

RIGHT: Green and golden forms of purslane have succulent crunchy leaves that add texture and freshness to salads. When mature, the shoots can be used for stir-fries.

"The Purselane is one of the Garden herbs, served first in Sallets, with Oyle, Vinegar, and a little Salt as well at the mean, as rich mens Tables, yea this for a dainty dish with many served first at Table in the winter time, preserved after this manner."

The Gardeners' Labyrinth, (1577) Thomas Hyll

Purslane was first described in Chinese literature c. 500 BC. The Romans used it as a salad plant that would also sooth and heal toothache. Pliny added two more exotic outcomes: one being that it checks lust and amorous dreams, the other that if you rubbed it on your head you would not suffer from catarrh that year. All these uses emphasize the cooling, refreshing qualities of the plant. Apart from its early culinary and medicinal uses in Europe, it was strewn around a bed to protect the sleeper from evil magic. Medieval herbalists recommended eating or drinking it if you were suffering from gonorrhoea. Yet another medicinal use was as a cure for "blastings by lightening or planets and burning of gunpowder."

It fell out of favor in British kitchens, not helped by writings such as that of William Cobbett in *The English Gardener* 1833: "A mischevious weed, eaten by Frenchmen and pigs, when they can get nothing else. Both use it in salad, that is to say, raw." Hence its common name of little hogweed. In France it was prepared like spinach or in a gratin whereas in the south it was an important soup ingredient.

Purslane enjoys the same conditions as lettuce and they grow well together; the golden form can also be raised from seed. It is very attractive with light golden succulent leaves on red stems that are decorative in salads or in omelettes and stir-fries.

TASTING NOTES

Peach and purslane salad

Fruit is the perfect accompaniment to purslane when sliced into a delicious salad.

Preparation time: 10 minutes
Serves: 1 person

You will need:

· 1 peach (peeled) or nectarine (with skin)

· Handful of fresh purslane leaves

· 3–4 hazelnuts, toasted and roughly chopped

· ¼ tsp freshly milled coriander seed

· 1 tsp hazelnut oil

Peel and slice a peach finely and arrange on a plate in two rows of a semicircle.

Place the leaves of purslane (golden leaves if available) in curved lines to complete the circle of salad. Use the smallest leaves to decorate the spaces between the slices of fruit.

Toast the hazelnuts in oil in a pan until golden brown, then roughly chop.

Trickle oil over the salad and sprinkle hazelnuts on the top.

Roses
Rosa

ABOVE: The *Rosa* x *alba* strains are ancient and those with good scent are ideal for infusing in vinegars or nonalcoholic drinks. Try steeping rose petals in sparkling white wines.

Common names: Apothecary's rose, gallica rose

Type: Shrub

Climate: Hardy, cold to very cold winter

Size: 3¼–6½ft (1–2m) or more

Origin: Northern hemisphere

History: Tablets excavated at Chaldea appear to record that Sargon, King of Sumer (2350–2300 BC), triumphantly brought back roses as well as vines and figs from his campaigns. The ancient Egyptians grew roses in commercial quantities; Cleopatra had the sails of her barge washed in rosewater.

Cultivation: Roses are supplied either in containers or bare rooted. They should not be replanted in soil that has already been used to grow roses. Ideally, prepare the ground well in advance. Dig deeply and dress with well-rotted manure or compost and bone meal—never allow fresh dung to touch the roots. If bare rooted, soak the roses for an hour before planting to plump up the roots.

Storage: Dry rose petals or layer with sugar and store in an airtight jar. To make rose petal vinegar and oil, see p.75.

Preparation: Choose well-scented roses. Nip out the heel at the base of the petal, and layer petals with superfine sugar, as per lavender sugar (see p.111).

Rose petals can be candied, made into jam, jelly, and desserts or simply used for decorating. For jam you can follow the quote on the next page of 1lb (450g) petals to 1lb sugar, with two tablespoons of water and one dessert spoon of rosewater. Sprinkle rosewater over fresh pomegranate seeds for a fragrant dessert or as an accompaniment for rich fruit creams and pound cakes. If you can, ensure unbruised or undamaged rosehips, otherwise the fibrous centers must be removed.

For a scented jam, simply simmer 1lb of rosehips in 30floz (1½ pints) water for two hours. Then add to 1lb peeled apples, simmer until soft, then boil to setting point with ¾lb (20g) sugar. Pot and seal in usual way for jam.

"Rose petals make a pleasant jam. Damask roses have the most aroma.
Cook, with as little water as possible, then measure 1lb of pulp to 1lb of
sugar and finish as usual. If liked, half apple jelly and half rose pulp may
be 'set' together, but this mixture will not keep so long."

Food in England, (1954) **Dorothy Hartley**

The ancient Egyptians created beautiful and productive gardens along the flood plains of the River Nile, where a system of canals kept them irrigated through the dry season. The Egyptians' gardening skills were imported by the Romans along with the discovery of the heady perfumes of roses, their oil and petals. Apart from their beauty and scent, roses were grown for their medicinal oil.

The earliest cultivated roses were, in chronological order, the Gallica, Damask, and Alba, all of which have petals that can be used for cooking. The apothecary's rose, *R. gallica* var. *officinalis*, is the oldest known form, which was introduced into France from the Near East around the early 14th century. French apothecaries developed rosewater and oil, which were also used to flavor vinegar and conserves. *R. gallica* was one of the parents of the Damask roses, *R. × damascena*. *Rosa × alba* is an ancient hybrid of European gardens, and the oldest Albas are "Maiden's Blush" (see next page) and "Alba Semiplena" (the white rose of York).

The extremely hardy Rugosa roses were introduced from Asia in the 19th century and, having highly fragrant flowers and generous hips, are invaluable for the gourmet gardener. Rosehips were known as "Shrouts" or "Rose Shrouts." There are recipes for vitamin C-rich rosehip syrup for babies dating back to 1730, a practice that was popularized some 200 years later during and after World War Two.

Dig a hole large enough to spread out the rose's roots and cut off any damaged roots with a clean cut. If space is restricted, consider planting elsewhere or as a last resort trim the roots so that they have room

to grow and properly establish new root development. Note where the soil level is on the stem and plant at the same depth, firm in, water well during the first growing season, and mulch.

Roses can be grown from hardwood cuttings taken when they are not in flower. Prune for shape in late winter or early spring, and unless you want the rosehips, remove the dead flowerheads on a regular basis to encourage further flowering (only on

TASTING NOTES

Roman-style rose wine

This recipe is based on one by the Roman gastronomer Apicius, though this wine and violet wine were used as a laxative.

Preparation time: 21 days
Serves: 4–6 people

You will need:

• 2 handfuls of rose petals, white parts removed

• Honey, to taste

• 30floz (1l) dry white wine

Remove the lower white parts of the petals.

Sew into a linen bag; add to wine for 7 days.

Remove the old petals and replace with new petals; leave for another 7 days. Repeat.

Strain the wine through a colander.

Add honey to sweeten before served.

LEFT: The dark pinky red of *Rosa gallica* is enhanced by crystallizing. Do not deadhead if you want the hips.

repeat-flowering varieties). For the larger garden, the *Rosa rugosa* is ideal for the herb garden. It has highly fragrant flowers, large fleshy red hips, and is very hardy.

ROSES TO GROW

When viewed as herbs, historical use is evoked by the Gallica, Damask, and Alba groups and, as they effectively only flower once, they are ideal for hips. Modern-scented hardiness, some repeat flowering, and good hips are the virtues of the Rugosa roses, and climbing and rambling roses are perfect for arbors, trellis, and walls.

Gallica roses are descendants from *Rosa gallica*, a wild rose native to southern and central Europe, Asia Minor, and the Middle East. Apart from the apothecary's rose, there are other highly scented types to consider, such as "Agatha," whose pale pink blooms have a darker center, and whose petals are excellent scattered through fruit salads. "Cardinal de Richelieu" has the rich, velvety, purple flowers that equate with high ecclesiastical office, looking sensational when crystallized. The decorative and delicious "Tuscany Superb" is another recommended Gallica rose with large, deeply crimson purple, semidouble blooms.

Damask roses are said to have been brought back into Europe by the Crusaders on their return from Damascus. First to come to mind is Kazanlik, the *R. × damascena* "Trigintipetala," widely grown in Bulgaria for the rose perfume industry. It is highly scented, the original "attar of roses" rose, with warm pink flowers. "Blush Damask" is a highly scented, little rose with pale pink blooms; the flowerbuds are excellent for decoration and drying. "Celsiana" is a classic antique rose that has clusters of semidouble pink flowers set against attractive gray foliage. It will grow in a pot in the shade of a tree, or in poor soil, and can be cut into a hedge. The very fragrant "Madame Hardy" has glorious white double blooms, with an elegant habit; it is ideal for planting near outdoor seating.

Alba forms have a distinctive scent of which the following are excellent. One of the oldest varieties is "Maiden's Blush", which has a strong sweet scent and double blush-pink flowers. It is known in French as *cuisse de nymphe*—nymph's thigh, which says something about the cultural differences between France and Britain. There is "Alba Maxima," known as the Jacobite rose, with excellent large rosehips. "Amelia," with its large, semidouble pink flowers with pronounced golden anthers set against gray-green foliage is versatile and will grow in a pot in the shade of a tree or in poor soil, and can also be cut into a low hedge. "Königin von Dänemark" has a rich Alba scent, with bright pink blooms.

ROSA RUGOSA

These are excellent multipurpose roses. Apart from a heady scent, they can be grown as an almost impenetrable hedge and have attractive and useful rosehips. They thrive in a moist, well-drained soil and are best pruned by the renewal method in winter, i.e. remove one third of the oldest canes to the ground. This keeps the new canes in production. They can grow to 6½ft tall and are also extremely resistant to black spot and mildew as well as being very tolerant of exposure, even on coasts. There are several varieties: two of the best are "Alba" and "Hansa". The former has bright green foliage that turns an attractive yellow in the fall and single white blooms that are highly fragrant; the later flowers contrast well with the huge red hips. "Hansa" was introduced in 1905 and has medium red blooms with an intense clove fragrance. It is repeat flowering and sets a heavy crop of hips.

CLIMBING ROSES FOR ARCHES, ARBORS, TRELLIS, AND WALLS

Many climbing roses can be successfully grown with scented honeysuckles to make a doubly scented screen and prolong flowering interest. Good climbing roses include the vigorous "Crimson Glory Climber", which has shapely, deep and velvety, vibrant red blooms and can attain 14¾ft in height. The deep maroon-red "Guinée" is a climbing Hybrid Tea rose that will grow in poorer soils and can also reach 14¾ft tall. One of Gertrude Jekyll's favorite roses, "Madame Isaac Pereire" is a Bourbon rose whose double blooms are a dark vibrant shade of purple. It is best if trained on a sunny wall where it can reach 5ft tall.

Like climbing and rambling roses, many of the shrub roses will also respond to being trained against a trellis, arbor, or wall. Prune back any outward facing buds and tie in branches. Be aware that most roses prefer a sunny aspect, so plant against a south- or west-facing wall or fence, although some roses are more shade tolerant than others and will tolerate a north- or east-facing position. If in doubt, always buy roses from a specialist nursery where you will get the best

advice. An alternative, devised at the Helmingham Hall gardens in Suffolk, England, is to train a rose up a central support that has wires attached at the top then arched to the ground like an umbrella. As the rose grows the branches are tied in, which greatly encourages flowering. Not only does this achieve the effect of a fountain of roses, but it also provides some protection from its thorny branches.

ABOVE: Petals of any of the highly scented roses, such as the pictured purple velvet rose (an historic form of *R. gallica*), can be used for culinary preparations. A finger bowl of rose petals raises eating with your hands to elegant heights.

Rosemary
Rosmarinus officinalis

NUTRITION

Modern research indicates that rosemary does enhance cognitive performance as well as facilitating and aiding metabolic changes.

Common names: Rosemary, dew of the sea, sea dew, elf leaf, guardrobe, incensier, compass weed, polar plant

Type: Shrub

Climate: Hardy, average winter

Size: 18in–5ft (45cm–1.5m)

Origin: Mediterranean

History: A maritime herb, *rosmarinus* translates as "dew" or "rose of the sea," and its silver-lined leaves thrive both in the wild and in gardens along seashores. The common saying, "Rosemary thrives where the woman rules" has nothing to do with power, but ruling in the sense of understanding the needs of a domain.

Cultivation: Although it can be raised from seed, ready-rooted plants grow better and you can ascertain the variety. Rosemary needs to be warm and well-drained; it will thrive against or growing down a wall. For the latter choose prostrate varieties. Rosemary and sage enjoy the same conditions so can be grown together in a large terracotta pot.Potted rosemary is susceptible to root rot, so never overwater. The containers can be brought in for Christmas and decorated.

Storage: Although not necessary with this evergreen, you can dry small branches. Break off dried leaves as needed and crumble before adding to food. Freeze if necessary.

Preparation: One of the *herbes Provençales* (see p.138), rosemary is a truly evergreen herb, providing year-round fresh pickings. The leaves are spiky so make sure you chop or crumble them into small pieces. When following recipes, three tablespoons of fresh chopped leaves are equal to one of dried.

A classic for lamb in combination with garlic, chop finely together and push into incisions in a leg or shoulder of lamb; this can also be done with lavender leaves. Sit lamb joints or chicken on rosemary leaves for roasting and remove before making gravy from the herb-flavored meat juices.

Chopped leaves are good in shortbread cookies, which can be served with cold desserts and crème brulée. Using scissors, finely cut tips and flowers into salads; they are excellent with tomatoes and in vinaigrette. Strip leaves from woody branches and use as skewers for kebabs as the wood imparts an aromatic taste. Smaller woody stems can also be used to thread on olives in lieu of sticks for cocktails. Rosemary is also good for tisanes.

The Romans recognized that rosemary was a herb of primary medicinal and culinary importance, as well as being decorative. It was used as hedging for the magnificent seaside villas of the great and the good and is listed in Charlemagne's *Capitulare in Villis Imperialibus*. In French medieval hospitals it was burned with juniper to ward off contagion, hence the common name *incensier*. It was finally reintroduced into England by Philippa of Hainault in the early 14th century, and like the Romans, good medieval and Tudor housewives nurtured it as the health of their community relied on its successful growth throughout the year. Sir Thomas More grew rosemary over the walls of his Chelsea Manor, both for the bees and the fact that it was a symbol of remembrance and friendship.

In Googe Barnaby's 1578 translation *The Whole Art and Trade of Husbandry*, he wrote: "sette by women for their pleasure to grow in sundry proportions, as in the fashion of a cart, a peacock, or such by things as they fancy." Historical references abound, praising its value, savor, and symbolic associations. In the words of Shakespeare's Ophelia in *Hamlet*: "There's rosemary, that's for remembrance; pray you, love, remember." Rosemary is doubly for remembrance because eating it reputedly aids your memory, not to mention improving your circulation.

When growing, think Mediterranean hillsides and replicate them with warm, dry conditions and well-drained soil. Rosemary is hardy along more northern coasts and tolerates salt-laden winds. It will not survive wet winters and prolonged freezing conditions. In warm, dry

BELOW: Traditionally, rosemary has blue flowers but there are several attractive white-blossoming forms that taste just as good with lamb, finely chopped in salads, or in cookies.

conditions, rosemary can be clipped into an attractive hedge or as part of a garden knot. It is also a good subject for topiary, albeit not as ambitious as Googe quoted on the previous page.

Tip cuttings (see p.203) taken in early summer from new shoots will root readily, or take larger heel cuttings in the fall. In late spring after flowering, clip or prune back to new growth, cut out dead wood, and clip into shape. There are two examples of good species: *R. eriocalyx* in southeastern Spain and *R. tomentosus* in southern Spain.

THE MANY FORMS OF ROSEMARY

Christian legend recounts that rosemary never grows taller than six feet, because this height is associated with Jesus Christ, and that the blue flowers are a remembrance of his mother Mary throwing her cloak over a rosemary bush when they sheltered during their flight to Egypt. However, there are both taller and shorter varieties, with flowers in many shades of blue as well as pink and white. The silver variegated rosemary has been lost to cultivation, but golden-striated varieties have been reintroduced, although they can be temperamental. When rosemary is grown over walls it exudes its scent as the stone or bricks warm up in the sunshine.

The flowers of "Severn Sea" are an attractive dark blue set against dark green dense foliage. As the leaves are softer than the standard type, it is good for fresh chopping. It responds well to being trained along a wall, as does "Tuscan Blue." The latter has tall, softer leaves, with dark blue flowers, and has a good culinary profile because it contains less pine and camphor oils. From experience, the most floriferous of all rosemaries, with a mass of bright blue flowers set against soft green leaves is "Sudbury Blue," bred in

ABOVE: The young branches of mature rosemary bushes, such as *F. albiflorus*, can be used to make kebab skewers, which are attractive to serve and infused with added herbal flavor.

the 1970s by Suffolk Herbs in the UK. The variety "Benenden Blue" grows very densely to about 3¼ft, so is ideal for hedges and topiary. It has bright deep blue flowers in late spring and early summer, sometimes repeating in the fall. Also of interest is the pale blue-flowered "Green Ginger," which grows to 24in tall and makes a beautiful and interesting plant.

Two interesting American varieties are "Arp" and "Shady Acres." The first is reputedly the most cold hardy, surviving temperatures as low as −18°F. It forms an upright hedge, is good for small topiaries, has a good flavor and clear-blue flowers. "Shady Acres" grows to 5½ft tall and was introduced in 1999 by Shady Acres Herb Farm in Minnesota. Although it rarely flowers, the dark green leaves are produced close to the stem and are up to 1in long.

As the name suggests, "Marjorca Pink" has pink flowers, but with an underlying mauve hue, and they often bloom throughout the winter. It is a freestanding, upright small shrub growing to 5ft that can be trained into a standard. It is hardier on dry, well-drained soil. White Rosemary, F. *albiflorus*, is covered in white flowers in spring and summer. It has small, dark green needles and grows to about 31½in tall. Another attractive white form is "Lady in White."

For the dedicated rosemary grower prepared to experiment, golden varieties are of interest. "Aureus," with its gold variegation splashed across its leaves, is also known as the Golden Variegated Rosemary. It has small pale blue flowers and grows to about 31½in tall. "Gold Dust" has bright green and gold-edged leaves and is very heat tolerant. Lastly, there is "Joyce DeBaggio," which is also known as "Golden Rain."

PROSTRATUS GROUP

Rosemaries of the Prostratus Group are readily available and popular, as they can be planted to tumble over a wall or creep as ground cover shrubs. Prostrate varieties include "Capri," "Freda," "Gethsemane," "Jackmann's Prostrate," and "Rampant Boule." Thought to be a sport of the excellently trailing "Capri," the first leaves of "Wilma's Gold" are bright gold, darkening as they age with pale blue flowers.

"Fota Blue" is among the smallest prostrate lavenders, growing to only 15¾in, with blue flowers. It has an arching, trailing habit, ideal for small pots, but it tends to be short-lived. Take cuttings every year as insurance.

TASTING NOTES

Toasted walnuts

A truly gourmet salted snack, the rosemary and sage flavor both the nuts and the salt. Any leftovers can be stirred into a risotto.

Preparation time: 10 minutes
Cooking time: 20–30 minutes
Serves: 10 people (as a snack)

You will need:

· 1 tbsp olive oil

· 1 tbsp butter

· 2 tbsp fresh rosemary, finely chopped

· 1 tbsp sage, finely chopped

· 1 tsp paprika

· ¾ tsp salt

· 12oz (245g) walnut halves

Preheat a conventional oven to 325°F (160°C / gas mark 3 / fan 140°C).

Heat the oil and butter in a pan. Stir in herbs, spices, and the salt. Add walnuts and toss until coated in the mixture.

Toast on a baking tray for 20–30 minutes.

Store in a sterilized, airtight jar.

VITAMINS AND MINERALS

THE ADDED VALUE OF EDIBLE HERBS

In prehistoric farming, the weeds that sprung up among the cereals were reaped and harvested along with the grain. This was no bad thing for several reasons. First, the weeds were tougher than the cereals and could be relied upon in a bad season if the cereal crop failed. Second, the large weed seeds, roughly ground, had a food value of their own. Third, weed seeds, along with wild herbs, supplied natural protein when meat and fish were in short supply. For very different reasons, this final point is as important today for those trying to cut back their salt intake. Edible weeds and herbs were valued as they provide seasoning as well as healthy supplements.

The World War Two "Dig for Victory" slogan *Eat Your Greens* was a reminder that plants are rich in vitamins and minerals, and this includes most herbs, notably parsley. There are other health advantages, such as boosting your immunity with elderberries or garlic, and controlling the calories in your diet. One of the hardest elements of dieting is the need for taste. Great ancient examples were and are fennel seeds, chewed to alleviate hunger during times of fast. They effectively anesthetize the taste buds and give a welcome aniseed breath freshener—sweet cicely seeds do much the same. Garlic is renowned for its health-giving properties; peel cloves and leave for 15–20 minutes before cooking because this increases its immune-boosting enzymes.

Herbs provide an array of trace elements and minerals to lubricate the body and mind's many functions. Many health scares and contraindications have arisen through the marketing of herbal medicines and essential herb oils, such as rosemary and sage, which are powerful and should be used with caution both internally and externally. The fact is, it would be hard to overdose on any of the 60 or so herbs in this book if eaten fresh, and to an even lesser extent when they are dried. Dandelion leaves are rightly known to be a potent diuretic. However, the good news is that unlike the side effects of many medicinal diuretics that drain the body's potassium, dandelion leaves are very rich in potassium.

So eat your herbs while following the seasonal and culinary advice given for each. Relish delightful traditions, such as rosemary improving your memory or ground elder alleviating gout, and choose whether you want to have eternal life by eating sage in May, or slow down your ageing process by consuming fresh thyme. As Erasmus wrote, "folly is the seasoning of pleasure."

RIGHT: Under the World War Two "Dig for Victory" banner, potatoes and onions are munitions of war as surely as shells and bullets. The wartime diet included parsley, mint, and thyme. Rosehips and elderflowers and berries picked from the wild.

A GUIDE TO VITAMINS AND OTHER PROPERTIES IN HERBS

If you plan to take herbs medicinally, in sustained quantities, it is essential to seek medical advice. However, eaten fresh in reasonable amounts as part of a balanced diet the outcome is positive.

Vitamin A — Cumin (*Cuminum cyminum*)

Vitamin B$_1$ — Eryngo (*Eryngium foetidum*), cumin (*Cuminum cyminum*)

Vitamin B$_2$ — Eryngo (*Eryngium foetidum*), cumin (*Cuminum cyminum*)

Vitamin B$_6$ — Horseradish (*Armoracia rusticana*), elder tree (*Sambucus* fruit), cumin (*Cuminum cyminum*)

Vitamin C — Ground elder (*Aegopodium podagraria*), chervil (*Anthriscus cerefolium*), horseradish (*Armoracia rusticana*), cumin (*Cuminum cyminum*), salad arugula (*Eruca vesicaria* subsp. *sativa*), Eryngo (*Eryngium foetidum*), perilla (*Perilla frutescens*), parsley (*Petroselenium*), rosehips, elder tree (*Sambucus* fruit), dandelion (*Taraxacum officinale*), nasturtium (*Tropaeolum majus*), nettle (*Urtica dioica*)

Vitamin E — Cumin (*Cuminum cyminum*), dandelion (*Taraxacum officinale*)

Vitamin D — Chervil (*Anthriscus cerefolium*)

Vitamin K — Salad arugula (*Eruca vesicaria* subsp. *sativa*)

Iron — Cumin (*Cuminum cyminum*), salad arugula (*Eruca vesicaria* subsp. *sativa*), Eryngo (*Eryngium foetidum*), perilla (*Perilla frutescens*), purslane (*Portulaca oleracea*), dandelion (*Taraxacum officinale*), nasturtium (*Tropaeolum majus*), nettle (*Urtica dioica*)

Calcium — Horseradish (*Armoracia rusticana*), cumin (*Cuminum cyminum*), salad arugula (*Eruca vesicaria* subsp. *sativa*), Eryngo (*Eryngium foetidum*), perilla (*Perilla frutescens*), dandelion (*Taraxacum officinale*), thymes (*Thymus*), nettle (*Urtica dioica*)

Copper — Cumin (*Cuminum cyminum*)

Manganese — Cumin (*Cuminum cyminum*)

Magnesium — Horseradish (*Armoracia rusticana*), cumin (*Cuminum cyminum*), dandelion (*Taraxacum officinale*)

Phosphorus — Horseradish (*Armoracia rusticana*), dandelion (*Taraxacum officinale*), thymes (*Thymus*)

Potassium — Horseradish (*Armoracia rusticana*), cumin (*Cuminum cyminum*), salad arugula (*Eruca vesicaria* subsp. *sativa*), perilla (*Perilla frutescens*), dandelion (*Taraxacum officinale*), thymes (*Thymus*), nettle (*Urtica dioica*)

Zinc — Cumin (*Cuminum cyminum*)

Omega-3 fatty acids — Purslane (*Portulaca oleracea*), dandelion (*Taraxacum officinale*)

"There is no herb, nor weed,
but God hath given virtue to them,
to help man ... a good cook
is half a physician."

Andrew Boorde (c. 1490–1549)

The list of individual properties in the table opposite indicates that a healthy number of herbs contain vitamin C, iron, calcium, and potassium, a foursome comprising the most important for our well-being. In themselves they form a chain reaction for the stylist's drive for hair and skin to look good, feel good, and the old adage that it will do you good. Cumin, perilla, dandelion, and nettle contain all four.

The body cannot store vitamin C because it is water-soluble. Vitamin C can be available daily from fresh herbs year round but be mindful not to destroy with overcooking. It is something of a wonder vitamin—it protects cells and keeps them healthy, is active in the support and structure of tissues and organs such as the skin, bones, and blood vessels, and aids wound healing. It is also crucial in increasing the amount of iron the body absorbs from plant sources, so is excellent in combination with the iron herb list. Iron in the diet is associated with robust good health as it provides life-giving oxygen to our organ systems. It alleviates fatigue and insomnia, strengthens not only the immune system but also the ability to concentrate and muscle function, and it helps regulate body temperature.

Calcium puts strength in your bones and teeth, important for children and post-menopausal women. Modern research indicates that calcium promotes more fat to be burned and less to be stored, thus having slimming effects on the metabolism. Salmon, chicken, milk, and almonds are sources of potassium, so double up the intake by preparing them with potassium-rich herbs: horseradish mayonnaise with salmon; chicken broiled with cumin seeds served with a mixed salad of arugula, purple perilla, and young dandelion leaves. Rabbit cooked in thyme and milk is fragrant and easily digestible. For an unusual appetizer, sauté young nettle leaves with almonds and black olives in virgin olive oil—serve warm or cold.

ABOVE: Dandelion is packed with nutritional value. It contains vitamin C, iron, calcium, and potassium.

Sorrel
Rumex acetosa; also *R. scutatus*

Common names: Sorrel, sourock, green sauce; also French sorrel, buckler-leaved sorrel

Type: Perennial

Climate: Hardy, very cold winter

Size: 24in; 12in (60cm; 30cm)

Origin: Europe

History: Pliny recommended eating wild harvested leaves with pearl barley. In *The Englishman's Flora* Geoffrey Grigson lists no less than 36 common names for *R. acetosa*—the last being from Kent, the splendidly descriptive "Tom Thumb's Thousand Fingers."

Cultivation: Sow seed in spring, direct into moderately fertile and well-drained soil in a semi-shaded position. Thin to 4–10in spacings. It will readily self-seed so to prevent this cut off flowering stems. The very hardy *R. acetosa* grows in Arctic regions.

Storage: Leaves can be frozen but are available almost year round.

Preparation: Wash and cook in the water clinging to the leaves. Sorrel soup is a traditional French staple often thickened with potato—an alternative is in combination with lettuce. In France, carp is presented on a bed of steamed sorrel leaves, while hake is served on sorrel purée mixed with two egg yolks, a teaspoon of French tarragon

ABOVE: Sorrel should be prevented from flowering and going to seed. Instead, trim back the stems to encourage the production of more leaves.

mustard, and fresh French tarragon leaves. Mix shredded with apples, sauté in butter, then add cider for a fruity, slightly sharp sauce for roast goose. In Provence, sorrel is mixed with spinach to make green gnocchi. The leaves of sorrel are excellent shredded into white sauces for fish and veal—add cream and egg for a richer taste. Sorrel can be substituted for spinach in combination soups, and the smaller buckler-leaved sorrel provides a lemony bite in green salads and can be scattered like salad arugula over pizzas and pasta.

> "Sorrel is well known for the grateful acidity of its herbage, which is most marked when the plant is in full season, though in early spring it is almost tasteless. The plant is also called 'Cuckoo's meate' from an old belief that the bird cleared its voice by its agency."
>
> *A Modern Herbal*, (1931) Mrs. M. Grieve

Before the ready availability of lemons, sorrel's acidic, cooling taste was much used with fish, and English botanist and herbalist John Gerard wrote that it cooled the stomach. Sorrel was slowly cooked, strained, and then packed into stone jars and sealed with clarified beef fat for winter use. In *Culinary and Salad Herbs*, Eleanour Sinclair Rohde suggested when serving roast duck, stew in a quarter pint of sorrel leaves, mix with an equal quantity of gravy plus six gooseberries, add sugar to taste, and serve hot.

Although sorrel will grow almost anywhere, in dry conditions the leaves become increasingly acidic, as do the older leaves. To prevent this, keep picking to keep a constant supply of fresh leaves. In milder areas, leaves are available year round. Try sowing in late summer for an early spring crop. Although edible, the wild sheep sorrel, *R. acetosella*, is an invasive weed that spreads by runners and is best kept out of the garden.

TASTING NOTES

Sorrel varieties to try

Sorrel leaves have a distinctive "acid" lemon-vinegar flavor, but are appetizing.

R. acetosa "Abundance"	Does not produce flowers and gives a good crop of salad leaves. Recommended for soups.
R. acetosa "Blonde de Lyon"	Has the largest leaves. Although hardy it is best resown and replanted every five years.
R. sanguineus	The more ornamental red-veined sorrel can also be eaten. The stems are red and its bright green leaves, with blood-red veins, have a velvety texture.
R. scutatus	Known as buckler-leafed sorrel because of its small and attractive, arrowhead-shaped leaves. It is sharply lemony and more tolerant of drought.
R. scutatus "Silver Shield"	An attractive form with a metallic urnish.

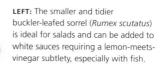

LEFT: The smaller and tidier buckler-leafed sorrel (*Rumex scutatus*) is ideal for salads and can be added to white sauces requiring a lemon-meets-vinegar subtlety, especially with fish.

Sage
Salvia officinalis

Common names: Common sage

Type: Perennial

Climate: Hardy, average to cold winter

Size: 12–31½in (30–80cm)

Origin: Mediterranean, Northern Africa

History: Pliny derived *Salvia* from the Latin word *salvere,* meaning "to heal" or "save." The Romans gathered it with some ceremony and were aware that iron salts react with the chemicals in sage, so they never harvested it with an iron blade. Sage features on the earliest surviving garden plan, that of St. Gall c. AD 816 and on Charlemagne's list *Capitulare de Villis Imperialibus.*

Cultivation: Sow seeds in spring. Green sage from seed will flower prolifically, however many new varieties have been bred for their leaves so they tend not to flower at all. A native of the Mediterranean, sage thrives in sunny, dry conditions or in a terracotta pot with rosemary—good to look at and convenient. Sage makes an attractive ground cover spaced at 12in apart.

Storage: Dry leaves whole and store in an airtight jar; never keep longer than a year.

Preparation: Fresh sage leaves are excellent cooked with onions, cheese, pork, duck, veal, and chicken. Dip in batter and deep fry. Alternatively, melt sage butter over lamb, veal, or broiled tomatoes—mix 12 sage leaves with 2½oz of butter, pound and add two teaspoons of lemon juice, salt, and pepper to taste. Apples cored and filled with chopped sage and onion can be roasted around pork as a lighter alternative to sage and onion stuffing. When making bread, especially Italian-type loaves kneaded with olive oil, to every 1lb of white flour add 12 fresh green or purple sage leaves or two teaspoons of dried leaves. Scatter sage flowers in salads.

From earliest times, sage has been valued for its health-giving properties that lie at the root of the Arab proverb "How can a man die who has Sage in his garden?" and the English version of "He that would live for aye must eat of Sage in May."

Under Beeton's recipe for Genevese sauce for salmon and trout, there is a line drawing of sage, noting that it has long been cultivated in English gardens. She recommended the red or purple sage as being the best for cooking, followed by the green, and included a recipe for the traditional sage and onion stuffing served with pork and duck in Britain. Beatrix Potter's children's book, *The Tale of*

Jemima Puddle-Duck of 1908, recounts the hapless tale of a stupid duck who picks sage and onion for a "sandy whiskered gentleman." He is a fox with cunning plans to eat her and knows (as would the young readers) that these are the perfect flavorings for roast duck. As this is a children's story, Kep the wise collie dog saves Jemima from a gruesome end.

Sage establishes quickly in a sunny position to form an attractive green, purple, or variegated ground cover, or edging. It can also be grown in blocks, in geometric beds, or in paving. The violet-lavender flowers appear in summer. In spring, cut out dead wood and trim back, and through summer pinch all the shoots back regularly to keep the plant bushy and within bounds. It is easy to root from cuttings in early summer or fall. In the garden it is useful as additional plant interest around new shrubs in sunny beds, but after three or four years it tends to become leggy so that is the time to lift it out and leave the shrubs to develop. A simple way to propagate and renew sage is to mulch up to the leaves with a light compost in fall. The following spring, draw away the mulch and you will find that some of the stems have roots. Lift the sage, cut off the ready-rooted cuttings, and replant them. They can be used to renew other sage plantings if they are becoming leggy.

Among the tender salvias, the pineapple sage (*Salvia elegans*) has strongly pineapple-scented leaves that can be used to infuse a fruit flavor. They are, unfortunately, not good to eat.

SO MANY SAGES

There are over 900 species of *Salvia*, many with scented leaves or flowers, but the best culinary sages are varieties of *S. officinalis*. Within this species there is still plenty of variation in leaf shape and flower color as well as variegation.

"Purpurascens" is the purple-leaved sage that has long been considered to be superior for culinary use as it has a stronger flavor. It is also hardier. The purple leaves have the deepest color in spring, gradually becoming mauve-green. The flowers are

BELOW: Sage flowers have a beautiful blue color but rarely appear on modern varieties, which are bred for their foliage.

a purple-blue. It will tolerate some shade but is best in full sun. There is also the striated form "Purpurascens Variegata," with pink and creamy white markings. The most ornamental is "Tricolor," or variegated sage, which has gray-green leaves marbled with white and purple markings, and pink and lavender-blue flowers. It is the least hardy of these sages, but grows well in pots.

Many cooks, however, prefer green-leaved sages. One of the largest leaved is the rarely flowering "Berggarten," which is also known as mountain garden sage and giant German sage. The generous oval leaves have serrated edges that turn a soft gray as they mature unless they are planted in full sun when they take on a purplish hue. The leaves dry well. "Extrakta" is an improved strain that can be raised from seed; originally bred for commercial production, it has a high oil content ensuring a good flavor when dried. The elegant leaves of "Albiflora" are truly sage-green; the white flowers last from late spring into early summer. Research has been undertaken on its potential antioxidant activities.

There are golden cultivars that will provide a bright contrast to the purple or green forms as well as looking good in pots. "Aurea" has colorful, fragrant green leaves with marginal gold splashes and is freely flowering. The growth habit is compact, to 24in tall and wide. Also known as golden leaf sage, "Icterina" has fragrant gray-green leaves that are mottled with yellow. It will grow in, and is useful for brightening up, semishaded areas. The leaves of "Kew Gold" are almost entirely golden. It has pale violet-blue flowers in early summer and a compact dwarf habit, growing to only 12in.

Finally there are several sages that have ornamental value with some culinary uses for the enthusiast. Spanish or lavender-leaved sage, *S. lavandulifolia*, has the same flavor as the leaves of *S. officinalis*. As a native of hot rocky places, it is ideal for a sunny spot or on a drystone wall. As the name implies, it has narrow, almost lavender-like leaves. Sounding fruity, the apple-bearing sage, *S. pomifera*, has leaves that can be used as substitutes for *S. officinalis* or infused with the Greek sage *S. fruticosa* to make the fragrant tea, fascomiglia. The leaves of Greek sage are also infused to make the Cypriot chanomilia; the plant is also known for its woolly galls, which form on the plant in its native habit. These are known as "apples" and are crystallized into sweetmeats in Greece.

Although it is mostly grown as an ornamental in hot climates, the seeds of *S. hispanica* exude a nutritious jelly that is used for flavoring fruit juices and the tonic chia in Mexico. Geographically close is the Californian white sage, *S. apiana*. If it is grown in sufficient quantities, bees will work the flowers and produce a clear, pale superfine honey. A dramatic flourish can be created with the painted sage, *S. viridis* var. *comata*, which should not be mistaken for "Tricolor." It is an annual with striking red, blue, pink, and sometimes white-tinged green bracts that can be used for cooking but it is inferior to the *S. officinalis* sages.

Elderberry
Sambucus nigra

Common names: Common elderberry, elderflower, bour-tree

Type: Tree, deciduous

Climate: Hardy, very cold winter

Size: 20ft (6m)

Origin: Europe, Northern Africa, Southwest Asia

History: British folklore says that summer starts when the elder flowers and finishes when the berries are ripe. In Scotland, the ancient custom was to plant the bour-tree or elder at the back of the house and the rowan, *Sorbus aucuparia*, at the front to ward off evil spirits and witchcraft. The bark and leaves were much used for dyeing in Harris tweed manufacture, while the berries were applied by the Romans as a hair dye.

Cultivation: A native of woodlands and hedgerows, it is easy to grow the species from fresh seeds sown in the fall. Semiripe cuttings can be taken in summer. Elderberry will tolerate a wide range of soils. Control it by cutting back old wood and weeding out seedlings.

Storage: Dry or freeze flowers removed from their stalks. Berries can be frozen whole or as juice. Both flowers and berries make excellent vinegars (see p.75).

Preparation: The flowers infuse a fragrant muscat flavor. Steep them fresh to make a syrup with the addition of lemon juice and finely grated peel as an excellent base for cordial and sorbet. Add them when stewing gooseberries for fool, in pies or cobblers, or when making gooseberry wine. Dried flowers can be infused in white wine or cider vinegar, or in boiling water as a tisane. Flowers and berries can be brewed, the former as champagne and the latter to make a fortified port-like wine. Simplest is to steep the berries in vodka for at least two months, adding sugar to taste, then drain off the vodka for a deep purple port-like spirit. A syrup of elderberries and cinnamon is an excellent winter pick-me-up. Very young stalks can be peeled and sautéed in lots of butter for 45 minutes; add a squeeze of lemon before serving.

The flowers and berries should be eaten cooked. Not only will they taste better, but when raw these also have low concentrations of toxic chemicals that are destroyed by cooking. The leaves are poisonous.

Elder was a potent symbol of sorrow and death. Although not a native of Palestine, it was believed that Judas Iscariot hanged himself from it. Such was the fear it engendered, the use of its wood was so restricted it was not even used for firewood. Norse legend tells a different story: Hulda, the mother of the good fairies, lived under its roots. The good news remains that the elderflowers and berries have a multiplicity of medicinal uses and are both delicious and fortifying. A project called Ethnomedica or Remembered Remedies is a collaboration between the Royal Botanic Gardens, Kew, the National Institute of Medical Herbalists, Chelsea Physic

RIGHT: When using elderflowers, only leave the stalks that are actually holding the flowers because they have an acrid flavor that diminishes the muscat scent of the blossoms.

"Towards the end of spring, the elder comes into bloom, and makes wonderful fritters. Mix the blossoms with ricotta, Parmesan, egg, and powdered cinnamon, and shape the mixture into little crescent shapes. Flour them lightly and fry them in butter, and send to table sprinkled with sugar."

The Fruits, Herbs and Vegetables of Italy, (1614) Giacomo Castelvetro

TASTING NOTES

Elderberry sauce

This sauce is based on British author Dorothy Hartley's recipe. It is excellent added to red cabbage stewed with apples, onions, and raisins.

Preparation time: 1 hour
Cooking time: 3–4 hours
Serves: makes 10oz (280g) Kilner jar

You will need:

· 1lb (450g) elder berries, picked from the stalk

· 1 pint (600ml) vinegar

· 1 shallot, minced

· Piece of root ginger, bruised

· 1 tsp cloves, whole

· 2 tsp peppercorns

Preheat a conventional oven to 325°F (160°C/ gas mark 3 / fan 140°C).

Slowly bake the berries in a covered, ovenproof jar with ½ pint of vinegar.

Leave to cool and strain the juice into a pan.

Add the shallot, root ginger, cloves, and peppercorns. Boil up well in the remaining vinegar.

Pour into a sterilized jar and seal.

Garden, Neal's Yard, the Eden Project, and the Natural History Museum to collect data about local uses of plants for medicine in Britain. The use of elder (flowers and berries) for treating coughs and colds appeared among the top ten remedies.

Elderberry is a versatile tree that has many ornamental cultivars. These include variegated, serrated, gold- and purple-leaved forms as well as weeping, dwarf and double-flowering varieties. Stratification (see p.37) will be required if raising from dried seed. In the garden, it makes an attractive shrubby addition to large borders if well maintained with judicious pruning, and it can also be grown in a mixed hedge or as a standard tree. It is said to be resistant to deer. The white muscat scented flowers grow in flat-topped clusters from late spring into early summer; the dark purple fruits ripen in late summer.

There are 40 cultivars of *S. nigra* including:

Eva "Black Lace"—bred at East Malling Research Station, it has finely cut, velvety black leaves with pink flowers.

Gerda "Black Beauty"—an English cultivar with pink flowers set against dark purple, almost black, foliage.

"Guincho Purple"—has dark purple-green leaves in the spring that gradually turn to green.

NUTRITION

Elderberries are antioxidants, rich in vitamins A, B, and C and are used to lower cholesterol, improve vision, and boost the immune system.

LEFT: The elder is a small tree with many attractive cultivars suitable for small gardens. Do not harvest all the flowers if you want some superfood berries.

Salad burnet
Sanguisorba minor (syn. *Poterium sanguisorba*)

Common names: Salad burnet, garden burnet, pimpernel, Drum-sticks, Old Man's Pepper, red knobs, God's little birds

Type: Rhizomatous perennial

Climate: Hardy, very cold winter

Size: 24–35in (60–90cm)

Origin: Europe, North Africa, Southwest and Central Asia

History: A native of English chalk downs, it provided greenery for sheep throughout the winter. Early settlers took it to North America.

ABOVE: The cucumber-like flavor of salad burnet has long been used for infusing in red wine, straight or as a punch.

Cultivation: Raised from seed, preferably freshly harvested, it is best sown in the fall. Seedlings and plants can be transplanted in spring at spacings of 12in.

Storage: Dry leaves before flowering to add to drinks. For salad burnet vinegar, see p.75.

Preparation: If you wish to add the delicate leaves to salads, there is only a small window of opportunity in spring before they become too dry and paperlike. For drinks, you can use fresh or dried leaves all year round.

Salad burnet grows in dry places and makes a pretty, almost evergreen, fern-like edging to herb beds. The Latin name *Sanguisorba* stems from the word *sanguis*, meaning "blood," and *sorbeo* "to soak up," as it was believed to have styptic qualities and was used as an infusion to stop bleeding resulting from dysentery.

As the quote, right, and common names suggest, this herb was prized for its hot, dry taste, and the aromatic cucumber-like flavor it infuses into drinks. The 16th-century herbalist William Turner advised adding it to wine and beer as a cure for gout and rheumatism. The name "God's little birds" derives from the Dutch *Hergottes berdlen* because the red tufts of flowers sit on two little leaves that look like birds.

Salad burnet will colonize under roses and other deciduous shrubs. The young leaves that spring from the base mature on stems that become increasingly angular, and the round juvenile leaves develop into lanceolate leaflets, almost frilly in the marginal serrations that cup the flower stems. The bird-like flowers are actually a cluster of square calyces and it is the red of the pistils that first appear, followed a couple of weeks later by stamens around the base of the flowerhead. It is not only a herb for drinking cups, but one that also imbibes what little moisture there is through its own structure, making it a great survivor of dry summers.

LEFT: Salad burnet is pretty and very hardy in dry conditions. The young, serrated leaves are good and attractive for salads but for only two or three weeks in the year.

" … A most precious herb, … the continual use of it preserves the body in health and the spirit in vigour … Two or three of the stalks with leaves put into a cup of wine, especially claret, are known to quicken the spirits, refresh and clear the heart, and drive away melancholy."

Complete Herbal, **(1653) Nicholas Culpeper**

Savory

Satureja montana and *S. hortensis*

Common names: Winter savory, mountain savory; also the annual summer savory

Type: Subshrub (*S. montana*), annual (*S. hortensis*)

Climate: Hardy, cold winter

Size: 6–15in (15–38cm)

Origin: Mediterranean

History: The Latin name *satureja* was used by the ancients. In the *Georgics,* Virgil noted it to be one of the most fragrant of herbs, which he recommended growing around beehives. The Romans used it for flavoring vinegars. Summer savory was one of the herbs in the English poet and farmer Thomas Tusser's 1557 book *Seedes and Herbes for the Kitchen*.

Cultivation: Both savorys can be raised from seed from spring onwards as they are slow to germinate. They grow to 30cm tall. Winter savory thrives in poor soil and can be propagated from cuttings. Summer savory requires a richer loam and grows well with French and haricot beans.

Storage: Winter savory should provide fresh pickings all year round but dries well. Summer savory is best frozen; break the stems into fresh and dried bean dishes or try vinegar, see p75.

LEFT: As their names suggest, the spiky leaves of winter savory are best used for cold-weather stews and soups while the heady, freshness of summer savory is excellent with new French or runner beans.

Preparation: As the name suggests, this herb adds an aromatic savoury flavor. The woody, winter savory (*S. montana*) has spiky leaves and is ideal for slow cooking, traditionally with cassoulet. Chop leaves with parsley for dumplings. Add to dried peas and pulses when cooking. The soft stems and fragrant flowers of the summer savory (*S. hortensis*) should be sprinkled over fresh bean dishes or forked through haricot bean salads; it is excellent in herb butters and is recommended for salt-free diets.

Thomas Hyll in his 1568 *Proffitable Arte of Gardening* recommended using winter savory with common thyme to create a low-clipped knot. English herbalist and botanist John Parkinson, writing in 1629, recommended adding chopped winter savory leaves to breadcrumbs for coating meat and fish. Both winter and summer savory were among the herbs John Josselyn took to New England in 1638 and 1666 (see box).

Winter savory should be planted at 10in spacings in well-drained, poor soil in a sunny position. It grows well in a clay pot or trough. Although small, the pale pink flowers attractively smother the small branches in the summer. Tip or heel cuttings (see p.203) should be taken in spring or fall respectively. Cut back after flowering and keep well trimmed to stop it becoming leggy. Replace every four to five years with rooted cuttings. As the name *montana* implies, winter savory is a native of mountainsides and is therefore extremely hardy. Hyll's suggestion of using it in knots would only work with small thymes, but winter savory is pretty as an edging on the dry margins of paving or paths.

Scatter the seeds of summer savory, instead of sowing in rows, to create a delightful and edible haze of small pink flowers in a block or drift. The herb is traditionally served with beans, and it can be successively sown in the richer soil around fava, runner, or French beans.

OLD HERBS, NEW WORLD

John Josselyn was born at Willingale Doe in Essex and probably trained as a surgeon or physician. He traveled to Maine to join his brother Henry and lived there from 1638–9 and again in 1663–71, after which he published *New England's Rarities Discovered* in 1672 and, two years later, *An Account of Two Voyages to New England.*

From these we have a list of herbs taken out such as savory and spearmint for gardens as well as a conserve of roses and fresh ginger that he took to prevent sea sickness. He also carried a hot-off-the-press, 1633 copy of John Gerard's *Herbal* that had been revised, enlarged, and improved by Thomas Johnson; it included the first description of a banana.

NUTRITION

Rich in volatile oils, it is one of the digestive herbs. It is said to soothe bee or wasp stings.

"Both Summer Savory *(Satureja hortensis)* and Winter Savory *(Satureja montana)* have a strong, very pleasant aromatic flavour, and it is strange that they are not more frequently grown. Before the use of the East Indian spices became common, these two herbs were the most strongly flavoured herbs in use in the kitchen."

Herbs and Herb Gardening, (1936) Eleanour Sinclair Rohde

CUPS

TISANES, WINES, CORDIALS, AND COCKTAILS

The volatile oils and aromatics of herbs are at the base of many drinks, to refresh and revitalize, to calm and comfort, and to savor and satisfy. Whether you are gardening or cooking, put fresh, lemon-scented herbs or fennel in a pitcher of cold water at the start of the day. Cover and leave the herbs to gently impart their flavors during the day and drink a glass as and when you need it.

What could be simpler than pouring boiling water over fresh or dried herbs or aromatic seeds and leaving them for 5–15 minutes to infuse to create a tisane? This is altogether lighter and more palatable when compared to the more medicinal alternative of boiling up the water with the herbs to make a stronger brew. Cordials were originally made to ease and stimulate the heart. Today they are fragrant, flavored syrups that are delicious and refreshing diluted with still or sparkling water. With a little adjustment they can form the basis of a sorbet, which is also perfect for refreshing the palate between courses or alongside antipasti, or tomato or fruit salads.

Shaken, not stirred, cocktails can range from the seriously alcoholic to innocently fruity and nonalcoholic. As herb oils are alcohol-soluble but not water-soluble, there is a far greater aromatic infusion when steeped in alcohol. Add herbal style by serving them with olives threaded onto a rosemary twig rather than a cocktail stick.

TISANES

To make a tisane, take one tablespoon of fresh or one teaspoon of dried herb, and/or one teaspoon of crushed, aromatic seeds to every 20floz of boiling water. Put it in a glass or ceramic teapot, pour over boiling water, and leave to infuse for at least five minutes. Alternatively, leave the kettle to stand for 30 seconds as this method is said to release the aromatics but not the bitters in herbs. Using a teapot is far better as it means that the

LEFT: The golden-orange petals of the traditional calendula marigold can be used for tisanes on their own. They can be mixed with other herbs such as mint or thyme, or simply to brighten up traditional blends.

volatile oils released by the boiling water do not disappear into the ether. A cup with a lid just requires one herb sprig.

Scented, refreshing, and often sweet, tisanes are strongly associated with Morocco, especially peppermint where the leaves are bruised with sugar before infusing. Moroccan tisanes also include lemon verbena leaves or saffron threads, which yield a dusky pink tea. Two further herbs, used individually or jointly, are chamomile and rosemary, with the fragrant addition of rosewater.

The best herbs are listed to the right. Use the leaves unless otherwise stated: angelica, chamomile, dill seeds, fennel stems, rose-scented geranium, hyssop, lavender flowers, lemon balm, lime flowers, marigold flowers, mint (especially apple, *Eau-de-Cologne*, ginger, peppermint, and pineapple varieties), rose hips, rosemary, sage, sweet cicely, verbena, vervain, and violet flowers. Apart from taste, tisanes are also taken for their therapeutic properties.

TASTING NOTES

Tisane properties

Digestive	Chamomile flowers (*Chamaemelum nobile*) and peppermint (*Mentha × piperita*) are the best known.
Lemon refreshers	Lemon verbena (*Aloysia citriodora*), lemon balm (*Melissa officinalis*), lemongrass (*Cymbopogon citratus*)—a mere detail, but how about stirring punch with a lemongrass stick? Mix lavender (*Lavandula*) and basil (*Ocimum*), and infuse, allow to cool, top up with lemonade, and serve chilled with slices of fresh lemon.
Soothing	Chamomile flowers (*Chamaemelum*), lime flowers (*Tilia*), vervain (*Verbena officinalis*).
Pick-me-up	Lavender flowers (*Lavandula*), lemon balm (*Melissa officinalis*), rosemary (*Rosmarinus*), sage (*Salvia*), thyme (*Thymus*).
Travel	Ginger root (*Zingiber*). See also Stone Ginger Beer, p.214. Cold peppermint steeped in hot milk is a great restorative.

LEFT: The scent and pale green of peppermint tea is inextricably associated with Moroccan food, but it is refreshing and invigorating after any meal.

WINES

Homemade wines are enjoying a comeback. Not just heavyweights like dandelion and burdock, but also subtle variations to elderflower wine with the more delicate gooseberry-infused elderflowers. Elderberries are described as the English grape—if well vinified it is hard to tell its wine apart from port—and bruised root ginger appears in many traditional recipes. Hot wine cups have long been enjoyed by northern Europeans to counteract the chill of winter days. The addition of bay leaves, which infuse a smoky aroma, was an English variation.

CORDIALS AND COCKTAILS

Simple cordials can be made either by pouring boiling syrup over herb flowers, leaves, roots, or seeds and leaving for two hours, or alternatively leaving them overnight to infuse in a cold syrup. The basic syrup mix is 1½ pint of water simmered with 12oz of superfine sugar. These cordials can be adapted for water ices and sorbets.

TASTING NOTES

Basic sorbet

This recipe is equally refreshing between courses, with fresh fruit or as a cool finale.

Preparation time: 10 minutes, plus infusing and freezing time
Serves: 4 people

You will need:

• 12oz (350g) superfine sugar

• 1½ pint (900ml) water

• 2 lemons, juice and peel

• 16 elderflower heads or 16 sprigs of mint (pineapple, Eau-de-Cologne) or 20 lemon verbena

• 2 egg, whites only (optional)

Add the sugar to simmered water, with a strip of lemon peel to make syrup.

Pour in the lemon juice.

Infuse the flowerheads, sprigs or leaves for 2 hours. Strain.

If you do not have an ice cream maker: Freeze the syrup until semifrozen, then whisk until the mixture becomes opaque. Fold in a stiff, beaten egg white. Refreeze.

ALCOHOLIC CONCOCTIONS

Juniper berries were valued both for their fresh taste and medicinal efficacy. They were often used in Elizabethan *aqua vitae* or *aqua composite*, while more famously in Holland, the Dutch created genever, the ancestor of gin. During the 17th century, a simple *aqua vitae* was created by using four parts of proof spirit to one of water, with aniseeds for flavoring. A more strongly flavored aniseed water was made as "an excellent water to strengthen the stomach." The liquor was sweetened with sugar or sugar syrup and this was colored by a tincture such as red roses.

Angelica water—actually proof spirit redistilled with the roots and green parts of angelica, aromatic seeds, and water—was reputed to strengthen the heart wonderfully. A similar process was used for rosemary water, "an excellent cephalic and stomachic," as well as the health-giving (alcoholic) waters of caraway, marjoram, saffron, and spearmint. They were marketed as cordials and sold as drams by the distillers, doctors, and apothecaries, as well as being produced by housewives using home-distilling apparatus. Home-produced spirits were probably unadulterated and more wholesome, but they also contributed to increased drunkenness in late 17th-century England. The availability of cheap spirits culminated in signboards for gin, such as "Drunk for a penny; dead drunk for two-pence; clean straw for nothing."

RIGHT: Coriander seeds may be small but they are packed with flavor. After harvest they can be stored until you have time to experiment with cordials and other delights.

TASTING NOTES

Coriander cordial

This cordial is aromatic and alcoholic.

Preparation time: 5 minutes
Cooking time: 10–15 minutes
Serves: makes 20floz (600ml)

You will need:

• 15 tsp coriander seed

• 4 tsp caraway seed

• Stick of cinnamon

• 20floz (600ml) gin or brandy

• 9oz (250g) superfine sugar

Steep spices in gin or brandy for 3 weeks.

Make a syrup by boiling the water with the sugar until reduced to 20floz.

Strain off the spices and pour the alcohol into the syrup. Store in a sterilized bottle.

Gin forms the base of many cocktails into which the leaves and flowers of borage add a cooling cucumber flavor and pleasing appearance. In 1840, James Pimm mixed up a house cup to serve in his Oyster Bar in Poultry Street in the City of London. The secret blend became known as Pimms No. 1 cup, which he sold in pints. It was based on gin, quinine, and a secret mix of herbs. The company changed hands several times and after World War Two, Pimms Nos 2 to 6 were added, based on Scotch, brandy, rye, and vodka respectively. The choice is now back down to Pimms No. 1, No. 3, and No. 6, but, regardless of which number is being mixed, they can all benefit from one or all out of bruised mint leaves, borage leaves, and borage flowers.

The best spirit for infusing herbs is vodka as it does not have a distinct flavor of its own and is cheaper than brandy or gin. Try experimenting with any of the aromatic seeds or stems of angelica, fennel, or lovage. Put them in a bottle or wide-necked jar, cover with vodka, and leave for a month. Britain's wild food forager John Wright infuses both rose petals and rose hips into vodka, his first choice for this is *Rosa rugosa*. The flower recipe could not be easier or quicker: simply steep the petals in vodka by filling a sterilized glass jar with petals and topping up with vodka—and leave overnight. The next day, drain the liquid, squeezing out every last drop from the petals, and you will have a fragrant pink vodka. The hips take longer, imparting a less fragrant but pleasantly scented, vitamin C-enhanced tipple.

LEFT: Rose petals and hips from *Rosa rugosa* will impart their scent and a delicate pink into vodka. Prepare one weekend and serve the next.

TASTING NOTES

Bloody horse cocktail

A tempting and delicious alcoholic beverage that is great to wow dinner guests with.

Preparation time: 5 minutes
Serves: makes 2½ pints (1½l)

You will need:

· 1½ tbsps horseradish, thinly cubed

· ¾ tsps Worcestershire sauce

· 46floz (1,300ml) tomato juice

· Tabasco, to taste

· 7floz (200ml) vodka

· Sea salt, for decoration

Mix all of the ingredients together—shake or stir.

Serve in a coarse salt-rimmed glass.

(You can add a stick of lovage for a garnish.)

Dandelion
Taraxacum officinale agg.

Common names: Dandelion, blowballs, pissabed, priest's crown, swine's snout

Type: Perennial

Climate: Hardy, very cold winter

Size: 12in (30cm)

Origin: Northern hemisphere

History: The Persian name *talkh chakok* translates as "bitter herb" and in Arabic this became *tarakhshagog*, the root of the medieval Latin *tarasacon* and hence *Taraxacum*. Its medicinal properties were recorded by Arab physicians from the 10th century.

Cultivation: Wild dandelion is so easy to grow that it is very often considered a pernicious weed. It has a strongly bitter taste but with better medicinal properties. However, there are many cultivated forms that are more esculent. Sow seeds in spring, thinning plants to 14in spacings.

Storage: Leaves are best eaten fresh. Roots can be left in the ground and lifted, washed, and eaten as required. Dandelions can be dried whole, then carefully stored or ground down to a powder.

Preparation: Fresh leaves have a chicory-like flavor. Young dandelion leaves tossed with fried bacon is a popular spring salad in France. Mix with green herb leaves such as arugula, purslane, and dill for a strongly flavored green salad. Roots cleaned, dried, and roasted to a coffee color in the oven can then be ground to make a caffeine-free coffee substitute. Just add boiling water.

ABOVE: The leaves are the easiest part of the dandelion to eat, preferably young. Health purists advise against blanching (see p.190) but it means a larger and more palatable leaf.

RIGHT: There are many improved cultivars of dandelion that are equally hardy, providing leaves as a tonic from early spring.

NUTRITION

Bitter tastes have a tonic effect on the body and should not be sweetened with fruit if their digestive tonic action is to be fully enjoyed. Dandelion has the highest levels of lecithin from any plant sources; lecithin is important for cell membrane protection and replacement, reducing cholesterol, converting fat into energy, prevention of strokes and heart attacks. It also has vitamins C, E, and traces of B_1, B_2, B_6, B_9 as well as potassium, calcium, and iron.

TASTING NOTES

Dandelion varieties to try

Dandelion has a leafy, bitter taste somewhere between the vegetables endive and chicory. Improved cultivars include those listed below but they may be hard to source:

"Coeur Plein"   Reputedly the most nutritious. Good for blanching. Very rich in minerals and vitamins.

"Ameliore Geant"   Numerous, highly serrated leaves whose formation is reminiscent of endive.

"Arlington"   Mild flavor more like endive.

"Mayses's Trieb"   Best variety for forcing.

"Tapeley"   Variegated leaves.

In the 13th century, the Welsh physicians of Myddfai recommended *Dant y Llew*, or dandelion, as a general stimulant to the body and more specifically for jaundice, pounded with parsley in a good strong ale at the rather variable dosage of "four egg shellfuls" to a pint. The "dent de lion" or lion's tooth-shaped leaves are nature's way of channeling rain to the root. As one of its common names implies, *Taraxacum pseudoroseum*, dandelion is a noted diuretic and it is advisable not to eat or drink it after midday.

Growing dandelions in the shade will make the leaves less bitter, as will harvesting them young. The central white midrib is the most bitter bit to eat, so tear off the green parts into a salad, but this bitterness can be lessened by blanching (see box below).

If you find a dandelion growing in the garden, harvest the leaves by cutting it just under the top of the rootstock. Remove dandelion flowers to prevent the plants self-seeding; they can be used to make wine.

BLANCHING

Shifting sands around a plant or soil covering plant stems encourages more tender growth in a bid to find the light.

In spring, sow dandelion seeds direct in a line into a trench; thinning to 12in spacings. Allow them to establish through the summer, picking leaves but cutting off flowering stems. Then in late fall, start to draw earth up around the leaves. As they continue to grow, ensure that only the tips of the leaves are above the earth. This will both blanch and protect them, providing additional salad leaves through the winter and into the spring.

Thyme
Thymus

Common names: Thyme

Type: Subshrub

Climate: Hardy, cold winter

Size: 4–12in (10–30cm)

Origin: Eurasia

History: The name is derived from the Greek *thyo*, meaning "to perfume." Just smelling thyme was believed to give you courage and strength. As a homonym with time in English, there are countless examples of word play. The poet William Shenstone described thyme as "pun provoking." One of the favorite design puns was growing thymes around sundials.

Cultivation: Many varieties can be grown from seed sown in spring or fall, but do not cover the seed as they need the light to germinate. Pinch out tips of seedlings to encourage them to bush out. Grow in well-drained calcareous soils in a sunny position.

Storage: Thymes dry well, harboring the scent of summer. Harvest just before flowering and once dried keep in a dry, dust-free place. Infuse in vinegar or oil (see p.75).

RIGHT: The 15th-century thyme seller depicted in a Latin manuscript of Dioscorides's *Tractatus de herbis* knows all about keeping dried herbs in a dry, dark place and only breaking them up when ready to use.

Preparation: One of the main herbs in the bouquet garni (see p.99), the woody varieties impart an aromatic savory fragrance, especially associated with chicken as well as pizzas and ratatouille. When used in winter soups such as pumpkin or parsnip, thyme evokes memories of hot, balmy days, and the soft leaves of the cushion-forming thymes are ideal sprinkled over salad, or chopped into dressings and salsa. They can be chopped finely and rolled into pastry for quiches or into bread or pizza dough.

Flowers from any variety of thyme can be snipped off with scissors and used for decoration and salads.

In Europe, the creeping thyme, *T. serpyllum*, was prized for its medicinal qualities and for flavoring the meat of the sheep. This is mentioned by Bardswell in the quote on the next page, and thyme forcemeats were a popular accompaniment while the commoner mint sauce was initially created to accompany the sheep that grazed on wild mints on the Romney Marshes in Kent, England. The creeping thyme is not great for cooking as the leaves are tough and it is invariably very gritty whereas the stalwart common and lemon thymes are ideal. In addition, the more colorful, ornate cultivars have softer leaves that can easily be trimmed and added to salads. Thyme flowers are a rich source of nectar, so it was planted in abundance near beehives. Gervase Markham recommended, "You shall perfume the Hive with Juniper, and rub it all within with Fennel, Hyssop, and Time-flowers, also the stone upon which the Hive shall stand ..."

As natives of stony hills, thymes thrive in gravel or on terraces. Make a feature of them by selecting different leaf shapes and colors as well as flowers that range from white through pink to purple and red. This will involve some ground cover varieties that are less suitable for culinary use. They are all well flavored, but will need careful washing before culinary usage. On a smaller scale, if they are planted in pots and old sinks it will enable you to orchestrate a collection as the season demands. To stop the plants from becoming woody, trim back to new shoots within ¼in of old growth. Thyme roots easily from cuttings taken in spring or fall—look for the nodules on the stems that indicate embryo roots and sink in a fibrous, well-drained medium from April to July or September and October.

The leaves and flowers from all varieties are scented and pretty for all manner of foods.

BUSH THYMES

Top of the list is common thyme, *T. vulgaris*, which is easily raised from seed and once established will freely self-set. It is excellent with almost all cooked foods—put underneath meats and chicken before roasting, use in marinades for barbeques, and chop over tomatoes for baking. It also dries well.

There are many different types, such as *Thymus carnosus* (syn. *T. erectus*), an upright species with white flowers that is ideal for container growth, and "English Winter"—claimed to be be the hardiest of culinary thymes. It can be raised from seed and spreads rapidly with its dark green leaves. As the name suggests, "Provence" is a French strain that can be raised from seed and is said to have the strongest and sweetest flavor. It looks very much like the orange thyme, *T.* "Fragrantissimus," which

NUTRITION

Recent research with rats revealed evidence that eating quantities of thyme slowed down their ageing process, which conjures up visions of wrinkle-free, frisky rodents. That said, it is high in calcium, phosphorus, potassium, and beta-carotene and you will lose nothing by trying.

RIGHT: The traditional bush thymes tend to get woody, but this does not matter if using for bouquet garnis. If just the leaves are needed, remove them by sliding a thumbnail down the stalk.

"Thyme! What a lovely thing to write about, to think of! Lemon Thyme, so clean-smelling, so fragrant, such a pleasant seasoning; Wild Thyme on the bank, 'with oxlips and the nodding violet'; Common Thyme on heath and down ... helps ... to make the plump Down-sheep into such delicious mutton."

The Herb Garden, (1911) Frances Bardswell

is gloriously fragrant, with silvery green foliage and tiny pink flowers. Put its stems under the skin when roasting chicken or mix tiny leaves into pastry. Orange thyme can be raised from seed and its naturally globular form makes it an attractive subject for a container.

The caraway thyme, *T. herba-barona*, was traditionally cooked with baron of beef and game. It has large leaves and forms a cushion. There is also a lemon-scented variety. Broad-leaved thyme, *T. pulegioides*, has, as the name suggests, broad leaves with soft stems. It is good cooked with chicken, tomatoes, and chopped in dumplings. Its very young leaves can also be added to salads. Its large leaves are easier to handle and there are a number of different varieties (see below).

ABOVE: Lemon thyme has larger leaves than the common variety; they are virtually evergreen and, in a sheltered spot, should provide fresh leafy shoots year round.

COLORFUL THYMES

Thymes of the Coccineus Group, including "Coccineus Major" and "Purple Beauty" have glorious red flowers and tinted leaves. Apart from cooking, the new young leaves are excellent in salads; grown together the different varieties make a colorful summer display.

For a golden-leaved thyme with tidy growth and interesting leaves, try *T. vulgaris* "Golden Pins" or the variety simply known as "Aureus"; both are excellent and can be used for cooking or salads.

LEMON-SCENTED THYMES

Lemon thyme, *T. citriodorus*, is the classic gourmet thyme with a flavor that enhances any simple chicken-based dishes or broiled fish. It is the best thyme in a bouquet garni, but also good as a tisane and it dries well too.

There are also a couple of *T. × pulegioides* cultivars with a lemon scent. "Archer's Gold" is compact and excellent when young for salads, and it also has very golden leaves. As the temperatures drop in the fall, the leaves and stems take on a reddish tinge, as do those of another golden, broad-leaved thyme with the advantage of a lemon scent, *T. × pulegioides* "Aureus." It is good with chicken, broiled tuna, and salads.

A personal favorite is the very ornamental but short-lived "Silver Posie"; its young, soft leaves are delicious in tomato, cucumber, and avocado salads. Just take cuttings every year to ensure you always have vigorous young plants. Similar "Silver Queen" is less hardy and tends to revert to green.

Lime
Tilia cordata

Common names: Littleleaf linden, small-leaved lime, linden tree

Type: Deciduous tree

Climate: Hardy, very cold winter

Size: 65½–130ft (20–40m)

Origin: Europe

DE STIRPIVM HISTORIA

De Tilia. Cap. LXXIIII.

Lindenbaum.

ED AGE TILIAM NVNC CONTEMPLEMVR, CV-
ius duo apud nos extant genera. Tilia sativa elegantissima est,
quod

ABOVE: A jolly sight of German peasants dancing round the linden tree c. 1552, and maybe an idea for allotment holders. Garden limes need to be carefully trained.

History: Pollen deposits in lowland England dating back 6,000 years show that littleleaf lindens were one of the commonest flowering trees. However, this changed as the climate cooled around 3000 BC. Unable to set seeds in the same quantities, it survived and spread by layering. During the medieval period its wood was prized for coppicing.

Cultivation: Although slow growing, the trees can grow to 130ft. *Tilia cordata* maintains itself almost entirely by vegetative reproduction in cool maritime climates, ripening seed only in the hottest summers. Littleleaf lindens tend to sucker and these basal shoots are the easiest to root. Prune and thin in early spring before leaf break.

Storage: If you keep bees, make limeflower honey. Only harvest and use the young flowers, which can be dried.

Preparation: Littleleaf linden tisanes are famously associated with French novelist Marcel Proust and his remembrance of drinking limeflower tea with madeleines: use 4g dried flowers to one pint of boiling water and infuse for 10–15 minutes. It is reputed to be a blood cleanser. The French also make a limeflower cordial: follow the same instructions for elderflowers (see p.184). The young leaves, shoots, and fruits are all edible—nibble and see if you like them. Use young leaves as saladings.

The word linden means made from lime-wood and the inner fibrous bark was formerly used by gardeners as ribands and matting. Stand and listen when the littleleaf linden comes into full flower in July when the noise of bees working the blossoms makes it

ABOVE: Hand-colored plate from Johann S. Kerner's 18th-century book *Beschreibung und abbildung der baume und gestrauche*. The youngest of the lime tree leaves can be eaten in salads or placed in a sandwich. Not to be confused with the unrelated citrus fruit.

sound like a factory. The tea made from their young blossoms is known as *tilleul*, from the French word for the lime, and the volatile oil carries an aromatic, scented taste. Curiously, littleleaf linden trees and cocoa plants are actually in the same family: the *Malvaceae* and the fruits are said to have a cocoa-like taste, which is not surprising given that *Tilia* are related to *Theobroma cocao*.

Unless you vigorously train or pleach them (see box), an art enjoying popular revival at garden shows and private gardens, you need either a large garden, community project, or borrowed landscape. Underplant with square or round beds of sweet

woodruff or clipped golden variegated lemon balm. The upright "Greenspire" is a hardy cultivar with a narrow oval crown, attaining 49ft. "Winter Orange" is a variety with beautiful orange young stems, which is ideal for pleaching.

The littleleaf linden tree is one herb under whose canopy you will be able to sit and sip a cup of tea made from its blossom, knowing that even if the rest of the garden gives you dyspepsia, the nervine properties of lime flowers will soothe your anxiety, calm indigestion, and make it worth the heartache.

PLEACHING

Pleaching is a method of training trees to produce a narrow screen or stilted hedge by tying in and interlacing flexible young shoots along a supporting framework. Lime is the traditional subject and you can buy them ready pleached or with the initial structure in place. This is recommended if you need to keep them in large containers.

If you are planning to start pleaching from scratch, trees should be planted 4ft apart, using 1–2 year-old trees. Identify the main trunk, initially leaving the side shoots to strengthen the tree, gradually pruning them off to their collar. You will need to create a light support framework from three vertical canes, one centrally lined up with the trunk,

and the other two spaced 24in to the left and right. At 5ft above the ground, tie in horizontal canes or wires between the three canes, repeating upward at 12–18in spacings.

Training or pleaching the tree's branches starts at about 5ft above the ground. Encourage shoots from horizontal buds and tie in along the horizontal canes evenly on each side. As they grow, weave these branches with those from adjoining trees. Rub out forward- and backward- facing buds, tying in leafy laterals over the summer.

In early years, prune while the tree is dormant in winter. Once established, prune back after flowering. In time, the framework can be removed.

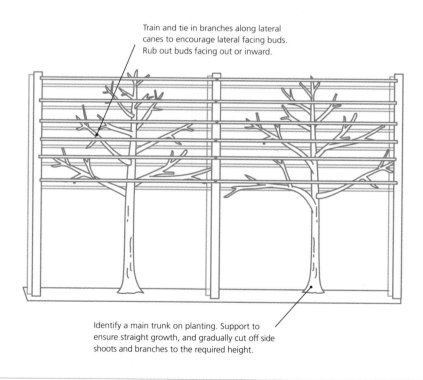

Train and tie in branches along lateral canes to encourage lateral facing buds. Rub out buds facing out or inward.

Identify a main trunk on planting. Support to ensure straight growth, and gradually cut off side shoots and branches to the required height.

Fenugreek
Trigonella foenum-graecum

Common names: Fenugreek, methi, Greek clover, Greek hay

Type: Annual

Climate: Frost tender, warm temperate

Size: 12–24in (30–60cm)

Origin: Southern Europe, Asia

History: A native of the dry grasslands and hillsides of Southern Europe, the triangular appearance of the off-white flower's corolla lead to its generic name, *trigonos*, meaning "three" and *gonu* "joint," while *foenum-graecum* translates as Greek hay.

Cultivation: Sow directly into drills in well-drained, loamy soil in spring. Germination is excellent and seeds dried for spice can be sown. It grows rapidly and can flower after six weeks, reaching maturity in 16 weeks.

Storage: Dry young leaves for mild flavoring, dry and keep seeds.

Preparation: A ready supply of sprouting seeds requires temperatures of 55–70°F. Germinate in a glass jar with a calico top, rinsing with fresh water once or twice daily; the young shoots will be available in 2–4 days and can be added to salads. Seeds are commonly used in curry powder and fresh leaves can be used as a spinach substitute.

One of the oldest of culinary plants, fenugreek has a host of medicinal associations as a fever soother, a carminative, an aphrodisiac, and a contraceptive. With a slightly fetid taste, the ground seed is one of the key curry spices while the whole seed can be used in pickles and chutneys. It can be grown year round as a sprouting seed or microsalad and has a reputation as a superfood.

If you do not crop the young fenugreek shoots too heavily, in summer they will have pea-like flowers that are creamy and richly scented. However, only the young leaves and tender shoots are suitable for cooking and when chopped they can be added to dal or other lentil or chickpea-based dishes. Fenugreek or methi is a key ingredient in Indian dishes such as Aloo Methi, Saag Paneer, and the Gujarati Methi Muthiya. Not only is consumption reputed to improve the human complexion, but it is also fed to horses to achieve a glossy coat.

Last but not least, you can grow fenugreek as a green manure and, as it is fast growing and vigorous, you can still enjoy the leaves. Sowings can be made up until August. The crop will absorb nitrogen from the air and surplus soil nutrients and these are then released in the soil when they are dug back into the ground or hoed down before flowering. A fall frost will do this for you and leave the leaves as a protective mulch. It is a good alternative to mustard and is said to help where clubroot is a problem.

LEFT AND ABOVE: Fenugreek leaves are a friend to both the cook and the gardener. From germination onward, eat the shoots and then, before it flowers, chop down and dig in the whole plant as a green manure.

Nasturtium
Tropaeolum majus

Common names: Nasturtium, Indian cress

Type: Annual

Climate: Half-hardy, unheated glasshouse, mild winter

Size: 65½–98ft (20–30m) in height, but spreading and will climb if supported

Origin: South America, Colombia to Bolivia

History: A plant only known in cultivation, or as a garden escapee, *T. majus* was introduced from Peru to Europe in 1684. The botanist Carl Linneaus created the name *Tropaeolum* from the Greek *tropaion* as he thought the way the leaves and red flowers hung over a post resembled a classical trophy on a battlefield.

Cultivation: Sow seeds in spring either in pots or directly into moisture-retentive soil in a sunny position. Avoid over-fertilizing the soil as this encourages leaves rather than flowers. Once established, they will self-seed and survive in drier conditions. They can also be grown in window boxes and hanging baskets.

Storage: The seeds can be pickled as a caper substitute.

Preparation: Pick young leaves, flowers, and flower buds for salads: they taste like young radishes. The leaves can be used to roll around soft cheeses. Use the older leaves for lining a cheese basket or serving a pàte. The seeds can be used in place of capers in sauces and cooked dishes.

Check the points of open flowers for unwanted protein because they are a favorite resort of earwigs!

LEFT: Once they start to flower, nasturtiums will continue until the first frosts. Nasturtiums will scramble over other plants or a support and can cover a fairly large area over the growing season.

"*T. MAJUS* (Large Indian Cress). A showy annual, coming into flower more quickly, and few bloom longer. In poor soil the *compactum* forms bloom best. Their rich colours are superb in masses, and they are never without flowers from first to last. All who love rich masses of colour will find these dwarf Nasturtiums worth a place in some of the many fine sorts now obtainable."

The English Flower Garden, (1883) **William Robinson**

Thomas Jefferson sowed nasturtiums on "35 little hills" at Monticello (see p. 49). In *The English Gardener* Cobbett included them in the kitchen garden for "a seed enveloped in a fleshy pod, and that pod, taken before the seed becomes ripe, is used as a thing to pickle." Botanists originally named it *Nasturtium indicum*, or Indian cress, from which the English common name derives. This perfectly describes the peppery taste of the leaves, while the Latin *nasturcium* translates as nose-twister or nose-torturer. Torture is an exaggeration but the older the leaves the hotter the sensation. From the 1890s Monet annually carpeted the path down his grande allée at Giverny in northern France with nasturtiums, creating a river of color in late summer and fall.

On a more modest scale, nasturtiums make a colorful annual edging for vegetable gardens. They should flower within 70 days of sowing and can spread several feet. Once established they will freely self-seed. The seedlings are instantly recognizable and can be left to come up in the spring.

GARDEN PAINTBOX

There are a myriad of cultivars that can double as a feast for the eyes and stomach. The climbing hybrids can also be left to scramble across the ground, as seen in Monet's garden at Giverny, or used to camouflage unsightly dry parts of the garden, such as a compost heap. The dwarf varieties will give pockets of color in dry places and are best if space is at a premium.

NUTRITION

Rich in sulfur; also iron and vitamin C.

ABOVE: Nasturtium flowers vary in color from cream to red through various shades of yellow and orange. They are perfect for enlivening salads.

Nasturtiums offer a colorful feast. For leaf and flower color, the Alaska Series have light green leaves marbled with cream and flower colors that range from cream through yellow to orange. It is tidy and suitable for small pockets. Many adore the depth of color in the deep-blue green to almost purple leaves of "Empress of India" with its brilliant scarlet flowers. It is more spreading than the Alaska Series but also tidy. The modest spreaders are ideal for hanging baskets, where they happily trail over the edge. The butter-yellow flowers of "Moonlight" are indeed great by the light of the moon. The more vigorous varieties can be trained over rocks, walls, and tree stumps or be left to scramble as seen in Monet's garden at Giverny. "Tall Single Mix" is a vigorous variety with large and fragrant, orange, gold, and red flowers. It can attain a spread of over 6½ft. Deep scarlet-flowered "Fiery Festival" is abundant and fragrant. "Darjeeling Double" has fully double flowers but they do not set seed.

PROPAGATION

INCREASING YOUR STOCK

Methods for raising herbs from seed were outlined in the introduction (see p.9). This is a good way of propagating annual and some perennial herbs, but it is not a great way for cultivated varieties (cultivars) with specific characteristics as many seeds do not "come true to type." This means that the valued characteristics of the parent (such as leaf variegation or flower color) may be lost or diluted in subsequent generations. Many of the woody herbs are best replaced after about five years as they have a tendency to become leggy, sparsely leaved, and sprawling. The good news is that most will readily root from cuttings.

The advantage of taking cuttings from a herb rather than sowing seeds is that you are creating a clone and know exactly what it will look like. It is also an excellent way of increasing your herb stock. Some herbs do the work for you, such as mint runners, which can be cut off and moved ready rooted. It is worth checking the undersides of the lower stems or branches of chamomile, lavender, rosemary, sage, thyme, and sweet woodruff for root nodules; you can then gently layer them, i.e. fix them to the ground and surround with fibrous compost. Layering was the traditional way of rooting sweet bay. In principle the lower branches of shrubs and trees are easier to root successfully. Once a small root system has established itself, cut the rooted section away from the parent plant and replant elsewhere.

ABOVE: Illustration of women picking hyssop from *Tacuinum Sanitatis (Medieval Health Handbook)*, dated before 1400, based on observations of medical order detailing the most important aspects of food, beverages, and clothing.

SELECTING YOUR PLANT

First, always ensure that you choose a healthy, disease-free herb to take the cuttings from and select a vigorous, well-formed shoot or branch from which to prepare the cutting. With pruning shears, cut the raw material from the parent plant and put it into a polythene bag or wrap in damp cloth and keep cool. This material should be taken to the kitchen or potting shed for further preparation. It might seem like stating the obvious, but if taking cuttings from several herbs, especially cultivars of the same herb, make sure you make a note of their names on a label and put it in the bag. You should always take more than one cutting to insure against inevitable losses.

When it comes to preparing the cuttings, a clean cut is essential, so only use a sharp, clean propagating knife or razor blade and wipe the blade between cuts. If you are worried about your thumb, cuttings can be made on a piece of clean glass. Good clean pruning shears can be used but ensure that the stems to be rooted are not crushed or damaged.

PRACTICAL CUTTING TIPS

Two key rules are to avoid touching the cut edges of the cuttings with your fingers, as this can contaminate them, and to avoid pushing the cuttings into the growing medium—instead, make a hole for them first with a pencil or dibber.

Remember that until the cutting roots it cannot draw up moisture or nutrients, and yet it will continue to transpire water from its leaves. You need to keep it in suspended animation. The horticultural ditty is misty tops, cool middles, and hot bottoms. This is easy to achieve if you have an electric propagator, but a simple alternative is to put the cuttings in a terracotta pot filled with moistened, fibrous compost and sharp sand, then seal the whole pot in a white polythene bag. Left in a warm, light place, it will form its own microclimate. Gradually open the bag to harden off the cuttings when they are rooted. Fall heel and root cuttings will take in a cold frame or glasshouse over winter.

It is important that effective rooting compost should have sharp sand for drainage and consider fibrous compost for the young roots, though a multipurpose potting compost is fine. Moisture

and nutrients are imbibed through the hairs on a root so a fibrous compost encourages root hair development and is good at getting the roots growing and creating a sturdier plant for when the time comes to plant out.

HERBS FOR SOFTWOOD CUTTINGS

Softwood cuttings are good for lemon verbena, French tarragon, hyssop, lavender, bergamot, oregano, marjoram, scented geraniums, rosemary, sage, thyme, and winter savory. The advantage of softwood cuttings is that rooting is rapid, although the young plant will be smaller and need hardening off. Cuttings are best taken as soon as the new softwood shoots are long enough, usually in early spring.

A nodal cutting is best, so make a straight cut directly under the node or bud of the leaf joint, where the stem is harder, to create a 4in

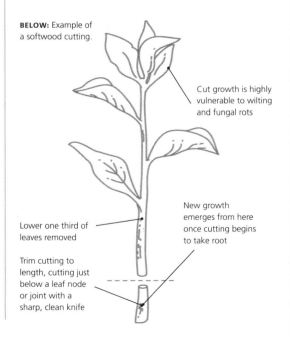

BELOW: Example of a softwood cutting.

Cut growth is highly vulnerable to wilting and fungal rots

New growth emerges from here once cutting begins to take root

Lower one third of leaves removed

Trim cutting to length, cutting just below a leaf node or joint with a sharp, clean knife

ABOVE: Lime trees (*Tilia*) root well from suckering shoots that sprout from the base of the plant. They should be taken as semiripe cuttings.

cutting. This exposes the embryo roots under the bud. Make a pencil-sized incision in compost, gently push the cutting in, lightly water so that the compost is damp but not soaked. Cover them to reduce moisture loss (in a propagator, plastic bottle, or plastic bag tent), and applying a bit of bottom heat helps if you have a heated propagator. Rooting should be established within six weeks, after which it will rapidly produce new leaves. If rooting is successful, pot them on.

HERBS FOR SEMIRIPE CUTTINGS

Semiripe cuttings are good for bay, juniper, myrtle, rose, and sage. These cuttings are usually taken in late summer while the stems are still growing. The growth will have started to harden and so the cuttings are a lot less prone to wilting than softwood.

Using the same method as for softwood cuttings, *Tilia* shoots cut from the base of the tree root more readily and the cutting can be 6in long. The disadvantage is that rooting will be slow but as the initial cutting is bigger, the final plant will be larger and should be hardier.

Place in a cold frame or cool glasshouse over winter where they should be left for the entire next season for their root systems to develop fully. The following fall, one year after taking the cuttings, those that have successfully rooted can be transplanted.

Semiripe cuttings do not benefit from any bottom heat and some or all of the leaves can be cut in half to reduce water loss.

HERBS FOR HEELED CUTTINGS

Heeled cuttings are good for hyssop, juniper, bay, lavender, myrtle, rosemary, thyme, and winter savory. Take cuttings in the late summer and leave until the following fall before planting out.

Select a healthy, well-formed small branch from which to take your cuttings. Remove it by making a straight cut just above a bud. From this branch, choose suitable side shoots for your cuttings, pulling them sharply away from the branch so that a strip of the branch remains attached. This is the heeled cutting and the older wood on the heel will help the shoot root. When the shoot is pulled to make a heel, it sometimes is quite long so it can be neatened with a sharp clean knife to about ½in. The stem-tip of the cutting should be cut off to make each heel cutting about 4–6in long. Make an insertion in the rooting compost and follow the previous instructions.

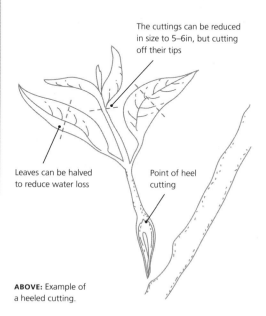

The cuttings can be reduced in size to 5–6in, but cutting off their tips

Leaves can be halved to reduce water loss

Point of heel cutting

ABOVE: Example of a heeled cutting.

Nettle
Urtica dioica

Common names: Nettle, Naughty Man's Plaything

Type: Perennial

Climate: Hardy, very cold winter

Size: 29½in–3¼ft (75cm–1m) or more

Origin: Northern hemisphere

ABOVE: Harvest nettle tops well before there is any sign of an inflorescence. Whereas ground elder has a carrot-meets-spinach taste, nettles are creamier and marry well with fish and olives.

NUTRITION

Nettles are highly nutritious, containing vitamins A and C as well as the minerals calcium, potassium, iron, and manganese. Apart from soup, nettle tea and beer are brewed as a stimulating tonic.

History: After bathing, the Romans indulged in urtication, or flogging, with nettles as a cure for rheumatic joints. This continued to be a traditional remedy for chronic rheumatism and the loss of muscular power. Walter Scott wrote of nettles being forced under glass for "early spring kale" in *Rob Roy* (1817).

Cultivation: Why would a gardener today, albeit a gourmet, grow such a weed? Nettles can draw phosphates out of the richest soil, acting as a clear indicator of where the good soil is in a garden. If you do not already have nettles in the garden, then transplant a root in spring.

Storage: Freeze nettle soup.

Preparation: Only harvest the young, top 2–2⅓in of the nettle and wear thick rubber gloves. Dried leaves do not lose their sting; readers of herbaria have been stung by samples that are over 200 years old!

The steaming, green soup rivals that of Alice's Mock Turtle. Nettles can be used in the same way as ground elder leaves and as a spinach substitute. Sauté in olive oil with black olives or in butter with garlic and green sage, and season to taste (nettles need little or no salt). Serve with gnocchi.

> "If they wad drink nettles in March
> And eat muggons in May
> Sae mony braw maidens
> Wadna gang to the clay."
>
> *Popular Rhymes of Scotland*, (1847) R. Chambers

The good news is that nettle stings help clear toxins from the body and the pain can be assuaged by dock leaves. The sting lies in the downy hairs, each of which has a sting in a sharp, polished, hollow spine. Its base is formed of small cells that contain bicarbonate of ammonia: the venomous, acrid fluid that makes them sting. Its beneficial uses against rheumatism are currently the subject of research. Nettle tea was drunk as a spring tonic, especially in colder regions where green leaves were in short supply during the winter. The fresh juice and the infusion, sometimes in white wine, are traditional stimulants to the digestion and help promote lactation. Muggons in the quote above is mugwort, *Artemesia vulgaris*, a relative of French tarragon that was used for boiled herb puddings, fattening poultry, and flavoring ale.

Nettles are one of the few plants not nibbled by rabbits as the stings attack their sensitive noses. Incidentally, a mulch of chopped blackthorn twigs does the same at the other end. A patch of nettles is a haven and food source for the caterpillars of small tortoiseshell and Red Admiral butterflies. Unwanted leaf tops can be used as a compost activator; just make sure it is not after they have set seeds. The roots are relatively easy to dig out if they become too invasive, but choose a wild part of the garden to grow them, or let them colonize fallow ground.

TASTING NOTES

Nettle soup

Try nettle soup during spring and early summer, when young nettle buds are collected.

Preparation time: 10 minutes
Cooking time: 30 minutes
Serves: 4 people

You will need:

· 1lb (450g) peeled potatoes

· Handful (wear gloves!) of nettle tops

· 1¾oz (50g) butter

· 32floz (900ml) chicken or vegetable broth

· 4 tbsp crème fraiche or sour cream

· Salt and pepper, to taste

Peel the potatoes, cut into thick slices and cook for 10 minutes in salted water. Drain.

Wear gloves for this next step: Wash the top 2–2⅓in of the nettles and chop them coarsely.

Melt butter in a saucepan, add the nettles, and stew gently for 10 minutes.

Heat the broth, add to the nettles with the drained parboiled potatoes, and bring gently to the boil, simmering for another 10 minutes.

When all is soft, cool slightly and blend.

Gently reheat. Season and serve with crème fraiche or sour cream.

Vervain
Verbena officinalis

Common names: Vervain, common verbena, holy herb, herba veneris, Simpler's Joy, ashthroat

Type: Perennial

Climate: Hardy, cold winter

Size: 31½in (80cm)

Origin: Southern Europe

History: The quote opposite was illustrated in the 11th-century *Herbarium of Apuleius*: a man is clutching a vervain stem in his left hand while thrusting a sword into an arching serpent with his right. A protective holy salve was made from vervain along with powerful herbs such as rue, dill, periwinkle, mugwort, and betony.

Cultivation: Sow directly onto cultivated soil in spring or summer, then thin to 6–12in. Established plants can be divided in the spring and stem cuttings taken in the late summer should root well.

Storage: Cut plants as flowering begins and dry flowerheads and young leaves.

Preparation: Use dried plants for tisanes. The Druids purified their sacred places with lustral water infused with vervain. It was also reputedly an aphrodisiac and today it is promoted as a calming tisane, especially if you are suffering from writer's block. Verveine is a popular antidepressive and calming tea in France.

The tiny flowers are echoed in two ancient names: "Tears of Isis" and "Juno's Tears," but there are dozens of others, especially in France. The name verbena comes from the Roman for sacred foliage and altar plants in general, and vervain comes from a medieval corruption meaning sacred bough. Vervain's reputed magical and medicinal properties were legion and out of all proportion to this modest free-seeding herb. In contrast to the 18th-century literary Druid mania, Philip Miller gives a more sober description in *The Gardeners' Dictionary*: "... very common in most Parts, and is rarely cultivated in Gardens." He acknowledged that physicians still used it and indeed it is still widely used medicinally. The flowers were also used as a flavoring agent in alcoholic drinks.

It is an upright herb with insignificant pale lilac flowers on terminal spikes, but the early leaves are attractive in the spring. In rich soils it can attain a height of 35in. Lemon verbena (*Aloysia citriodora*) was named for its similar flowers, and it yields the highly scented verbena oil. The scentless oil from vervain is known as Spanish verbena oil. As it is very hardy and self-seeds easily, let it colonize around flowers and under roses, where it adds interest. Though perhaps not a culinary herb, its digestive, relaxant properties make it an ideal infusion after gourmet consumption.

Why *officinalis*? It translates as "sold in shops"—to be precise, ancient Roman shops that specialized in medicinal products. When used in nomenclature, it is an indication that in history this plant was grown and marketed for its medicinal properties. Modern research suggests that vervain contains chemicals that reduce inflammation.

"For bite of adder, whatsoever man hath on him, this wort verbenaca, with its leaves and roots, he will be firm against all snakes."

Rev. Oswald Cockayne *Leechdoms, Wortcunning and Starcraft of Early England* 1864

RIGHT: Vervain will quietly self-seed in the garden. The leaves and flowers are used to make tisane, while a vervain and mint tea is recommended as a substitute for coffee.

Sweet violet
Viola odorata

Common names: Sweet violet, garden violet, English violet

Type: Perennial

Climate: Hardy, cold winter

Size: 4–6in (10–15cm)

Origin: Europe

History: The name *Viola* is taken from the Greek *ion*. Its sweet fragrance and delicate flowers have colonized Europe for millennia. According to Theophrastus, they were cultivated commercially in Attica for sale in Athens by 400 BC.

Cultivation: In many respects, it is important not to be too tidy a gardener. Once you have one plant it will self-seed in shady, moist corners, if the seedlings are not weeded out. If raising them from seed, ensure they have a period of stratification; i.e., exposure to winter cold (see p.37).

Storage: Steep flowers in white wine vinegar for up to two weeks, then strain and store in a dark, cool place. Crystallize the flowers (see p.59).

Preparation: Washed young leaves can be added to salads. Simply graze on the flowers when spring gardening; they have a scented crunchiness followed by a saliva-drying sensation. In Scotland, violet petals were soaked in white wine to make a drink called "shrub." The marzipan topping of Simnel cake can be delightfully decorated with fresh or candied violet flowers. Steep the flowers in vodka for a highly scented liqueur.

LEFT: Sweet violets colonize easily, providing a mass of flowers in spring. These flowers can be eaten fresh, candied, or infused in sugar or alcohol.

The perfume, color, and flower shape of sweet violets have created contradictory symbolism: on the one hand erotic love as the flower of Aphrodite and her son Priapus, god of the garden; on the other the Virgin Mary, humility, and death of the young. This dual symbolism can be traced across the dream gardens of medieval tapestries. Oil of violets and syrup of violets were valued medicines, a memory preserved in today's candied violets. However, Parma violets were probably developed from *V. suavis*. English writer and gardener John Evelyn recommended dipping young leaves in batter, frying, and serving them with freshly squeezed orange juice.

The heart-shaped leaves provide attractive green cover. In early spring the flowers appear with, as English botanist and herbalist John Gerard wrote, "chiefest beautie, and most gallant grace." There are many good scented varieties readily available, and after the first main flowering, there are occasional further bloomings right up until December. The flowers defined the color violet, but the shades range from deep dark purple through to pale mauve, with many named cultivars. A personal favorite and a good historic variety with strongly scented deep purple flowers is "The Czar." "King of the Doubles" is double blue eye-candy as well as

TASTING NOTES

Tarte à la frangipane et aux violettes

This recipe is based on British cook Geraldene Holt's from *Recipes from a French Garden*.

Preparation time: 20 minutes
Cooking time: 30–35 minutes
Serves: 6 people

You will need:

· 4oz (115g) soft butter

· 4oz (115g) vanilla-flavored sugar

· 2 eggs

· 4oz (115g) ground almonds

· 1oz (30g) all-purpose flour

· 1–2 tsps orange flower water

· 6¼oz (180g) pastry

· 1oz (30g) confectioners' sugar

Preheat a conventional oven to 400°F (200°C/ gas mark 6 / fan 180°C)

Mix together the butter and sugar until light and fluffy. Beat in the eggs one at a time. Work in the ground almonds and the flour. Then add orange flower water to taste.

Roll out the pastry to fit an 8in tart tin. Brush inside the pastry case with lightly beaten egg white. Spoon in the cream and level off. Bake for 30–35 minutes until golden brown.

While still warm, trickle over confectioners' sugar mixed with warm water and orange flower water.

Decorate with crystallized violets (see p.59).

ABOVE: Sweet violet flowers come in an array of colors. Young leaves can also be put in salads but are not as exciting as the flowers.

being scented and magnificent. An early flowering variety dating back to 1894 is "Baroness de Rothschild," with large violet-blue scented flowers on upright stems. A final suggestion is "Saint Helena," which was introduced in 1892. Its origins are lost in the mists of Napoleonic legend but it has masses of sweetly scented pale blue flowers.

The pink hues in the light violet and mauve varieties are pronounced in "Madame Armandine Pagès," which is one of the most fragrant with very pale rose pink, carmine-centered flowers. "Rosine Violet" also has pink flowers with a very sweet perfume and was introduced in 1920. There are also white and double-flowering forms of which "Beechy's White" was an interesting discovery by Jacqueline Sarsby, who found it growing on former violet enthusiast Dr. Beechy's bank in Devon, England.

Ginger
Zingiber officinale

Common names: Ginger, African ginger, black ginger, race ginger, *Adrak* (Indian name)

Type: Perennial rhizome

Climate: Heated glasshouse, warm, temperate

Size: 5ft (1.5m)

Origin: India

History: Ginger has an international history: the Greeks and Romans obtained it as a powder from Arab traders, and it appears in Chinese medical literature during the Han dynasty (AD 25–220). The Spanish introduced ginger from the East Indies into Spain, where they grew it extensively before Francisco de Mendosa transplanted it to plantations in the West Indies.

Cultivation: Ginger needs high humidity and to be grown in a humus-rich, neutral-to-alkaline soil; it increases in tuberous joints. Ideally it needs 10 months of unchecked growth to produce rhizomes. The fresh, young shoots are called "green ginger."

Storage: Ginger becomes twice as pungent when dried, but it is unlikely that the home grower will try to dry and powder the root. Peeled fresh roots can be steeped in hot syrup to preserve them. Sections or "hands" of the fresh root can be kept in a cool place for several months.

Preparation: Remove the skin with care so as not to lose the volatile oil or rich resin. One way is to lightly score the skin and pour over boiling water, leave for one minute, and the skin (like that of a tomato) will lift away. Alternatively, use a fine-bladed potato peeler. If grating fresh ginger, make a horizontal cut, peeling as little as possible, and grate to the skin. Writing in 1851, Beeton recommended adding bruised ginger when pickling cucumbers.

Finely grated and chopped fresh ginger are good with baked sweet potatoes, and with Jerusalem artichokes. Grate into kedgeree, red lentil soup, stir-fries, or any savory dish needing a little livening up. See also the recipe for Bengal chicken on p.219. Pickle stems in vinegar to make *gari* or Japanese pickled ginger for sushi. Following the same method as angelica (see p.59), crystallize ginger for ginger cake and gingerbread.

ABOVE: Much of ginger's flavor lies just under the skin, so peel carefully or grate to the skin when preparing the roots. The skin thickens with age.

"Stone Ginger Beer. Boil for twenty minutes in a large pan one ounce of hops, three pounds of sugar, two ounces of whole ginger, and four gallons of cold water. Strain it, and before it is quite cold add one ounce of good yeast. Skim off all the yeast the next day, and bottle it and cork well. See that there is no sediment in the bottles. This will be ready for use in a week."

Summer Drinks and Winter Cordials, (1925) Mrs. C.F. Leyel

Ginger became such an important commodity in the Roman Empire that it was taxed from AD 220. After introduction into the West Indies, the finest roots were grown in Jamaica, from whence it naturalized into the Americas. During the 16th century the Spanish exported it throughout Europe. The rhizomes are sold as "races" or hands of ginger, race being the old name for a hand, which they resemble. In fact, the hot, lively flavored ginger root is the origin of the word racy. Its efficacy in Ayurvedic medicine is such that it is known as *vishwabhesaj* or universal medicine. Reputedly half of all Chinese and Ayurvedic medicines include ginger. Among other southeast Asian gingers is the bergamot-tasting *Z. mioga*—Japanese ginger.

It can be grown for interest as a summer annual in temperate climates, where it should provide a few new shoots, and possibly a ginger-scented, pale yellow flower with a purple lip. When buying a rhizome, if you see a bud breaking on the surface, cut through ½in on each side and try to grow it on in moist compost in a humid, heated glasshouse.

Ginger has a warming, antichilling effect on the body's circulation, not least promoting circulation to the extremities, so it is perfect for hot toddies and teas. Curiously it also promotes perspiration and so is doubly cooling in ginger beer.

Some will recall from childhood the relentless progress of fecund ginger beer plants, but it is still worth a try. Armed with the necessary symbiotic ginger beer plant jelly-like substance and a piece of ginger root, you are well on the way to making real ginger beer.

NUTRITION

Ginger in any form allays simple travel tiredness as well as motion sickness. It is said to be equally good for morning sickness. It can be taken in any form: as a tisane, ginger beer, gingerbread, or ginger cookies.

ABOVE: All parts of the ginger exude its scent. It is worth experimenting with growing the rhizome even if you do not have a glasshouse.

HERB FLAVORS

SIMPLE AND COMPOUND

The art of simpling is learning and identifying the individual properties of one herb or simple; the art of cooking is knowing when to use the flavor of one herb, or a compound of complementary aromatics. It is as important to identify and use a simple variant of lemon as it is to combine them, as described under *salads*, *fine herbes*, *bouquet garni*, or *herbes Provençales*. The list below acts as a flavor-first guide to the individual aromatic qualities that herbs provide in each mouthful or infusion in cooking.

LEMON

Most of the lemon-scented herbs indicate in their common names that they have this property, not forgetting the lemon vinegar taste of sorrel leaves. The lemon fruit with its thick rind and many segments within seems to equate with the myriad notes of lemon in woody and soft herbs. The quintessential lemon-scented herb has to be lemongrass, where all parts of it can be consumed for this taste, acting deliciously either as a main component in a dish or as a mere flavoring. The favorite for my sense of smell is the gloriously scented lemon verbena, where every part exudes the fragrance of the finest lemon bath products. Its leaves and bark impart a citrus fragrance to tea, tisane, and pot pourri.

The easiest and hardiest must be lemon balm, *Melissa officinalis*, which has plenty of attractive cultivars: "All Gold," "Aurea," and "Gold Leaf."

The young fresh leaves have the best zing but the stems can be used on barbeques or when broiling or baking fish. Almost as vigorous and useful is the lemon mint, *Mentha × piperita* f. *citrata* which gives a new twist to sorbets and Pimms. The American cultivar "Hillary's Sweet Lemon" was named for the former US Senator Hillary Clinton.

There are several cultivars of lemon-scented thyme, *Thymus pulegioides* , which often prove to be longer lived than the common thyme. Apart from the reliable cushion-forming type, there are the gold-leaved "Archers Gold" and "Aureus" as well as the delicately candid white variegated "Silver Posie" and "Silver Queen."

Basil and bergamot, both tender annuals, have a delicacy of scent that matches their cultural requirements. There are several lemon basils: the *Ocimum basilicum* "Mrs. Burns' Lemon" of Mexican parentage; and "Sweet Dani," of which the pure and clean citrus-lemon flavor is described as being "like a growing field of lemon drops." Also, there is Indonesian Kemangie (*Ocimum × africanum*) and the Thai lime basil (*Ocimum americanum*). The light green-leaved and mauve-flowered is the only lemon-fragranced bergamot (Monarda citriodora).

ANISEED

Apart from its namesake, the anise (*Pimpinella anisum*), the fresh green seeds of sweet cicely taste like traditional aniseed balls. There are anise variations to be found in the leaves of chervil, fennel, and sweet cicely. The anise basil (*Ocimum basilicum* "Horapha") carries the flavor in both its reddish purple leaves and flowers and has a dwarf form called "Horapha Nanum."

PERFUME

Fragranced food is redolent of Middle Eastern cuisine where rose petals and rosewater are frequently used, and the sun-ripened herbs used in Provençal food are imbued with a characteristic woody perfume. Apart from thymes, especially the orange-scented *Thymus fragrantissimus*, the aromatics of hyssop and lavender are key ingredients in Mediterranean summer perfumed dishes. The heady, sweet muscat grape taste of elderflowers and orangey spice of bergamot leaves are excellent infused into drinks. And let us not forget the elusive perfumes of the humble sweet violet.

HOT AND PEPPERY

This description links four very different herbs. There is the radish-hot and peppery bite in the leaves of salad arugula, whereas nasturtium leaves and flowers have more of a dry pepperiness. Horseradish sauces are marketed on scales of hotness and it is at its hottest when simply served with vinegar. The flowers have a gentle afterburn. Freshly grated ginger has a taste that heats you up when it is cold and conversely cools you down in hot weather.

GINGERY

Apart from the qualities of ginger, its taste can be gently appreciated in gingermint, *Mentha × gracilis*, and a cultivar of rosemary "Green Ginger" whose normal resinous taste has additional spicy notes.

COOL

The cucumber qualities of the green and golden purslanes make them invaluable cooling additions to a salad—green, mixed, couscous, or rice. The lemon tang of the small, buckler-leaved sorrel makes a refreshing contrast with cold fish salads.

SMOKY

Smoking salmon and other fish is a delicious tradition, and there is something similarly smoky but more aromatic in the difference between the leaves and seeds of dill. French tarragon imparts a more smoky flavor when cooked than when raw.

ABOVE: The flavor of the true aniseed seen here is replicated in many herbs, each providing their own variation on a theme—chervil, fennel, French tarragon, sweet cicely, as well as the basil "Horapha."

217

CHOCOLATE

Food of the gods, *Theobroma cacao* is the source of that most comforting of treats, chocolate. Its warm scent and flavor are often combined with mint. They can be jointly enjoyed in the mint *Mentha × piperita* "Chocolate Mint," and the chocolate-mint-scented geranium, *Pelargonium* "Chocolate Mint."

CILANTRO BY ANY OTHER NAME

Vietnamese coriander, *Persicaria odorata*, is one herb whose flavor associates it with the true *Coriandrum sativa*. The other being culantro, *Eryngium foetidum*.

OREGANO BY ANY OTHER NAME

The signature sharp, pungent flavor of oregano is due to a creosote-scented phenol, carvacrol, curiously not found in some species. Other herbs that have it include Jamaican oregano (*Lippia micromera*); Cuban oregano (*Plectranthus amboinicus*); and Mexican oregano (both *Lippia graveolens* and *Poliomintha bustamanta* are known by this name). Research suggests that carvacrol has antibacterial, antifungal, and antimicrobial properties.

COMPOUNDS

Having identified individual flavors and fragrances, it is interesting to experiment with combinations of them to create a compound; not a relish to be served separately, but a paste, salt, or pickle that gives a dish a signature taste. Classics include green curry paste that originated in Asia where garlic, ginger, onions, chilli peppers, lemongrass, cilantro, Kaffir lime leaves, Brazilian peppercorns, ground coriander, and cumin with salt and toasted sesame oil were pounded together and stored short term in a cool place. This glorious compound could then be added to an array of savory cooked dishes. It can be adapted to western products and/or tastes by substituting lemongrass with lemon verbena leaves, cilantro with flat-leaved parsley, and Kaffir lime leaves with rosemary.

Antonin Careme (1784–1833), arguably the world's first celebrity chef who prized having his own savory mixed spice to hand, dried and pounded thyme, bay leaves, basil, sage, a little cilantro, and mace, to which he added finely ground pepper. Elizabeth David wrote that we should "forget not the salt." Even nicer was her spiced salt compound that can be rubbed onto meats or put in marinades. She pounded together salt, peppercorns, dried bay leaves, ground cloves, grated nutmeg, cinnamon, dried basil, and coriander seeds. Salt, sugar, peppercorns, and brandy with dill are the primary ingredients for gravadlax (see p.34).

Dorothy Hartley's writings in *Food in England* (1954) ooze hands-on self-sufficiency, not least for pickles and chutneys. Her compound-spice pickle embraced bay and common salt, sugar, saltpetre, sal prunella, and juniper berries, which were boiled up in a quart of strong old ale. Then a generous faggot of herbs including bay leaves, thyme, sweet basil, marjoram, sweet briar, tarragon, a small clove of garlic, and spices was added. Once cool it could be stored for later use. It makes the standard malt vinegar seem very tame.

Bengal chicken

Two recipe suggestions that can include spices harvested from the garden, one for a spicy mixture and the other for a curry, are taken from the excellent *Cooking for Crowds* (1974) by Merry White. As the title suggests, the book shows you how to cook for large numbers—all recipes are tabulated for 6, 12, 20, and 50 people.

Curry powder

Grind or blend the following spices, store in a sterilized, airtight jar, and use within 2 weeks: 30 tsp coriander seeds, 30 tsp cumin seeds, 30 tsp fenugreek, 4–6 small dried red chillies, 20 tsp turmeric, 5 tsp cinnamon, 4 tsp cloves, 3 tsp nutmeg, 3 tsp mace.

Bengal chicken

Ingredients	For 6	For 12	For 20	For 50
Frying chickens, cut in 8 serving pieces	2	4	6 ½	11
Plain yogurt	½ pt	1 pt	1½ pts	2½ pts
Garlic cloves, minced	2 tbsp	4 tbsp	7 tbsp	1–2 bulbs
Fresh ginger, finely chopped	1 tsp	2 tsp	1½ tbsp	3 tbsp
Butter	1oz	2oz	6oz	15oz
Cooking oil	2 tbsp	4 tbsp	7 tbsp	10 tbsp
Medium onions, minced	2	4	7	10
Spices—ground				
Cloves	3	5	8	14
Fennel seeds	1 tsp	2 tsp	3½ tsp	10 tsp
Coriander seeds	4 tsp	8 tsp	12 tsp	20 tsp
Turmeric, ground	1 tsp	2 tsp	3½ tsp	7 tsp
Cumin seeds	1 tsp	2 tsp	3½ tsp	10 tsp

Place chicken in a mixing bowl and add the yogurt, half the garlic, salt, and fresh ginger.

Mix well and leave for a minimum of 2 hours or overnight in the fridge.

Melt the butter in a heavy pan. Add the oil and onion; cook stirring over medium heat until the onion is soft and golden. Add the remaining garlic and spices. Continue to cook over a low heat for about 5 minutes.

Add the chicken and marinating liquid, cover and simmer until the chicken is tender. Serve with rice.

BIBLIOGRAPHY

Bown, Deni. *The Royal Horticultural Society Encyclopedia of Herbs & Their Uses.* Dorling Kindersley, 1995.

Boxer, Arabella & Back, Philippa. *The Herb Book.* Octopus, 1980.

Castelvetro, Giacomo. *The Fruit, Herbs & Vegetables of Italy 1614.* Prospect, 1989.

Cockwayne, Oswald. *Leechdoms, Wortcunning and Starcraft of Early England.* Eyre & Spottiswode, 1864.

Crocker, Pat. *The Vegetarian Cook's Bible.* Robert Rose, 2007.

Crocker, Pat, Amidon, Caroline, and Brobst, Joyce. *Scented Geranium— Pelargonium 2006 herb of the year.* Riversong Studios Ltd. HSA, 2006.

David, Elizabeth. *Mediterranean and French Country Food.* The Cookery Club, 1968.

Darwin, Tess. *The Scots Herbal—The Plant Lore of Scotland.* Birlinn, 2008.

Grieve, M. *A Modern Herbal.* Jonathan Cape, 1931.

Hartley, Dorothy. *Food in England.* Macdonald, 1954.

Holmes, Caroline. *A Zest for Herbs.* Mitchell Beazley, 2004.

Holmes, Caroline. *Why do violets shrink? Answers to 280 questions on the thorny world of plants.* The History Press, 2007.

Holt, Geraldene. *Recipes from a French Herb Garden.* Conran Octopus, 1989.

Hyll, Thomas, Maybe, Richard ed. *The Gardener's Labyrinth.* Oxford University Press, 1987.

Lawton, Barbara Perry. *Mints: A Family of Herbs and Ornamentals.* Timber Press, 2002.

Lousada, Patricia. *Culpeper Guide: Cooking with Herbs.* Webb & Bower, 1988.

Ryley, Clare. *Roman Gardens and their Plants.* Sussex Archaeological Society, 1995.

Sass, Lorna. J. *To the King's Taste.* Metropolitan Museum of Art, 1975.

Turner, Paul, ed. *Pliny's Natural History.* Centaur Classics, 1962.

Wilson, C. Anne. *Food and Drink in Britain.* Cookery Book Club, 1973.

REFERENCES:

Culantro: A Much Utilised, Little Understood Herb by Christopher Ramcharan, 1999.

Walters, S. Alan. *Horseradish Production in Illinois.* HortTechnology, Vol. 20, No. 2, April, 2010.

INDEX

PICTURE CREDITS

5, 53, bottom 73, 108, 111, top &
bottom 120, bottom 145, 147, 195,
196 © RHS, Lindley Library

12, 15, 16, top 32, 40, 47, bottom
50, 55, 82, 85, 92, 100, 104, bottom
113, 115, 134, 135, 136, 178, 191 ©
Getty Images

31, 38, 56, 62, 75, 78, 81, 83, top
84, 94, 102, top right & bottom
right 107, top 113, 119, 130, 131,
144, 146, top & bottom 149, 152,
154, 180, top and bottom 183, top
and bottom 184, top & bottom
187, 188, 194, 207, 213, 214, 216 ©
Shutterstock

With thanks to Encore Editions
and PlantIllustrations.org

All images in this book are public
domain unless otherwise stated.

Every effort has been made to
credit the copyright holders of the
images used in this book. We
apologise for any unintentional
omissions or errors and will insert
the appropriate acknowledgment
to any companies or individuals in
subsequent editions of the work.

3 1270 007 9614